Planning and Managing ATM Networks

Planning and Managing ATM Networks

DAN MINOLI
Teleport Communications Group (TCG)
Stevens Institute of Technology

TOM GOLWAY
Fore Systems

with
Norris Smith

MANNING

Greenwich
(74° w. long.)

This book can be browsed and ordered electronically at
        http://www.browsebooks.com

The publisher offers discounts on this book when ordered in quantity.

For more information please contact:

        Special Sales Department
        Manning Publications Co.
        3 Lewis Street
        Greenwich, CT 06830
        or
        orders@manning.com
        Fax: (203) 661-9018

Copyediting: Margaret Marynowski

Typesetting: Donna Collingwood

Cover design: Peter Poulos with Leslie Haimes

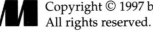
Recognizing the importance of preserving what has been written, it is the policy of Manning Publications to have the books they publish printed on acid-free paper, and we exert our best efforts to that end.

Many of the designations used by manufacturers and vendors to distinguish their products are protected as trademarks. Wherever these designations appear in this book, and we have been aware of the trademark claim, they have been typeset in initial caps of all caps.

Library of Congress Cataloging in Publication Data

Minoli, Daniel, 1952-
    Planning and managing ATM networks / Daniel Minoli, Thomas W.
  Golway, with Norris P. Smith.
       p.   cm.
    Includes bibliographical references and index.
    ISBN 1-884777-12-0
    1. Golway, Thomas W. II. Smith, Norris Parker, 1929-   .
    III. Title.
    TK5105.35.M37 1996
    004.6'6--dc20   96-6033
                                                           CIP

1 2 3 4 5 6 7 8 9 10 — CR — 00 99 98 97 96

For
Gino, Angela,
Anna,
Emmanuelle, Emile, and Gabrielle
and for
Elyse and Alexandra

contents

preface

Data processing in the late 1990s and beyond will be established around workgroup computing, whether the workers are in a building, on a campus, around town, around the nation, or around the world. To achieve the desired worker productivity enhancements sought through communication technology, workgroups will increasingly be interconnected over an enterprise-wide high-speed backbone network. Asynchronous Transfer Mode (ATM) technology and cell relay service are likely to play a major role in enterprise networks of the mid and late 1990s. ATM technology not only supports cell relay service, but also other fastpacket services, such as frame relay service, Switched Multimegabit Data Service, circuit emulation service, LAN emulation, and video/multimedia services. It is anticipated that ATM services will transform the enterprise network—from a data-only network to an integrated data, voice, video, image, and multimedia corporate infrastructure.

Specifically, many large corporations now have a growing need to extend high-speed communications beyond key sites, to support applications such as distributed cooperative computing, business/scientific imaging, video conferencing, video distribution, multimedia, (corporate) distance learning, etc. ATM presents itself as a viable, perhaps optimal, approach to meet these evolving corporate needs. However, because of the expense of high-speed networks, and the fact that in an ATM environment, most, if not all, of the corporate information flow may be aggregated over one or a few integrated broadband links, effective network management becomes very critical.

Therefore, such transformation of the enterprise network to an ATM-based infrastructure will result in an ever-increasing need for optimal management of information processing and communication resources and services, whether these services are locally based or wide-area-based. Users expect rapid reconfiguration of the services they are using, to help them meet market demands on the products they produce, since many of these products utilize, in one way or another, communication and computers. Corporate financial monitors expect cost-effective communication, low outage time, and few work disruptions. Communication and computing expenditures can represent as much as 10% (5% on the average) of the total revenue of a corporation. This can equate to tens of millions of dollars a year. Communications managers want tools to facilitate planning, monitoring, operation, maintenance, administration, and reconfiguration of the enterprise network, to satisfy their customer base.

The purpose of this book is to familiarize ATM and network planners in the user community with the network management challenges, opportunities, and capabilities that ATM presents. The technology is just beginning to be deployed, but as soon as the equipment is taken out of the box and powered up, the question immediately presents itself to the user: "How do we manage—in a cost-effective manner—this thing?" A network technology without a mechanism for the user (and the provider, for that matter) to manage it, is like a car without a steering wheel—of limited or no value.

Detrimentally, there has been a feast of hyperbole about ATM during the past couple of years. Some in the trade press imply that ATM is "magical" in its support of bandwidth on demand, scalability, and other features. These people attribute to ATM features that have never existed and never will exist. The definition used by many neophytes—that ATM will fix whatever significant networking problems you have today, be they staffing; complexity; inability to reach remote exurban, rural, or third-world locations; expenditures; the need to keep up with technology, the need for analytical design; the need for tight operational discipline; or security, is absolutely positively wrong. This book seeks to expunge these misleading accretions. They have no place in a rational discourse of what can be done to next-generation corporate networks.

So what is good about ATM? It is not a panacea. It is only the best technology to come along so far. It can be put to effective use in meeting high-speed connectivity requirements, particularly at the backbone/WAN level, where the tributary bandwidth requirements have been aggregated well beyond the bandwidth needed by a single desktop user. For example, on the assumption that 1.5 Mbps dedicated is adequate to support (e.g., by using MPEG-1) video to each desktop, a company with 100 desktops may see an aggregate requirement of 155 Mbps (if all users must access a remote video server containing some information of interest). As a straight connectivity technology at the WAN level, ATM presents itself as a good candidate, in this example, to support this bandwidth need.

Some also look to ATM to support legacy LAN requirements at the premises level (we don't mean here new ATM services to the desktop, but a hybrid of a premises-based ATM-made-to-look-like-Ethernet suite of transitional equipment). This may or may not occur. In the past, new technologies have failed to win over the *legacy support* market. For example, when satellite links for data applications first appeared, they were not able to support mainframe links; a whole new application (VSAT) had to emerge. When ISDN standards were published (e.g., Q.931), three-quarters of the protocol state machine (as measured by the thickness of the standard) was dedicated to the interworking of traditional packet services over the D-channel (only one-quarter of the standard related to supporting circuit-switched services). This legacy support never occured in ISDN. Similarly, no frame relay service now available is offered in conjunction with ISDN as originally conceived. Numerous other examples can be cited. Naturally, it is the market (but not the vendors) who will decide.

After debunking the hype, users will deploy ATM services for those (new) applications that really need it. Several studies have shown that network management can take as much as 40% of the total communication budget. To ensure that the network management methodology, and the tools that may be selected by an organization, provide for efficient network operations, several issues need to be addressed:

- Is it easy to manage ATM?

- How does the organization define ATM network management?

- What ATM network management services are provided? By whom?

- What are the ATM performance metrics and objectives?

- What are the requirements for the support staff in charge of ATM?

- How does one integrate the management of the new ATM technology with existing LAN/WAN network management systems?

- What features are available in commercial ATM network management products? How easy is it to extend these products if needed?

- Are there standards for ATM management?

- Can one use SNMP for ATM management?

- How does one go about supporting an integrated ATM data, voice, video, image, and multimedia corporate infrastructure?

These and other issues are treated in this text. We hope it will assist corporations early on, in making the necessary decisions about ATM. The text takes a pragmatic approach. It is aimed directly at communication professionals and corporate network managers and planners.

After an overview of the field (Chapter 1), an assessment of the importance of ATM in enterprise networks is provided (Chapter 2). This is followed by a primer on key ATM technologies that will play significant roles in the near future and which corporations expect their communication planners to manage (Chapter 3).

Chapter 4, provides a detailed technical analysis of ATM network management capabilities. Chapter 5, discusses the management of the protocol stack at the physical and ATM level. Chapter 6, looks at models to support Customer Network Management of ATM services. Chapters 7,8, and 9 cover the Open Systems Interconnection Network Management Specific Management Functional Areas (fault management, accounting management, configuration management, performance management, and security management) in the ATM context. Chapter 10, covers some of the network management issues faced by carriers offering ATM services, as they contemplate managing their own ATM networks.

The chapters that follow look at specific user environments, and assess the issue of managing ATM overlays to these embedded networking architectures—which clearly organizations cannot obsolete overnight in favor of an all-ATM enterprise network. Chapter 11, looks at emerging computing environments and the specific management requirements these impose on ATM. Chapter 12, examines the issue of establishing corporate network management goals. Chapter 13, addresses the predecision issues related to technology assessment for the deployment of ATM. Chapter 14, assesses management issues in Virtual LANs. People-related issues are covered in Chapter 15, along with a description of other collateral tools for effective network management. Finally, Chapter 16, provides an assessment of the industry in terms of commercial tools that have emerged and are expected to emerge in the next couple of years. Typical features and functions are discussed.

In addition to its professional market target, we believe that the book can be used for an undergraduate or graduate course, particularly from an enterprise network perspective. This material has, in whole or in parts, been used for teaching ATM technology at Stevens Institute of Technology to students already familiar with fastpacket communications.

The authors hope that this book will be of value to early adopters of ATM in selecting an appropriate network management strategy that provides a path of cost-effectiveness that goes beyond technical innovation. In the experience of the authors, corporations seek technology for productivity enhancement rather than pure academic pursuit of abstract technical advancement and sophistication.

acknowledgments

For Mr. Minoli, some portions of the material (specifically, Chapters 5–8 and 16) were originally done while at Bell Communications Research (Bellcore). Mr. Minoli also wishes to thank McGraw-Hill for allowing him to expand a network management chapter in the book *Cell Relay Service and ATM in Corporate Environments*, 1994, by Mr. Minoli and M. Vitella, into this more inclusive treatment.

Mr. Minoli wishes to thank Dr. Roy D. Rosner, Vice President and General Manager Data Service and Private Line LOB, Teleport Communications Group Incorporated (TCGI) for the support provided in the development of this treatise, based on the high-quality ATM services offered by TCGI.

Mr. Golway wishes to thank his clients for providing the opportunity to build advanced networks such as those described in the book. He also wishes to thank Ed, Mike, Bob, Domminic and Vinnie for their encouragement and freedom to go beyond conventional wisdom and push the envelope.

PART I

Introduction to ATM

chapter 1

Overview

Network planning and operations managers find that their networks are entering a period of significant transformation in the latter part of the 1990s. A network technology called Asynchronous Transfer Mode (ATM) will be in the forefront of this transformation and the ensuing corporate and public infrastructure transition. The need for change is evident. During the early decades of data networking, complicated, expensive, and often duplicative solutions were created in isolation. Strenuous efforts led to some form of network interoperability. Increasing adoption of standards and open systems philosophies have reduced, to some extent, the interworking complications. Nevertheless, these solutions are barely adequate to meet evolving requirements for integrated, ubiquitous, and cost-effective connectivity.

This chapter explores the motivations, opportunities, and challenges faced by this evolving technology for corporate networks.

1.1 Asynchronous Transfer Mode

An explosion in demand for enterprise-wide connectivity is now taking place. It is certain to accelerate in coming years. The networks that have been glued together over the years are not capable of meeting this demand adequately. In addition, it is becoming increasingly difficult for network managers to maintain cost efficiency and respond fully to their customers' requirements. Some view data networking as an unloved stepchild of a telecommunications establishment that has been preoccupied with voice transmission. Perhaps this has been justifiable, until now, when one considers that voice represents a yearly US expense of over $200 billion. Nevertheless, the data portion of many telecom budgets continues to increase significantly. Networks to support high-speed transmission of images—broadcast television and cable—have remained, at the practical level, in a separate domain.

No single technology can resolve all interworking, integration, and network simplification issues. It seems certain, however, that ATM will play a central, strategic role in the networks of the future. ATM is an open solution, based on international and industry standards. ATM technology provides the following capabilities:

- Much higher transmission capabilities than existing packet or frame-based technologies. From the start ATM will support LAN speeds 10 to 20 times faster than current systems. By the late 1990s, ATM will be able to operate at gigabits per second.

- Flexibility and versatility. Voice, data, video, and images can be transmitted simultaneously over a single, integrated corporate (or carrier) network.

- The ability to meet the needs of each segment of the corporate network, supplementing and eventually supplanting the different networking solutions that now prevail at the work group, at local area networks (LAN), at campus or metropolitan area networks (MAN), and at the wide-area networks (WAN).

- Adaptability to a wide variety of physical media, from ordinary twisted-pair wire to high-capacity optical fiber.

- The ability to support qualitative as well as quantitative changes in the corporate landscape. ATM will change how networks are used. Specifically, it will enable new applications that could transform the entire computer/network/user environment.

- Universality. ATM technology has the potential to become a ubiquitous, multiservice platform handling a range of traffic types.

- Support of virtual networks, leading to independence with respect to physical topology and decreasing user-perceived dependence on specific pieces of hardware.

On the negative side, ATM has been the subject of much hyperbole and many overwrought vendor claims. On another level, vendors who in the past decade have concentrated on legacy equipment, such as routers, seem to have a hard time grasping the principles and benefits of ATM; often they trivialize, undervalue, or bad-mouth the technology. In fact, ATM is already a working reality, serving the real-world requirements of many kinds of users. At press time one already finds hundreds of users who are in various stages of ATM pilots, early deployments, and initial production use.

ATM implies far-reaching institutional as well as technological changes. Such changes do not propagate through an organization as rapidly as some would think or hope. To be honest, ATM is not yet a fully mature technology, specifically in regards to a commodity status of the various constituent components. Effectively, ATM is today where LANs were in 1984: standards had been developed, and some basic equipment was available, but all the equipment breakthroughs, especially in the areas of high-performance cost-effective bridges, routers, hubs, switches, and Network Interface Cards (NICs), were still several years away. In fact, it took about a decade to achieve a commodity status. Standards-making bodies are still resolving some details of ATM specifications, particularly in support of video, voice, and multimedia. Data WAN technology is well-advanced, while LAN-based ATM technology is nearing completion of standardization. Timing is, thus, a crucial dimension of ATM evaluation, adoption, and implementation. Corporate network planners and managers must be conscious of the immediate realities of the next couple of years, as well as ATM's long-term potential. Specifically it appears that large-scale ATM deployment will take place first in the MAN/campus context, followed by WAN implementations and, eventually, at the work group and desktop level.

1.2 *About this Book*

This book aims to provide readers with the background, concepts, and strategies that they need to prepare for ATM technology deployment in their corporations. It focuses upon network planning and management as it pertains to ATM. Most observers recognize that the planning process will be the key to successful operation of ATM-based networks.

The book assumes that the reader has some basic familiarity with ATM technology, including the references. There are now a number of books on the market focusing on ATM technology, including Ref. [1]. This text covers other topics related to the effective management of ATM equipment, services, quality of service, traffic, and carriers' offerings.

Management, as used here, includes:

- Decisions and broad oversight by a corporation's senior executives.

- Planning and management of the structure, applications, procedures, and future course of the network.

- Operational management of day-to-day functions at the network's logical and physical levels.

This book addresses the needs of readers concerned with these and other dimensions of network management. Particular emphasis is given to corporate networks. Early implementers include major governmental and academic organizations, as well as Fortune 100 companies.

The content of the book is also relevant for small businesses and others that obtain ATM services from common carriers. This situation will become increasingly important as many more carriers in Europe and Canada, as well as the United States, adopt and implement ATM technology. In the US, service is already available from a number of alternative access providers, interexchange carriers, and regional Bell operating companies.

Special attention will be given in this text to the far-reaching changes that ATM technology and principles will bring about in network design, deployment strategies, physical and logical management, and other activities related to network operations, administration, maintenance, and provisioning.

This book emphasizes the human dimension. Too often, networking is defined primarily in terms of hardware and the process of making that hardware work. A network must reflect the requirements, structure, and objectives of the organization whose people use it to do their work. Along this direction, topics discussed include the importance of training, making efficient use of help desks, dynamic and interactive documentation, and the trade-offs between the use of in-house staff and out-sourcing services from contractors [2]. Issues such as proactive modeling, managing information flows, and setting and enforcing network policies are also examined.

Close attention is given in Part 1 to the issue of time, which is so important for an evolving technology like ATM. The book examines each step in the adoption cycle, from evaluation through the possible establishment of a specialized ATM lab, running a pilot, defining objectives, initial deployment, learning systematically from small as well as large crisis, and eventual production-level operation. In addition, ATM will require new procedures for management at the operating level. A full understanding of these fundamentals is essential to the quality and efficiency of ATM networks. Parts 2 and 3 of this book provide essential information for effective operational management. Topics covered include the management of the Physical and ATM Layers, customer network management, mechanisms to handle fault and configuration issues, performance management, accounting, and security management. Part 4 focuses on the gamut of collateral tools and techniques required to successfully plan and deploy ATM-based networks.

1.3   The Networking Environment

ATM technology can be placed in its broader context by examining the outlook for broadband demand, the anticipated requirement for tomorrow's networks, the expected evolution of networks, and management issues raised by the new networks. Specifically, we want to answer questions like:

- What is happening in networking?

- What is the place of ATM technology in the evolving network environment?

- What are the implications of ATM for network planning and management?

- How can managers prepare for the end of the decade while they strive to keep step with the requirements of today?

1.3.1 Merging of Islands

A decade ago, computers were thought of as machines operating in isolation. That view is now totally obsolete. Starting in the mid 1980s, computers began to become "socialized," especially in major businesses, government, universities, and other large-scale contexts. More recently, individuals and smaller businesses have connected with networks through the Internet. Computers and the networks in which they function have become integrated. Each is an extension of the other, within a total system whose common capability exceeds greatly the sum of its individual parts. Increases in the performance of computers, and hence their output into networks, have been the primary force behind a massive growth in demand for network capacity. Providing that capacity with existing technology has become more and more difficult. ATM will therefore play a crucial role in meeting the bandwidth demands of corporations and institutions. Indeed, some feel that ATM can provide more capacity than is likely to be required during the next five years; ATM's bandwidth scalability will help mediate this growth. However, it must be clearly understood that what makes this capacity available is advances in fiberoptic technology, not ATM proper; ATM is only a bandwidth manager that efficiently allocates the bandwidth of the fiber to multiple users/applications.

Demand for low-cost network bandwidth is also being generated by the rapid growth and widening reach of the Internet. The Internet itself, a conglomerate of local, regional, and global networks, will require new management capabilities as well as higher bandwidth if it is to support corporate applications of specified quality of service.

New functional tools like the World Wide Web (WWW)—which barely existed in 1993 and is now used by millions of people—will add significantly to demands for network capacity. These innovations have transformed the Internet hitherto restricted to mostly text-based information—into a multimedia environment that requires transmission of high-volume images and video, as well as data.

ATM must also respond to the requirements of telecommunications service providers. They will need greater capacity to handle growing demand for data, image, and video transmission, as well as traditional voice services. Efficient, reliable management is also essential for telecommunications companies.

Expansion of the user community in multiple dimensions will be accompanied by new security requirements. ATM is only part of the solution to today's complex security issues, but it can provide an essential foundation. If networks lag behind, they will become liabilities. Consider the Channel Tunnel between the United Kingdom and the rest of Europe. Its ability to compete with air travel and fast trans-Channel ferries assumes high-speed trains for the entire route from Paris to London. Yet this system's efficiency for many years to come will be hampered by poor tracks on the English portion, where trains capable of much higher velocity will be restricted to the speeds of 50 years ago.

In networking, this issue is even more evident. The overall throughput rate of a transmitting user to a recipient is constrained by the slowest portion—usually the smaller capacity network facilities at both ends—as well as by inadequacies in bridges, routers, gateways, and other equipment in between.

Before long—primarily after it has become routine for WANs and backbones—ATM is expected to be brought to the desktop. Thus, a single-architecture solution would prevail during the entire transmission from the sender's desktop to the recipient's desktop. Costs for ATM ports are decreasing steadily. Along with the flexibility of ATM, this will facilitate the way toward seamless solutions.

1.3.2 Who is Using ATM Already?

Looking from a mid 1990s vantage point, ATM has been primarily the concern of early users, especially technology driven companies, but other organizations are taking an active interest in this new technology. It should also be noted that as a multiservice architecture, ATM is being used to support frame relay and native LAN or FDDI (Fiber Distributed Data Interface) interconnections, sometimes invisibly to the end-user. Hence, ATM-based technology is entering the scene before native ATM services are deployed by user organizations.

The pioneers of native ATM services have included businesses like financial houses that are highly network-dependent and time-sensitive. In pursuit of an immediate competitive edge, they have been eager to take advantage of a faster, more versatile network architecture like ATM. They appreciate ATM's ability to provide better bandwidth management, varying service level "guarantees" and other advantages. Most businesses of this kind are employing ATM initially in longer distance networks (WANs). Some are experimenting with ATM in LANs and campus-level networks.

Interest in ATM is now reaching into additional computationally intensive industries like oil exploration, which require the timely transmission of very large datasets. Other mainstream businesses are adopting ATM. These include retailing, manufacturing, and transportation, where high volume, reliability, and reasonable costs, combined with adequately high transfer rates are more important than split-second speed advantages.

ATM is also being investigated by universities and far-sighted local, regional, and national governments that seek an information infrastructure capable of supporting up-to-date education, delivery of health services, and distance-learning [3].

1.3.3 High Bandwidth, Complexity, Diversity

In addition to supporting continuing increases in *bandwidth* (the carrying capacity of a network, usually described in terms of millions or billions of bits per second), the networks of the future will need to be more intelligent. They will be required to transport many kinds of media simultaneously—including high-quality images (especially moving pictures), as well as data and voice traffic.

These new types of information objects will be created and manipulated by new classes of applications. These applications should be network-enabled, designed and developed specifically for more intelligent networks. They will require various service classes and will generate unpredictable information flows. These networks must also be fully digital. Computers will almost exclusively communicate to other computers in their native digital language. The awkward and expensive conversion from digital to analog to digital once again (audible in the whines of faxes and modems) will become obsolete.

Forecasts like these are on solid ground, but they are not enough. The complexity, diversity, flexibility, and high speed of tomorrow's networks will be qualitatively different from today's network/computer partnership. They will open new prospects and create new challenges that cannot now be imagined.

1.3.4 The Unforeseen Future

This phenomenon can be illuminated by two examples: At first, the automobile was no more than a machine that was faster, cheaper to operate, and created less inconvenient waste products than a horse and carriage. Yet, over time, the automobile became ubiquitous, stimulating a vast infrastructure, from highway networks to malls, motels, and theme parks. In commercial terms, early aircraft were in effect super-sized carrier pigeons. Airmail was one of the first applications of flight, but aircraft were treated as a faster but otherwise identical carrier, like trains and trucks. Much later, Federal Express and its emulators established an entirely new kind of service, based on new technologies and new concepts that had not been foreseen when modern air transport began in the 1930s.

Networks have had a similar history, although at a much more rapid pace. In the last twenty years, one has seen networks evolve from simple asynchronous dial-up connections, to various LAN solutions, to ATM. ATM will, of course, not be the ultimate solution, but it is likely to predominate in networking for a substantial period. It has the potential for sweeping changes in the way networks are used. Its architecture makes it possible to classify types of information and provide varying levels of service for each type. It also allows for subsets of users to maintain their own views of the network.

One manifestation of intelligence is in virtual networks. Virtual networks allow great flexibility without the complications, uncertainties, and high costs that are typically involved in setting up a work group whose members may be located at a distance from one another. Whatever their locations, participants in ATM networks can be members of a virtual community. Public carriers will also be able to offer this kind of network intelligence using ATM.

1.3.5 Managing the New Networks

Managing a crowded airspace like the skies over the New York metropolitan area involves distinctive requirements. The demands are totally different from the casual flight supervision of the 1930s. For tomorrow's networks, the contrast with the past—and the management challenges—are even greater. Imagine the complexity of air traffic control if dozens of space craft, flying at the speed of the space shuttle, each as large as a cruise ship, were converging upon an airport from all directions every few minutes. It would be necessary to set priorities, identify and overcome difficulties, and manage traffic with almost perfect precision at extraordinary speeds. This can serve as an analogy for the management challenges created by ATM-based networks which are capable of speeds up to gigabits per second. The challenges are: to cope readily with multimedia, and to be able to adapt to the needs of applications that do not yet exist.

Network management has traditionally concentrated on the physical level, responding to crisis in wiring, switches, and other hardware. With ATM, network management will need to focus attention on the logical level. Watching for equipment lights, and monitoring the health or illness of ports will no longer be enough. Bandwidth is only one part of the solution. The preferred strategy will be to take full advantage of the multiple service levels and the loss prioritization mechanisms made possible by ATM. But these new features have significant network management implications.

1.4 Ubiquity, Intelligence, and Virtual Networks

ATM's broad capabilities derive in large part from one of ATM's distinctive characteristics: bandwidth is managed on the logical level rather than the physical level. Most practitioners predict that networks based on ATM will become ubiquitous. The consequences of ubiquity will not be limited to incremental improvements in performance. ATM's versatility, as well as its intrinsic power, could stimulate far-reaching qualitative changes in the way people define, configure, use, and pay for network/computer services.

How could one new technology be capable of such an impact? ATM's architecture differs significantly from existing enterprise networks because it supports high-speed switching as a way to accomplish any-to-any connectivity, rather than using pairwise sets of private lines. This makes it possible to consider new applications, while leading to new challenges for network managers.

The consequences of the increase in demand for network capacity cannot be satisfied with today's prevailing bandwidths in the dozens of million bits per second, and the associated management procedures of telecommunications networks based only on digital private lines. It has been argued that as bandwidth reaches very high levels, it becomes "nearly cost-free." However, nothing is ever free, and so communication resources must still be effectively managed. Some also envision universal configurations of global scope. The ideal of a global corporation whose in-house telecommunications are equally homogeneous is also appealing.

High bandwidth is not enough by itself because switching (and also propagation) delay mean that increases in effective throughput do not keep pace with increases in bandwidth. For example, the propagation time between New York City and Los Angeles is approximately 2500 miles/186000 miles per second = 13.4 milliseconds. If the information can be transacted between the network and the user at intervals less than this (e.g., sending a 1518-character Ethernet frame over a 155,000,000-bps ATM link, which takes about 0.1 milliseconds), then the propagation time becomes the dominating term in some applications. As another example, if the cell switching time is relatively high, say 10 milliseconds, then it becomes the dominating term. These considerations increase over longer distances, because of the higher propagation times and the fact that more switching hops will be found along the way. Fast ATM switches can minimize these effects. For full network efficiency, it is necessary to allocate bandwidth intelligently and manage traffic flow skillfully. ATM's capability for intelligent allocation of bandwidth will make it possible to exploit the full potential of additional bandwidth.

In addition, well-considered, carefully executed measures must be taken to manage traffic flows and adapt specifically to the requirements of applications. ATM affords multiple quality-of-service classes, but these also become more complex to manage. It will be necessary to choose among the many alternatives for policy implementation. If these steps are not taken, ATM's full potential will not be realized. Network management must develop the policies needed to accomplish these goals in the broadband/ATM context. Precedents may be of limited value because problems on this scale have not been encountered in previous networks. Even in today's environment, however, it is possible to improve traffic flow through prioritization and better management of applications.[1]

Specialists in operating system software and applications are now dealing with these issues. Program management must accelerate its efforts to catch up. The use of higher level, integrated, object-based management might be a suitable strategy. ATM's characteristics enable enforcement of policies that in principle can make it easier to manage at the higher levels of applications. This contrasts with traditional concerns, which have focused upon how to make legacy networks like Ethernet and Token Ring work effectively, or upon the management of a router or switch.

In most corporate environments that have deployed legacy networks, the planning function and the operations/program management function grew up separately. These are now tending to merge, and this should be encouraged.

Meanwhile, corporate networks have been adopting loose management policies because traffic has unintentionally been shaped by bridges, routers, and other network infrastructures that support the legacy network. In fact, whole networks (and corporate fortunes) have been built on the necessary evil of box-centric protocol conversion in the form of routers. With ATM, traditional routers can safely go away, although vendors with vested interests will make enough noise to foster their use in the networking industry for perhaps another 5–7 years. With the disappearance of routers, the whole box-centric view of network management must also change.

---

[1] As will be covered in Chapter 2, ATM per se does not support per-cell cell-treatment priority from a performance point of view. (There is a loss priority, but this is not directly related to expediting cells through the switch or rendering special treatment.) To compensate for this, implementers have developed an external mechanism for providing per-session traffic priority discrimination. In a Permanent Virtual Circuit environment, the cells belonging to a session are implicitly assigned a priority at the switch by (i) making a notation of the specific port on which the connection terminates; (ii) adding some supplementary cell-enveloping at the switch as the cell traverses the switch (this supplementary information is, however, removed as the cell exits the switch); and (iii) routing cells (based on the supplementary information) to different buffer pools. This implicit mechanism allows traffic flows to receive different switching treatment (e.g., Constant Bit Rate and Variable Bit Rate). For Switched Permanent Connections, the treatment of the block of cells associated with a connection is based on the kind of service class called for in the setup message sent by the user for that connection, at the start of the session. Again, the switch will have to use extensions of ATM to service the different requirements; in addition, the priority is not on a per-cell basis. Hence, the issue of priorities in ATM has to be carefully worded: one can say that mechanisms exist to support a kind of connection-level grade of service which gives the appearance of supporting, from a performance point of view, a weak kind of traffic priority.

ATM requires a new perspective. Applications appear radically different. The physical and logical topologies of ATM and of familiar networks must be considered separately. In addition to providing freedom from the conventional constraints of hard-wired, point-to-point connectivity, virtual circuits based on ATM will, in many instances, reduce the costs and inconvenience of moving or changing users' platforms, routers, switches, and other equipment. In current circumstances, such changes are costly, time-consuming, and can inhibit needed adaptation to changes in work groups. With permanent virtual circuits, Moves, Adds, and Changes (MACs) can be facilitated. With switched virtual circuits, these new connections can be undertaken automatically.

New management tools will be needed to accomplish this. Today's network analyzers that spot faults in a shared network's physical infrastructure will not work effectively on virtual networks in which the logical layer is the playing field. (In due course, however, low-cost ATM-based test and diagnostic equipment will no doubt enter the market.) Today's ATM testers are expensive. They can cost as much as a quarter of a million dollars.

In a network that exploits fully the capabilities of ATM, the distinction between client and server could become even more blurred. The new model will be a cooperative environment. There will be no clients and no servers. Each will share characteristics of both roles. The result will resemble a meshed topology at the application level.

These potential benefits are, however, prospects for the future—in the later years of this decade, perhaps later. During a fairly protracted transition period, it will be necessary for ATM to function in conjunction with existing network protocols like IPX, IP, and Appletalk.

1.5 *Into the Future*

Applications requirements may be difficult to foresee, but basic network management issues are easier to anticipate. In addition to continuing needs like traffic prioritization, traffic control, and dynamic allocation of bandwidth, additional issues will include the following (discussed in more detail in later chapters):

- Chargeback procedures and other accounting issues. For ATM the old assumption of flat charges based on arbitrary classes of computers could be replaced by different criteria, including business objectives and quality of service.

- Fault detection, correction, and bypassing. ATM will make it easier to undertake and to remotely operate these functions. In turn, this will allow some companies to outsource to contractors lower level element-oriented management functions like port failures; this would permit in-house management staff to focus on broader issues.

- Help-desk functions and trouble-ticketing procedures will require restructuring as larger scale operations develop virtual network operations centers (NOC). Response times and mean times to repair (MTTR) based upon the Physical Layer of networks have been increasing steadily as networks grow more complex. Measures need to be taken to reduce those delays and to adjust to virtual networks.

1.6   The OSI Seven-Layer Model

The architecture of a computer is relatively easy to diagram: a small number of boxes (CPU, active memory, disk memory, output to monitor or printer, etc.) are linked by channels and buses. Box and line diagrams can also map a network, but more is needed: a protocol architecture describing the behavior of peers in the network.

The most widely used depiction of the protocol stack was created in connection with OSI (Open Systems Interconnection), a protocol developed by the International Organization for Standardization. The OSI model, depicted in Table 1.1, will be referred to frequently throughout this book.

ATM can also be described by this model. In fact, ATM itself is a peer-to-peer protocol supporting a (small) sublayer of Layer 2 (Data Link Layer). In current parlance, the term *ATM* is taken to mean the entire infrastructure (protocols, physical transmission facilities, switches) supporting Layer 1 and part of Layer 2. (In the signaling plane, ATM supports up to Layer 7.)

Layers are numbered from bottom to top, because each depends upon the support of all lower layers, through the services supplied by the layer immediately below it. The upper layers tend to be implemented in software (Layer 3 or above), while the lower layers tend to be implemented in hardware (e.g., NICs or switch termination). In an ATM network environment, the user's end system (e.g., a client) needs to implement Layers 1 and 2 (ATM and ATM Adaptation Layer) with an ATM protocol peer in the network switch, and the ATM Adaptation Layer, along with Layers 3–7, at a protocol peer in the remote end system (e.g., server). The network switch provides a relaying function, generally at the ATM Layer. (Occasionally, the ATM Adaptation Layer is also supported at the switch; this occurs when service interworking takes place.) Then the far side of the switch supports a set of Layer 1 and Layer 2 peers to the destination end system (e.g., server).

Layer	Function
Application (Layer 7)	Support of user functions such as file transfer, transaction processing, etc.
Presentation (Layer 6)	Transfer syntaxes (character coding).
Session (Layer 5)	Coordination services, dialogue, synchronization.
Transport (Layer 4)	Reliable end–end communication.
Network (Layer 3)	Delivery within a single subnetwork. End-to-end aspects, such as addressing and internetworking.
Data Link (Layer 2)	Delivery of blocks of data (e.g., cells) between two points; the ATM and the ATM Adaptation Layers are sublayers within the Data Link Layer.
Physical (Layer 1)	Bit Transmission.

Refer to ISO 7498 or ITU-T X.200 for a more formal and complete description of these functions.

Table 1.1   OSI Seven-Layer model

References

[1] D. Minoli, M. Vitella, *Cell Relay Service and ATM for Corporate Environments* (McGraw-Hill, 1994).

[2] D. Minoli, *Analyzing Outsourcing, Reengineering Information and Communication Systems* (McGraw-Hill, 1995).

[3] D. Minoli, *Distance Learning: Broadband Applications* (Artech House, 1996).

chapter 2

The Emergence of ATM

*A*TM *is an evolutionary rather than a revolutionary technology, but it marks a major step beyond other existing network architectures. ATM technology takes full advantage of the large capacity potential of fiber optic circuits, while adjusting to the limitations of today's infrastructure, which will remain in place for a number of years. Specifically, interworking with legacy networks and protocols is a feature that has been built into ATM.*

Private networks have evolved over the past quarter century. Successive architectures—all still in use—include X.25, Ethernet, Token Ring, FDDI, and Frame Relay. ATM technology is capable of overcoming its antecedents' shortcomings. Advantages include bandwidth, simplicity, sophisticated traffic-handling capabilities (or traffic management), and suitability for combined data, image, and voice traffic. The ATM standards were originally based on Broadband Integrated Services Digital Network (B-ISDN) standards, which in turn evolved from ISDN. For LAN and campus environments, a number of newly developed standards have also evolved in the recent past. ATM is an enabling technology for new networking applications, but challenges—including efficient support of legacy networks, applications design, network management, and scalability—must be satisfactorily and fully addressed before ATM can be utilized comprehensively. This chapter explores these important facets of this evolving technology.

2.1 Introduction

Networks and computers rest on the same technological foundation: VLSI (very large scale integration). Just like computers, the crucial components in network hardware—adapter cards, switches, bridges, and routers—are based on high-density transistors, and other electronic devices. Both technologies deploy this hardware in similar ways, obtaining roughly comparable efficiency and performance. The history, defining factors, constraints, and other aspects of these sibling technologies show many common points, but there are also differences. To understand the nature of networks, and in particular, the distinctive capabilities of ATM, a brief comparison with computers is useful.

Computing has for the past dozen or more years followed *Moore's Law*: the density (and hence the potential performance) of silicon-based microprocessors doubles every eighteen months. This observation, named after its originator, Intel cofounder Gordon Moore, is governed by technology. Another way of saying this is that power increases by an order of magnitude every 4 or so years. The price/performance of computers, reflecting competition as well as technology, improves at about the same rate as the Moore's Law cycle. This is especially true now that an increasingly wide range of computers is based on commodity microprocessors.

Consequently, the obsolescence rate of computers, especially the desktop computers that respond most directly to Moore's Law, is very rapid. As every computer user is aware, however, the actual "mouse-end" utility of a computer is actually determined by software. Software—both operating systems and applications programs—evolves much more slowly, ascending a much lumpier curve with numerous flat spots. Part of this problem is that software developers have focused on constantly adding new features to programs rather than keeping the feature level constant but improving speed. For example, increasingly more complex word processing packages are being developed to add many point-and-click capabilities, rather than keeping basic programs. The latter should not preclude more user-friendly versions, but the option should exist for the advanced user to buy a compatible version of the software that focuses principally on speed. Many applications programs still in active use, often supporting billion-dollar industries, have remained fundamentally the same for ten or twenty years. Fast new hardware can thus be slowed down in actual execution by the need to adjust to the limitations and complexity of old-fashioned software.

How is networking different? Networking technology has advanced more slowly than computer technology, as measured by, say, user-available bandwidth. It was shown in [1], in what might be called an equivalent "law," that the bandwidth of a WAN increases by an order of magnitude every 20 years. (This "law" is based on an analysis covering 60 years.) This is not due to laggard networking hardware, which could have been developed much more rapidly. Networking systems must conform to constraints that do not hinder computers as severely. Some of the most important are summarized below.

Raw bandwidth growth has been governed principally by technological factors. Networking standards are needed to make it possible to connect systems of numerous manufacturers and to facilitate interoperability of networks having different specifications. The traditional gap between computers and networks has been influenced by the lack and ineffectiveness of such standards, their slow evolution, and their often-cautious adoption. As a result, ten-year-old networks are commonplace, and many are likely to remain in service for quite a while. Network software has, on the whole, advanced even more slowly than computer software.

A network is also limited by the capacity of the transmission media through which data and other signals are transferred. These physical channels have evolved from twisted-pair wire, intended initially only for voice traffic, through more advanced uses of copper, to today's fiber-optic circuits. Electronic switches have gradually displaced electromechanical equipment. These diverse physical foundations, spread all over the world, represent an immense investment. Telecommunications companies are accustomed to multidecade system lifetimes. Therefore, there is a tendency to retain embedded technology for a significant amount of time.

In most relatively wealthy countries, national backbones and other WANs may be replaced rather soon (which in practical terms means by the end of this decade, or later). The capacity and overall cost-effectiveness of fiber are attractive, giving impetus to the transition. Fiber is already predominant for long distance communication in the United States.

Installation of high-bandwidth circuits on a national- or full-system scale remains limited to aggressive private projects (especially for newer companies and those that place exceptional value on timely transmission) and compact, high-density countries like Hong Kong and Singapore that are anxious to gain a competitive advantage. The rest of the world may not catch up until well into the new century.

Many private networks are also moving to improve backbone as well as desktop capacity. Refinements in copper-wire technologies and the cost of replacing existing investments will, however, delay the introduction of fiber for private LANs at the desktop level. Four recent developments are extending the practical lifetime of existing media in private networks:

- Improvements in carrying capacity, and error reduction in copper-based LAN runs.

- Introduction of switching into the traditional shared media networks, such as Ethernet, Token Ring, and FDDI.

- Adoption and near standardization of data compression techniques that now reduce the bandwidth demands of images and video, as well as text, making 10Base-T and 100Base-T LANs at least marginally capable of supporting these media.

- At the backbone level, what has held back the introduction of dedicated fiber facilities is the availability of high-speed services from carriers, eliminating the need for companies to become their own carriers, outside of their core competencies. These days, given the international nature of the competitive horizon, companies have enough challenges in keeping up their own products and market postures, without having to themselves be technologically advanced mini-telephone companies.

2.1.1 Networking Potential

From the perspective of today's networks, the potential physical capacity of fiber wiring is very large: 10 Gbps now and 1 Tbps in a few years, using technologies like coherent modulation and wavelength division multiplexing. The challenges now facing network designers, operators, standards-makers, and hardware manufacturers are defined in large part by three contrasting and sometimes contradictory requirements:

- Taking full advantage of the possibilities created by fiber.

- Adjusting as well to the capabilities of existing infrastructure.

- Providing for optimal operation of networks that combine both older and newer physical foundations and systems technology.

These circumstances provide unique opportunities for performance improvements based on new networking technologies like ATM, which by and large, use fiber media.

Physics and mathematics require that the 18-month Moore's Law cycle for microprocessor technology will at some not-too-distant point begin to flatten out and then reach a ceiling. Networking will be affected by its roots in the same basic microchip technology. It is also limited by inescapable problems with transmission latency due to propagation delays imposed by distance. Nonetheless, distinctions between computing and networking will diminish and may eventually become minor.

Especially in WANs, the basic infrastructure is provided by telecommunications companies. Traditionally, data transmission has depended upon translation of the digital output of computers into the analog format of telecommunications facilities that were designed originally to support human voice. Now there is a significant migration toward digital, at least for corporate networking.

Digitalization means the expression of all communications payload, including voice, images, and video as well as data, in the fundamental format of computers. All over the world, digitalization is rapidly transforming the telecommunications scene. It will nevertheless be well into the next century before this process is complete.

Regulation in telecommunications has fewer effects on LANs and on leased-line WANs—except in the considerable number of countries where circuit leasing is still hindered by restrictive regulations or high prices.

Many potential solutions are being concentrated upon these constraints and challenges. ATM stands out, however, because of its ability to respond to a broad spectrum of these requirements.

2.2 ATM's Predecessors

ATM has evolved from previous network architectures. Much has been done in recent years to upgrade LAN and WAN technologies. Both were originally based on copper wire twisted-pair, or coaxial. The quality and carrying capacity of copper media have been improved steadily, and these solutions remain useful for smaller LANs and WANs (particularly for access to the WAN) that do not generate high volumes of traffic.

In a larger perspective, however, LANs and WANs are both approaching their limits. Ethernet, Token Ring and comparable networks are the foundation of today's routine network functions: sharing files, the client-server philosophy, and clustering workstations or other computers together to form a single distributed system.

FDDI, a technology based on fiber, went into use in the late 1980s. It is also based on a token ring shared-media philosophy. FDDI's nominal transmission limit, 100 Mbps, is ten times the capacity ceiling of traditional Ethernet. FDDI makes it possible for network managers to control traffic flow, but it does not carry this capability very far.

In the early 1990s it became clear that a faster LAN technology would be necessary to keep pace with in-building bandwidth demands. However, FDDI was deemed too costly. Two competing technologies were proposed, each of which was based on the idea that the fundamental philosophy behind Ethernet could be extended to provide more bandwidth. These technologies were thus known as Fast Ethernet. One, called *100BaseT*, was compatible with Ethernet (but running at 100 megabits/second). Then other, called *100Base-VG*, had additional functionality. These high speed LANs serve a niche market; but, each is little more than an extension of legacy technologies. They do not have the capability to be an enabling technology.

ATM is an enabling technology, delivering a capacity level that can change the nature of networking. As it has been elaborated over a number of years, ATM is the next step in a progression, drawing on past experience. What makes the difference between ATM and the solutions from which it has evolved? This issue will be explored throughout this book, but some preliminary points deserve emphasis:

- ATM's architecture is different. It offers integral features such as quality of service and traffic loss prioritization. (See Chapter 1.) ATM supports a connection-oriented service, rather than a connectionless service. With its guaranteed quality of service, it is better suited to carry video and multimedia.

- ATM's bandwidth scalability is capable of accommodating, with appropriate hardware upgrades, the expected growth in end-user bandwidth demand. This expected increase is driven by the rapid increases in performance and output of the computers served by the networks, and by the growth in numbers of users, as desktop systems are becoming almost universal.

- Desktop workstations based on the most powerful Reduced Instruction Set (RISC) microprocessors—like Digital Equipment's Alpha—can already swamp a FDDI connection when used for I/O-intensive functions. PCs will reach similar output in a generation or two. As desktop users have deployed applications like Microsoft Windows and Lotus Notes with appended voice and video, demand for network capacity has accelerated. ATM will be able to support these and similar applications more effectively than existing communication services.

- The demand curve will level off as Moore's Law reaches its physical limits. Networks will bump up against similar ceilings as propagation delays over longer distances become a major limiting factor. Nonetheless, ATM-based services are the best suited, compared to all other currently available alternatives, to support high-performance applications.

- As bandwidth is increased, the laws of physics, as they relate to transmission, become an important factor. Throughput does not increase in proportion to bandwidth at speeds in the hundreds of megabits/second. Because of this, it is imperative not to further add switching delays. Again, ATM technology is the best suited, compared to all other currently available alternatives, to support high-performance services because the switching delay is kept very small.

- It is essential that bandwidth be allocated intelligently and efficiently. This feature cannot be added as an afterthought, but must be part of the original architecture—one of ATM's strongest features.

- ATM makes it easier to carry out routine element layer management functions, permitting managers to focus upon higher layers.

- ATM's basic philosophy is scalability, hence technological longevity. In addition to commoditizing the physical layers, the much simplified infrastructure made possible by ATM's basic philosophy permits a longer productive life cycle for the cabling plant and networking hardware. The cost and inconvenience of performance upgrades are reduced. For example, a change from ordinary Ethernet to Fast Ethernet requires a comprehensive replacement of adapters and other hardware. The ATM and Synchronous Optical Network (SONET) interface permits increases in speed with fewer, less costly adjustments. However, it must be understood that if the user purchased a 51.84-Mbps card, it will likely not support 155 Mbps or 622 Mbps: A new card would be required. The advantage of this approach is that the entry-level price is small, in that the user is not buying features that will not be used immediately. On the other hand, the user may choose to purchase a more powerful (but more expensive) card which can, by design, support 51.84, 155, and 622 rates immediately. The user would initially use this card only at the lower rate. As needs increase, the user can then, without any hardware changes, upgrade the speed. It should be clear, though, that a tradeoff is required: nothing is ever free.

- ATM also strikes a balance between two related issues in network design— accommodation of traffic bursts and control of congestion caused by competition for resources among candidates for transmission.

  Ethernet in the LAN, and Frame Relay in the WAN can cope with surges in network traffic, but can become congested if too many computers on the network want to transmit at the same time. Token Ring has a monitor that controls access, but it can backlog computers, waiting until a token lets them on the network.[1] ATM, in contrast, supports a form of bandwidth on demand, up to the maximum speed of the access line or switch, and consequently can deal more easily with bursts.

  Some in the trade press seem to imply that ATM is "magical" in its support of bandwidth on demand. This could not be further from the truth. ATM, like anything else, has a limited bandwidth equal (at the switch level) to the bus speed, say 2 Gbps; also, there is a finite number of buffers, say 64,000 per line card. As soon as the user puts in more than a well-calculable number of inputs and arrivals, he or she can become "dead in the water," just as in Frame Relay and Ethernet. In addition, constraints arise from the access speed of the link (user/line side) and the speed of the trunk.

- Like any other technology operating at the Data Link Layer, ATM is independent of upper layer protocols (in principle so are Ethernet, Token Ring, etc.). This means that ATM will carry any Protocol Data Unit (PDU) that is handed down to it through the ATM Service Access Point (SAP). From ATM's perspective, it is immaterial what is contained in the cell: IP, IPX, SNA, etc.

---

[1] However, in Token Ring the delay is deterministic and bounded, while in Ethernet it is stochastic and (theoretically) unbounded.

From the upper layer protocol's point of view, however, there has to be protocol compatibility-matching: the protocol's PDUs must conform to the ATM's SAP; hence, the upper layer protocol must know how to hand off its PDUs to ATM. Having noted this tautological observation, there is a desire to retain existing upper layer protocol (applications) unchanged. Hence, the developers have designed appropriate ATM Adaptation Layers (AALs) to accommodate the interworking functions. AALs reside above the ATM Layer and below the Network Layer. Note that ATM is a connection-oriented technology. This means that connections must be established at the ATM Layer before information can be exchanged. There is also a desire to develop virtual LANs (VLANs), where the logical community definition is independent of the physical location of the user. A number of products already exist to support VLANs, but these are vendor-specific. Many hope that ATM (in particular LAN Emulation technology) will become a vehicle to deliver vendor-independent VLANs.

• In ATM, the view of the network is nearly the same, whether it is a LAN or WAN, public or private. Thus, although ATM is an evolutionary step forward from earlier networking technologies, it is a major step.

Throughout the history of technology, far-reaching advances have brought new functions and new economies, but they rarely have been completed quickly. ATM is no exception. Although ATM is already available (especially as a high-bandwidth connectivity between networks) many of its key features still require elaboration. The most important areas that are yet to be finalized lie in network management.

2.3   The Evolution of Broadband Connectivity

In today's headlines, the term *information highway* usually evokes two images: the first is the Internet, a rapidly growing federation of public networks used primarily for e-mail, file access, and file transfer. The second is essentially a set of visions for the fairly near but not immediate future: various concepts for interactive entertainment, video on demand, and video marketing that are still in the early stages of development.

This book concentrates on an earlier, more comprehensive definition of internet, with a small *i*—"any interconnected set of networks." It focuses specifically upon private networks and internets established by corporate users and other large institutions (these are now being called *intranets*).

Private networking started with technologies like SNA (System Network Architecture, developed by IBM) and X.25-based packet services. SNA reflects its history and parentage. It was designed to provide communications within a corporation or other organization between a limited number of large-scale hosts (usually a few dozen), and hundreds or thousands of users. Pathways are assigned to each data-transmission session. Routing is static, and the network must be reconfigured when a new host is added. This can be cumbersome, but it provides an efficient means to move large numbers of transactions to and from a mainframe computer, in a stable environment.

X.25 refers to the packet-based protocol interface between a type of device called *Data Terminal Equipment* (DTE), which connects with the user's computer, and *Data Circuit-Terminating Equipment* (DCTE), which feeds data into the network. This technology supports transmission by segmenting data into variable-length blocks called *packets*. After the packets navigate the network they are reassembled at the other end. In a process similar to the operation of SNA—but much more flexible—X.25 establishes a pathway to the recipient and guarantees distribution.

Typical implementations of X.25 are slow, generally around 64 thousand bits per second. X.25 can be used to send data over common-carrier circuits. It has consequently been popular in Europe and other countries in which telecommunications monopolies have been reluctant to lease dedicated lines and so give up the substantial revenues collected by charging their regular tariffs.

Processing and transmission overhead is high because X.25 was designed to deliver messages reliably in an era of low-quality connections having high error rates.

As LAN technologies, Ethernet and Token Ring both transmit data in the form of frames. Messages are encapsulated in packets, tossed into the transmission stream and delivered to the recipient. This strategy makes it easy to add or delete nodes. On the other hand, congestion can occur if too many nodes are trying to heave packets onto the network at the same time. Token Ring is more structured than Ethernet: it makes for a more orderly flow of data but increases overhead.

Both Token Ring and Ethernet are mult-iaccess, connectionless systems. Neither guarantees packet delivery. They are, however, based upon limited-distance cabling with very low error rates. Furthermore, they are intended for data transmission; most protocols can recover from some data loss without serious impact to the application. It must be noted, however that ATM also does not guarantee packet delivery.

FDDI is a more recent token ring system for LANs, based on fiber optic media, that has a nominal rating of 100 Mbps. Like Ethernet and Token Ring, FDDI is limited to relatively short distances—from a single building to a fairly compact campus—although extenders and other measures permit transmission over somewhat longer distances. Token Ring and FDDI both include a prioritization feature. Tokens can be utilized to accept packets with defined priorities in preference to other packets. Multiple packets with equal priority all obtain access. The prioritization feature, however, has been used rarely on Token Ring because it was poorly documented, was given little emphasis by IBM, the sponsor of Token Ring, and did not seem to involve an important business requirement. On FDDI, the token algorithm is much more complex, as are its prioritization features, making it less cost effective to implement. It must be noted, however that ATM also does not explicitly support priority from a performance point of view. (See Chapter 1 for a discussion of this point.)

Shifting attention to WANs, Frame Relay is another technology intended to supplant legacy networks. It features lower overhead than X.25 and can support higher speeds: in the range from 64 thousand to 1.5 million bits per second. It operates by transmitting frames (very much like packets) over virtual circuits. Frame Relay is viewed by some as a transitional technology. Some telecommunications companies and other vendors have embraced it because it can deliver increased bandwidth (compared to traditional packet switching) at relatively modest additional investment in infrastructure.

Other solutions, designed primarily to deliver improved bandwidth, include Fast Ethernet, capable of a nominal capacity of 100 Mbps. Like Ethernet, Fast Ethernet lacks the technological scalability of ATM as bandwidth demands escalate out of the low hundreds of megabits per second toward gigabits (billions of bits) per second.

A high-speed technology called Fibre Channel has emerged in the past few years. Implementation remains very limited at this time, but it has a potential role in LANs, primarily for functions like direct channels between large-scale computers and storage devices or other peripherals. Fibre Channel could supplant High Performance Parallel Interface (HPPI), yet another technology developed to meet similar requirements.

Both of these recent technologies, however, lack the versatility and flexibility needed for across-the-board competition with ATM.

So far, we have discussed lower layer protocols (all, with the exception of X.25, residing at the Data Link Layer). A brief discussion of upper layer protocols follows. Beyond the basic clocking rate/speed of the underlying media, the communication throughput is ultimately controlled by these protocols.

TCP/IP (Transmission Control Protocol/Internet Protocol), which was designed in the late 1970s, has been synonymous with the public Internet but has been extensively adopted by operators of private networks. It is a protocol intended to facilitate operation of transfer points (routers) between networks. TCP/IP was originally developed to meet Department of Defense requests for a network that could continue operation despite destruction of nodes on the battlefield. It thus tolerates low-quality, error-prone circuits. This also means, however, that overhead is relatively high.

TCP/IP operates with packets up to 65,536 bytes (octets) in length. It includes an important provision that permits packets to be disassembled into smaller units without degrading the message if a receiving or transit network cannot handle longer packets. IP by itself is a best-effort protocol, like third-class mail; delivery of the data is not assured, because it does not offer error detection and recovery features. (The responsibility for these functions rests upon TCP.)

In parallel fashion, the OSI stack is a set of protocols developed by the International Organization for Standardization to serve objectives similar to those of TCP/ IP. In the United States and on the global Internet, TCP/IP—not an international standard—has largely filled this niche, although OSI remains favored in Europe and some other areas.

In the world of private corporate networks, many users are turning to TCP/IP—which is now supported by virtually all workstations and larger systems, including mainframes—to replace earlier, vendor-specific protocols.

For a while, at least, all the network architectures described above will continue to play roles in private networks. Increasingly, however, ATM will displace these architectures or be utilized as an intermediate layer supporting other protocols, such as TCP/IP and OSI. ATM offers the following features:

- It is suitable for both long-distance and local networks.

- It adapts to a wide range of physical media.

- It accommodates voice, data, images, and video.

- It is capable of supporting quality of service, congestion control, and other network management features.

- It can adjust to bursty traffic and also avoid congestion.

- It scales to much higher bandwidths than Frame Relay or other competitive architectures.

2.4 The Standardization of ATM

Telecommunications could not take place without protocols, but it is difficult to live with our current predicament of a large gamut of incompatible protocols. For data transmission, the ideal would be a universal or near-universal standard. Although at face value it appears that the voice world has come up with a single standard, there are in fact many standards. However, there has been more emphasis to achieve interoperability, so as to guarantee the ability to call anywhere in the world and be heard, than has been seen in the computer world.

For data, hundreds of official or de facto standards for networks of various kinds are in wide use. This diversity may be tolerable within LANs, but local networks also provide the connections that lead to backbone circuits and thus to other computers all over the world. Negotiating internationally accepted communications standards takes time. Procedures have been accelerated, but standard-setting is still much slower than the operation of Moore's Law.

De facto standards have arisen, with TCP/IP being the most conspicuous example. Although they may bypass the international consultative process, widely used de facto standards generally reflect a great deal of structured discussion by support groups, users, vendors, and others.

Even if standards and other characteristics are different, bridges, routers, and associated software may provide interoperability and make it possible for networks to exchange data with other networks. These compromises, however, may slow everything down and cause complications.

2.4.1 *The ATM Standard*

ATM took shape through the full international standardization procedure, although the standard specifications do not resolve every possible issue. Researchers in the 1980s were looking at the best method to achieve high-speed packetized data transmission. ATM grew out of other well-established standards.

ATM began with ISDN standards activities. ISDN is fully digital, but is characteristic of its generation. Its Physical Layer (level 1) is based on copper wire, and its bandwidth is limited to hundreds of thousands of bits per second. ISDN has been popular in Europe and Japan.

The European Union has stimulated a program of universal or near-universal ISDN availability before the end of this decade. Adoption in the United States has been more spotty, although regional telecommunications companies are turning to ISDN as a relatively low-cost means to increase bandwidth to subscribers.

ISDN allocates the available bandwidth into three channels using Time Division Multiplexing (also known as *synchronous transfer mode*) technology: two 64 kilobit channels for data transport and one 16-kilobit channel for signaling (housekeeping messages.) The signaling channel is used to establish a connection; the data transport channels then supports transfer of the information.

ISDN is strictly a circuit-switched service of defined bandwidth capabilities (nx64, $1 \leq n \leq 30$). It was not designed to support broadband applications.

A decision was made in the mid 1980s to seek a new standard that could be based on ISDN principles and support optical fiber in the WAN; because of the media used, the supported speeds are much higher. The newcomer became known as B-ISDN (for Broadband ISDN).

Although both are digital, ATM technology differs from ISDN insofar that ISDN is a *synchronous transfer mode technology.* ISDN is a circuit-switched technology without any statistical multiplexing or gains; on the other hand, ATM is an asynchronous transfer packet technology with statistical multiplexing and gain. Because the user and the carrier gambles on statistical multiplexing, sophisticated traffic management capabilities are required in the switching hardware.

2.4.2 Background Research

ATM concepts arose from research conducted in the mid 1980s. This work established that data units of fixed length were easier to switch at very high speeds than frames (like Ethernet, Token Ring, and FDDI), which could vary in length.

This philosophy was influenced by research done at IBM on a device called the Paris (Packetized Automatic Routing Integrated System) switch, which serviced both variable and fixed-length packets. The Paris project assumed, however, that all traffic would consist of data. It was a system in which senders could transmit only if they had received a token, awarded on the basis of an average data flow. (IBM later abandoned Paris and embraced ATM.)

The B-ISDN debates were carried on between two factions. The X.25 faction was concerned, above all, about more efficient, versatile, and less costly data transmission. The data faction was relatively unconcerned about the time of arrival, and could tolerate some delay while packets are reassembled. They were very concerned with protecting the integrity of the information. The other faction, the public telephone network, emphasized time-sensitive information, like voice, in which consistent sequence and timely delivery are crucial. Limited information loss was acceptable to them.

There were, however, common grounds. For packetized video, packets must come through at a regular rate to avoid transmission jitter. This is easier to accomplish with relatively short packets.

The two factions resolved their differences by deciding on a fixed-length packet, called a *cell,* that could be transmitted in an orderly, high-speed fashion over a switched network. This solution would provide the cost advantages of data networks combined with the predictability of voice networks.

But how long should those cells be? The data faction advocated a 64-byte specification, while the voice faction demanded 32 bytes. An agreement was reached: each cell would contain a 48-byte payload, accompanied by five additional bytes to identify the cell and carry other transmission information.

For high-bandwidth networks based on fiber, ATM is frequently employed with a Layer 1 standard, called SONET. SONET defines a series of bandwidth levels for transmission over fiber networks (for twisted-pair campus/desktop systems other Layer 1 standards are used.)

SONET rates consist of multiples of a base of 51.840 Mbps. Current ATM technology supports bandwidths at the OC-1 (Optical Carrier - 1) level (51.840 Mbps), at the OC-3 level (155.520 Mbps), and at the OC-12 level (622.08 Mbps). SONET levels now targeted by systems developers would deliver 1244.160 Mbps (OC-24) and 2488.320 Mbps (OC-48). SONET standards are now nearly ready for OC-192 speeds (about 10 Gbps).

For user access, current ATM services support the 155.520-Mbps speed; the 622.080-Mbps speed is currently supported only at the trunk level. Outside the US, the SONET concept is described in the context of the Synchronous Digital Hierarchy (SDH); effectively, this hierarchy uses building blocks of 155.520 Mbps rather than building blocks of 51.840 Mbps. However, they are basically consistent for appropriate values of the aggregate bandwidth.

OC-24 and OC-48 would represent the gigabit network concept mentioned so often in public discussion. Applied with ATM technology, these bandwidth levels should be achievable later in this decade, in terms of actual services.

2.5 *ATM as an Enabling Technology*

As noted in Chapter 1, ATM's architecture, as elaborated by bodies like The ATM Forum, create possibilities beyond the reach of earlier technologies.

The ATM Forum has focused on issues of interoperability that also affect other networking technologies. It appears that ATM may resolve these issues more quickly than was the case for its predecessors. This is primarily due to two factors, focus and commitment. The ATM Forum consists of a large number of vendor, user, government, and academic representatives whose commitment to the success of ATM is, in some people's view, unparalleled.

FDDI, for example, encountered some early difficulties in linking workstations from different manufacturers. Token Ring also had problems of this kind; (Ethernet encountered fewer interoperability obstacles because of the inherent simplicity of its architecture.) This predicament was due to the lack of an organization focusing on implementation and deployment issues.

In the campus environment, ATM uses multimode fiber to derive 100 Mbps (using FDDI-like encoding) or singlemode fiber to derive 155 Mbps (using Fibre Channel Standard (FCS)-like encoding), thereby not utilizing the fiber to its full potential. Also, it uses UTP 5 twisted pair to support speeds up to 155 Mbps. Hence, ATM provides high speed when and only when it uses the underlying media to the full potential. These larger transmission capacities, used in conjunction with appropriate switching technology, make it easier to cope with bursty traffic. Ethernet, with its 10-Mbps ceiling, can also handle bursty traffic, but is hindered by the contention issue and the easy-to-reach ceiling. As we have discussed, there are transmission (now 622 Mbps) and switching (now 2-20 Gbps) ceilings in ATM, but these are, at this time, more difficult to overwhelm.

ATM's dynamic allocation of bandwidth makes it easier to offer different classes of service to support different application classes. The transparency of the upper layers in ATM, when appropriate adaptation is provided (in pertinent equipment), makes it possible for ATM to be employed in multiple types of LAN and WAN topologies, and thus in every segment of the end-to-end connection.

ATM can be economically deployed in specific corporate environments, and its cost-effectiveness will increase over time. Error checking is performed only on the header, and not on the payload. This means that error-free reception of payload is not guaranteed at the ATM Layer. (It will be guaranteed at the TCP/ IP layer.) This is based on today's high-quality, low-noise transmission media. Fiber media, used with the SONET Physical Layer protocol, makes available high capacity to the connected users. However, there is still a need to support statistical multiplexing and bandwidth overbooking, to obtain transmission efficiencies, particularly in the long haul. It follows that in ATM, sophisticated congestion control is needed to yield a very small probability of cell loss even under significant traffic levels. These characteristics add up to a technology that can permit users and applications developers to explore possibilities that have not been feasible in a cost-effective manner until now.

2.6 Challenges Facing ATM

It cannot be presumed, however, that ATM technology has been developed to the point where every possible open issue has been resolved. Issues that require further work include:

- *Support of legacy networks* In an interworking mechanism called LAN emulation (LANE), packets with length and characteristics differing from ATM's PDUs (i.e., Ethernet, or Token-Ring) transit an ATM network and are delivered to a legacy or ATM network on the receiving end. LAN emulation provides users with a migration path from existing architectures without passing through successive stages of large-scale reinvestment. To dispel some misconceptions, it must be noted, however, that the prospective user has to make immediate investment to acquire LANE technology to support some of the ATM functions at this time. The transition is then from Ethernet/Token Ring, to LANE, to ATM. Another approach would be for the user to save the funds invested in this partial migration to ATM, to better equip himself or herself to make the direct migration from Ethernet/Token Ring to ATM at a later date.

The LANE solution requires investments just to support today's relative low bandwidth requirements, but later it could be difficult to scale up to meeting the challenges of evolving network traffic patterns. Traffic concentration using ATM's higher capacity could overload tributary Token Ring and Ethernet networks by dumping bursts of information that choke the receiving networks.

In addition, there are two other ways to support legacy environments in ATM that have to be considered: support of classical IP over ATM (CIOA), and support of Multi-Protocols over ATM (MPOA).

The desire to protect investments must be traded off against the risks of poor overall performance. In addition, solutions must be found for problems of network addresses brought about by connections with legacy networks. Even within the ATM domain, problems raised by address resolution and flow control have not been solved completely.

It is also desirable to integrate Frame Relay into ATM. Alternatively, ATM circuits might have to be utilized at lower speeds than SONET speeds to accommodate legacy traffic.

- *Applications design*   Applications like traditional e-mail may run well on ATM but do not take full advantage of its capabilities. Managers may choose to confine such traffic to alternative channels like the public Internet.

- *Security levels and quality of service considerations*   These also need to be developed further in the context of ATM. Current capabilities are limited and some applications (e.g., transport of Motion Picture Expert Group 2 video), are utilizing their own security methods above the ATM Layer. These considerations border on the classical polemic as to who should provide security: carriers argue that the applications should implement security measures; application developers argue that carriers should provide security.

- *Management and the network environment*   Elementary management—when a port flashes red, etc.—on ATM is not much different from earlier technologies. In the past, however, crucial issues like traffic flows, prioritization, chargebacks, and other accounting procedures have not been addressed adequately. At this time there is little ATM management work underway in these areas.

Some users may be relatively tolerant of cell loss but require the fastest possible delivery. Others—pathologists and others who depend upon the resolution of medical images, for example—are very sensitive to cell loss (although correctable at the TCP Layer) but may be willing to permit somewhat slower transmission or higher price. These issues can be addressed via the service classes supported by the carrier or switch (e.g., Available Bit Rate, Variable Bit Rate, Constant Bit Rate, or Unspecified Bit Rate). However, equipment must be developed to support these service classes, in true accordance and in conformance with the standards. In particular, feedback mechanisms must be developed in both network and user equipment to support Available Bit Rate services.

Equipment vendors are focusing on product delivery, but traffic management issues related to the statistical management of the classes of traffic just enumerated are holding back the full implementation of ATM. In the opinion of many users, as well as service providers, the switch's ability to shape the traffic and support connections with specific class of service with minimal loss of cells is also crucial.

Problems that might occur during a transmission across multiple networks (e.g., a campus network and a WAN) are another issue. These relate to availability, quality of service, and alternative routing in case of failure. ATM should provide resiliency from multiple failure situations within the network. If a problem occurs on the network, ATM must be able to reroute virtual circuits which traverse the faulty path. This must be done transparently to the applications residing on the network. However, some problems remain. For example, is it best to remap a circuit to a different path, which might work but would not necessarily support the same grade of service? This could cause a loss of session. If that happens, what are the best recovery procedures? Some of these issues are being addressed by the Broadband Intercarrier Interface (B-ICI) work now underway.

- *Scalability* It is not yet clear how far ATM performance will be able to scale upward with large increases in the number of devices and geographical size. Scalability in speed is not an issue, but at very high speeds, switching and propagation delays could have consequences. ATM's scalability can adapt to the distances characteristic of ordinary WANs, but will ATM scale to global dimensions? Another unresolved question is: Do applications scale on virtual networks?

Questions like these are being addressed by The ATM Forum, by vendors, and by individual users. The search for solutions starts from the realization that ATM is a technology that can take many forms and be adapted to many uses. Until the implications of these complexities have been worked out fully, widespread adoption of ATM will take place only gradually. As this process advances, however, ATM will increasingly become the solution of choice for a growing number of users.

References

[1] D. Minoli, *Telecommunications Technologies Handbook* (Artech House, 1991).

chapter 3

ATM Architecture

This chapter outlines some of the principal features of ATM; later chapters will describe the characteristics related to the management of these features in greater detail. Topics addressed include:

- *The structure of its 53-byte cells, or labeled information containers.*
- *The Physical Layer, ATM Layer, and ATM Adaptation Layer (AAL) that organize appropriate Service Data Units (SDUs)/PDUs for transmission. Special attention is given to the Adaptation Layer, which governs the treatment of cells to accommodate the special requirements of voice, video, and data traffic. The Service Layer sits on top of the AAL and uses specific AALs (e.g., AAL 1 or AAL 5) to provide the appropriate services to the legacy protocols (e.g., IP) residing at the Network Layer.*
- *LAN Emulation, in support of legacy LANs.*
- *Different technology solutions for ATM switches.*
- *The remaining agenda in the ATM arena—what needs to be done by the standards-making bodies to resolve issues like traffic management in a large network, additional LAN emulation features, support for twisted-pair media (particularly at the higher ATM rates), interoperability, and congestion control.*

3.1 Overview

This chapter provides a short tutorial on ATM. It is assumed that the reader already has a working knowledge of the field, and so the description is limited in scope. The assumption is that the reader has investigated ATM and would be inclined to deploy the technology in his or her organization, but is not sure of the network management implications. If more background on ATM is needed, the reader may refer to a number of texts, including [1].

ATM is a set of standards, defined originally by the International Telecommunication Union, Telecommunications (ITU-T), formerly known as the Consultative Committee for International Telephone and Telegraph (CCITT). These standards establish basic specifications for ATM protocols and interfaces. The ITU-T standards for ATM specify the cell size and structure, and the User-to-Network Interface (UNI). Note that there are two kinds of UNIs—one for access to public networks, and one, called *Private UNI*, for access to a customer-owned ATM network (specifically to a hub, router, or switch). For the public UNI, the Physical Layer is defined for data rates of 1.544 Mbps, 45 Mbps, and 155 Mbps (SONET OC-3). For the Private UNI, different rates and media (UTP, STP, single mode fiber, and multimode fiber) are defined.

ATM can be described as a packet transfer mode based on asynchronous time division multiplexing and the use of small fixed-length data units known as cells. ATM provides a connection-oriented service (although in theory it can also be used to support connectionless services such as Switched Multimegabit Data Service, SMDS). Note that LANs such as Ethernet, FDDI, and Token Ring support a connectionless service. Each ATM connection is assigned its own set of transmission resources; however, these resources have to be taken out of a shared pool which is generally smaller than the maximum needed to support the entire population. This is the reason for the much-talked about traffic management problem in ATM. ATM nevertheless makes it possible to share bandwidth through multiplexing (multiple messages transmitted over the same physical circuit). Multiple virtual channels can be supported on the access link, and the aggregate bandwidth of these channels can be overbooked. (ATM relies on statistical multiplexing to carry the load.) Within the network, expensive resources are "rationed," and bandwidth must be allocated dynamically. ATM is thus able to maximize bandwidth utilization.

A connection is established through preprovisioning with the carrier or private devices (thereby establishing Permanent Virtual Channels, PVCs), or through signaling mechanisms (thereby establishing Switched Virtual Channels, SVCs). Connections supported by these channels (PVCs or SVCs) enable computers or other systems on the network to communicate with one another. A virtual circuit can be either switched (temporary) or permanent.

Network resources, bandwidth, quality of service, multipoint capabilities, etc., are requested as a connection is established. A connection is established if the network is able to meet the request; if not, the request is rejected. Once the virtual circuit is defined, the call connection control assigns an interface-specific Virtual Channel Identifier (VCI) and Virtual Path Identifier (VPI) to identify the connection. These labels have only interface-specific meaning. Two different sets of VPIs/VCIs are assigned to the two endpoints of the connection. Inside the network, as many sets of VPIs/VCIs as needed (along the path) are used by the network, invisibly to the end users.

As long as the connection remains active, the assigned VCI and VPI represent valid pointers into routing tables in the network; the tables (accessed via the VPI/VCI) are used to accomplish cell routing through the network.

3.2 The ATM Cell

The ATM cell has a 48-byte payload, accompanied by a five-byte header that is divided into fields. (See Table 3.1.) Headers are of two types: the User-to-Network Interface (UNI) and the Network-to-Network Interface (NNI).

8	7	6	5	4	3	2	1
Generic Flow Control				Virtual Path Identifier			
Virtual Path Identifier (continued)				Virtual Channel Identifier			
Virtual Channel Identifier (continued)							
Virtual Channel Identifier (continued)				Payload Type Identifier			Cell-loss Priority
Header Error Control							
Payload							

Table 3.1   ATM cell structure

Fields within the UNI cell are:

- The first field, of 4 bits, provides for Generic Flow Control (GFC). It is not currently used and is intended to support a local bus (extension) function to connect multiple Broadband Terminal Equipment to the same UNI as equal peers. (Note that multiple users can be connected to the UNI today by using a multiplexing—not peer—function.) This is equivalent to the SAPI function in ISDN.

- A 24-bit routing pointing field is subdivided into an 8-bit VPI subfield and a 16-bit space for VCI. It indirectly identifies the route laid out for traffic over a specific connection, by providing a pointing function into switch tables that contain the actual route.

- Three bits are allocated to the Payload Type Identifier (PTI), which identifies whether each cell is a user cell or a control cell, used for network management.

- A single-bit Cell Loss Priority (CLP) marker is used to distinguish two levels of cell loss priority. Zero identifies a higher priority cell that should receive preferred loss treatment if cells are discarded due to network congestion. One indicates lower-priority cells whose loss is less critical.

- Header Error Control (HEC) is an 8-bit cyclic redundancy code (CRC) computed over the ATM cell header. The HEC is capable of detecting all single-bit errors and certain multiple bit errors. It can be used to correct all single-bit errors, but this is not mandatory. This mechanism is employed by a receiving device to infer that the cell is in error and should simply be discarded. It is also used for cell-boundary recovery at the Physical Layer.

- The remaining 48 bytes are devoted to payload.

- The Network-to-Network (NNI) cell structure has one difference. The 4-bit GFC field is dropped, and the VPI field is expanded from 8 bits to 12.

3.3 Addressing

Addressing is a fundamental need in any network. The ITU-T ATM protocols call for a hierarchical ISDN telephone numbering scheme, specified in ITU-T E.164, to be used in ATM. The standard permits the ATM address to be divided into an address and a subaddress. The ATM Forum recommends that the address describe the point of attachment to the public network (if connected), and that the subaddress identify a particular end station within a private network [3]. Note that the VPI/VCI are just labels, not E.164 addresses; they are table pointers for the relaying of cells on to their destination, based on switch routing tables.

The ATM Forum specification permits two address formats to be used as private ATM address. One is the E.164 format, and the other is a 20-byte address modeled after the address format of an OSI Network Service Access Point (NSAP), as seen in Figure 3.1. The octets are assigned as follows: A) Authority and Format Identifier (AFI); B) Data Country Code/International Code Desig-

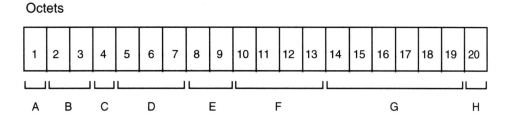

Figure 3.1 The ATM Forum's addressing format for private ATM networks

nator (DDC/IDC); C) Domain-specific part Format Identifier (DFI); D) Administration Authority (AA); E) Reserved; F) Routing Domain (RD) and Area (selected by organization); G) End System Identifier (ESI); and H) unused. *Note:* The end system contains a valid IEEE 802 MAC address. An alternative format allows the 8 bytes after the AFI field to contain an E.164 address. This option permits both public and private subaddresses to be combined into a single ATM address.

3.4 The Physical and ATM Layers

An extension of the conventional OSI seven-layer stack (Chapter 1) can be used to describe the structure of the ATM protocol: a reference model specific to ATM depicts its structure more clearly. This reference model distinguishes three basic layers. See Table 3.2.

Beginning from the bottom, these are the Physical Layer, the ATM Layer, and the ATM Adaptation Layer (AAL). Each is divided further into sublayers. The Physical Layer includes two sublayers:

- Like any other Data Link Layer protocol, ATM is not defined in terms of a specific type of physical carrying medium. Rather, it is necessary to define

Convergence Sublayer	AAL	CS	Data Link Layer
Segmentation and Reassembly Sublayer		SAR	
Generic flow control *(if/when implemented)* Cell VPI/VC translation Cell multiplex and demultiplex	ATM		
Cell rate decoupling HEC header sequence generation/verification Cell delineation Transmission frame adaptation Transmission frame generation/recovery	TC		PHY
Bit timing Physical medium	PM		

Table 3.2   ATM reference model

appropriate Physical Layer protocols for cell transmission. The Physical Medium (PM) Sublayer interfaces with the physical medium, and provides transmission and reception of bits over the physical facility. It also provides the physical medium with proper bit timing and line coding. There will be different manifestations of this layer, based on the specifics of the underlying medium (e.g., DS1 link, DS3 link, SONET, or UTP).

- The Transmission Convergence (TC) Sublayer receives a bit stream from the PM Sublayer and passes it in cell form to the ATM Layer. Its functions include cell rate decoupling, cell delineation, generation and verification of the HEC sequence, transmission frame adaptation, and the generation/recovery of transmission frames.

The ATM Layer, in the middle of the ATM stack, is responsible for one of ATM's most "trivial" functions: encapsulating downward-coming data into cells from a number of sources and multiplexing the cell stream; conversely it is responsible for de-encapsulating upward-coming cells and demultiplexing the resulting stream out to a number of sources. The ATM Layer controls multiplexing (the transmission of cells belonging to different connections over a single cell stream) and demultiplexing (distinguishing cells of various connections as they are pulled off the flow of cells). ATM, as a Data Link Layer protocol, is medium-independent: it is capable of performing these functions on a wide variety of physical media.

In addition, the ATM Layer acts as an intermediary between the layer above it and the Physical Layer below. It generates cell headers, attaches them to the data delivered to it by the Adaptation Layer, and then delivers the properly tagged cells to the Physical Layer. Conversely, it strips headers from cells containing data arriving from the Physical Layer, before passing the data to the Application Layer.

ATM supports two kinds of channels: Virtual Channels (VCs) and Virtual Paths (VPs). VCs are communication channels of specified service capabilities between two intermediary ATM peers. Virtual Channel Connections (VCCs) are a concatenation of VCs to support end system-to-end system communication. VPs are groups (bundles) of VCs. Virtual Path Connections (VPCs) are a concatenation of VPs to support end system-to-end system communication.

VCs and VPs are identified by their VCI/VPI tags.[1] The ATM Layer assures that cells are arranged in the proper sequence, but it does not identify and

---

[1] Do not confuse VCs/VPs with connections. VCs are channels; connections are instances of end-to-end communications. Connections are identified by Call Reference and Connection Identifiers included in the Setup message used in signaling. See [2] for a more extensive description.

retransmit mislaid or damaged cells. If this is to be done, it must be accomplished by higher level procedures. The ATM Layer also translates VCI/VPI information.

An ATM switch has its own routing table to identify each connection. In transit between switches, cell VPI/VCI identifiers (routing table pointers) will be different. Switches translate cell identifiers as they transfer cells onward to other switches.

Finally, the ATM Layer performs management functions. If the Payload Type Identifier (PTI) identifies a cell as a control packet[2], the ATM Layer responds by carrying out the appropriate functions.

3.4.1 Class of Service: The Adaptation Layer

The ATM Adaptation Layer (AAL) allows various Network Layer protocols to utilize the service of the ATM Layer. As discussed earlier, the ATM Layer supports only the lower portion of the Data Link Layer. Hence, for the Network Layer to use ATM, a "filler sublayer" is required. This is analogous to IP use over a LAN: the Media Access Control (MAC) Layer supports only the lower portion of the Data Link Layer; consequently, the Logical Link Control Layer is sandwiched in between.

Fundamentally, the AAL keeps the Network Layer *happy* by enabling it to use ATM transparently. The basic function of the AAL is to segment the downward-coming data (Network Layer PDU) into cells, and to reassemble upward-coming data into a PDU acceptable to the Network Layer.

It is critical to understand that AALs are end-to-end functions (end system-to-end system). A network providing pure ATM will not be aware of, cognizant of, or act upon AAL information. (In the case of service interworking in the network, there has to be network interpretation of the AAL information.)

In one classical view of the ATM protocol model, a service layer resides above the AAL, in the end systems. Hence, by further elaboration one can say that in a coincidental manner, the AAL differentiates in the end system the treatment of different categories of cells, and permits responses to user-to-user quality of service (QoS) issues. A number of AALs has been defined to meet different user-to-user QoS requirements. Again, however, a network providing pure ATM will not be aware of, cognizant of, or act upon AAL information. Therefore, the AAL-supported service differentiation is among end system peers, and is not the mechanism used by the ATM network to support

---

[2] The type of cells are: Idle, Unassigned, VP/VC traffic, and VC OAM traffic.

network QoS. We use the term *user-to-user quality of service* to describe the kind of end system-to-end system peer-to-peer connection service differentiation (this connection being viewed as external to the ATM network).

For example, an end system TV monitor needs a continuous bit stream from a remote codec to paint a picture; it may have been decided that an ATM network is to be used to transport the bits. Because of the codec/ monitor requirements, the bits have to be enveloped in such a manner that clock information is carried end to end so that jitter is less than some specified value. To accomplish this, the bits are enveloped using AAL 1. From the ATM network's point of view, this is totally immaterial: the ATM network receives cells and carries them to the other end; the network delivers cells. The network does not render a different type of QoS to these cells based solely on the fact that they had AAL 1 information in them: the network was not even aware of the content. Naturally, it is desirable for the network to provide reasonable QoS to this stream, based on some kind of knowledge or arrangement. How is that accomplished?

The different QoS requirements obtained via an ATM network are based on user-to-network negotiation, not by the content of a cell. In PVC, this negotiation is via a service order. Here, the user would tell the network (on paper) that he or she wanted to get reasonable service for a certain stream carrying codec video. The network provider would make arrangements to terminate this stream on a switch line card, where for example, a lot of buffers were allocated. The network provider then tells the user (on paper) to employ a certain VPI/VCI combination (say 22/33) for this stream. Here is what happens: the user sends cells over the physical interface terminated at the card's port. Certain cells arriving on the interface have VPI/VCI=44/66; these get some kind of QoS treatment. Then some cells arrive on the interface that have VPI/VCI=22/33; these cells get the agreed-to QoS by receiving specific buffer treatment by the switch. In SVC, a similar mechanism is in place, except that instead of communicating the information using paper, the call-setup message is used (with automatic call negotiation).

In any event, the QoS in the ATM network is not based on the fact that the cells carried a certain AAL. It is the other way around. The user needs a certain end system-to-end system QoS. He or she then needs to do two things: select the (network-invisible) AAL, and separately inform the carrier of the type of QoS needed.

AALs utilize a (small) portion of the 48-byte payload field of the ATM cell by inserting additional control bits. In all AALs, the ATM header retains its usual configuration and functions. Notice that the data coming down the protocol stack is first treated by the AAL by adding its own header. This AAL PDU must naturally fit inside the ATM PDU. Hence, the AAL header must fit inside the payload of the lower layer, here ATM. To say that quality of service definitions are obtained at the cost of reductions in payload is not exactly correct: AAL provides an appropriate segmentation and reassembly function—QoS is supported by the network switch. As discussed, AAL classes support peer-to-peer connection differentiation.

In some instances, users determine that the ATM Layer service is sufficient for their requirements, so the AAL protocol remains empty. This occurs, for example, if the Network Layer protocol can ride directly on ATM (this is unlikely for legacy protocols), or if the two end systems do not need additional coordination. In the majority of cases, however, this AAL Layer is crucial to the end system protocol stack because it enables ATM to accommodate the requirements of voice, image/video, and data traffic while providing different classes of service to meet the distinctive requirements of each type of traffic. See Table 3.3.

Two sublayers make up the AAL: the Segmentation and Reassembly Sublayer (SAR) and the Convergence Sublayer (CS).

	Class A	Class B	Class C	Class D
Application	Voice, video, clear channel	Packet video	Data	
Timing (source-destination)	Needed		Not needed	
Mode	Connection oriented			Connectionless
Bit rate	Constant	Variable		

The ITU-T specifications apply three broad criteria to distinguish four classes of ATM service, labeled A, B, C, and D; these end-to-end (network-external) criteria are:

- Time relation between source and destination.
- Bit rate.
- Connection mode.

To express these criteria in practical form, four AALs have been developed: AAL 1, AAL 2 (not yet defined fully), AAL 3/4, and AAL 5 (focused upon data transmission).

Table 3.3   ATM classes of service

The SAR Sublayer segments higher-layer information into a size suitable for cell payloads through a virtual connection. It also reassembles the contents of cells in a virtual connection into data units that can be delivered to higher layers.

Functions like message identification and time/clock recovery are performed by the CS Sublayer. The four end-to-end (network-external) classes of service are:

- *Class A*   (for example, clear-channel voice and fixed bit-rate video, such as movies or high-quality teleconferencing). A time relation exists between source and destination. The bit rate is constant, and the Network Layer level service is connection-oriented.

- *Class B*   As in Class A, there is a time relation between the source and the destination. Network Layer level service is connection-oriented, but the bit rate can be varied. Examples include audio and video with variable bit rates (e.g., unbuffered video codecs having motion compensation).

- *Class C*   The Network Layer level service is connection-oriented, but there is no time relation between the source and the destination; the bit rate is variable. This can, for example, meet the requirements of connection-oriented data transfer and signaling.

- *Class D*   Intended for applications like connectionless data transport; none of the three parameters applies: service is connectionless, there is no time relation between source and destination, and the bit rate is variable.

These classes are general descriptions of types of user traffic. They do not set specific parameters or establish values. Equipment from multiple vendors based on different parameters may thus find it difficult to establish connections. AALs are end-to-end and generally external to the ATM network; considerations on AALs relate to consideration of end user equipment. AALs are considered by the network only when there is service interworking. Examples include frame relay-to-ATM interworking in the network; legacy LAN-to-ATM interworking (LANE) in the network; and private line-to-ATM interworking in the network. For example, in the first case, frames come in and cells go out. There is another case where AALs are used in the network, but this is totally transparent to the user. This situation (called by some *network interworking*) is when the network supports a *carriage function* over ATM. Examples include frame relay carriage over an ATM network; ETHERNET carriage over ATM network (e.g., ETHERNET bridging); and private line carriage over an ATM network. For example, the frame relay user gives a relay frame to the (ATM-based) network. The network takes the frame and segments it into a stream of cells utilizing AAL 5 protocols. The stream is carried across the network, and in proximity of the destination, the cells are reassembled into a relay frame using AAL 5. The destination is handed a frame. This type of service is called *frame relay carriage over ATM* or *frame relay-to-ATM network interworking*.

So far, three AAL protocols have been defined to support the three classes of service in the end-system: AAL1, AAL 3/4, and AAL 5. Computers, routers, and other devices must employ the same AAL, to communicate with one another on an ATM network. The protocols provide the following functions:

- AAL 1 meets the performance requirements of Service Class A. It is intended for voice, video, and other constant bit-rate traffic, and its performance, to the upper layers of the end-system stack, is similar to today's digital private lines. Four bits in the payload are allocated to Sequence Number (SN) and Sequence Number Protection (SNP) functions. It is used in SMDS.

- AAL 2 aims at Class B requirements; it has not yet been defined.

- AAL 3/4 is intended for connectionless data services. Four bytes are devoted to control functions, including a multiplexing identifier as well as Segment Type (ST) and SNP indicators it issued in SMDS.

- AAL 5 is also intended for data communications, including services like Frame Relay. The ATM Forum and IETF recommend that AAL 5 also be used to encapsulate IP packets in the user's end system. See Table 3.4.

AAL 5 is specifically designed to offer a service for data communication with lower overhead and better error detection. It was developed because computer vendors realized that AAL 3/4 is not suited to their needs. In addition to the header, AAL 3/4 takes an additional 4 bytes for control information from the payload field, reducing its capacity by 8.4 percent. The vendors also maintain that the error detection method of AAL 3/4 does not cope adequately with issues of lost or corrupted cells.

Information payload	PAD	Control	Length	CRC-32
0 – 64K	0 – 47	1 Byte	2 Bytes	4 Bytes

Table 3.4   AAL Type 5 CS-PDU

With AAL 5, the CS Sublayer creates a CS Protocol Data Unit (CS-PDU) when it receives a packet from the higher application layer. The first field is the CS Information Payload field, containing user data. The PAD field assures that the CS-PDU is 48 bytes aligned. A 1-byte control field remains undefined, reserved for further use. The 2-byte length field indicates the length of information payload, and the CRC field is used to detect errors.

When the CS Sublayer passes the CS-PDU to the SAR Sublayer, it is divided into many SAR Protocol Data Units (SAR-PDUs). The SAR Sublayer then passes SAR-PDUs to the ATM Layer, which carries out transmission of the cell.

When passing on the final SAR-PDU within the CS-PDU, the SAR indicates the end of the CS-PDU transfer by setting to 1 the payload type identifier (PTI) in the header. By using the CS length field and the cyclic loss redundancy code (CRC) in the header's HEC (header error control), the AAL can detect the loss or corruption of cells.

3.5 LAN Emulation

3.5.1 Overview

Of the main specifications which The ATM Forum has developed to date for users in the LAN arena, is LAN Emulation (LANE). Traditional LANs provide a connectionless MAC service, supporting arbitration among end stations for access to a shared physical transmission medium (e.g., the twisted-pair cable). ATM, on the other hand, offers a connection-orientated communication service based on switched point-to-point physical media. To achieve connectionless MAC service over an ATM link, a protocol layer emulating the connectionless service of a LAN must be placed on top of the AAL. This layer, depicted in Figure 3.2, is called the ATM MAC. This layer emulates the LAN service by creating the appearance of a virtual shared medium from an actual switched point-to-point network.

Version 1.0 of LANE was adopted in 1995, and additional work is now underway. The purpose of LANE is to provide users with a migration path to ATM without immediately incurring the high cost of implementing ATM to the desktop. (However, LANE equipment must be deployed.) Figure 3.3 illustrates the LANE architecture.

In legacy LANs, the membership of an individual station in a LAN segment is dictated by the physical connection of the station to the shared medium. Membership of a station in an ATM LAN segment is identified by logical connections to the multicast ATM virtual connection. Hence, membership of an ATM LAN segment is defined logically rather than physically; the membership information is stored in a management database. This capability of ATM LANs offers terminal portability and mobility.

LANE provides transparent support for LAN-based applications since it functions at Layer 2, like a bridge. Effectively, it is a converting bridge technology be-

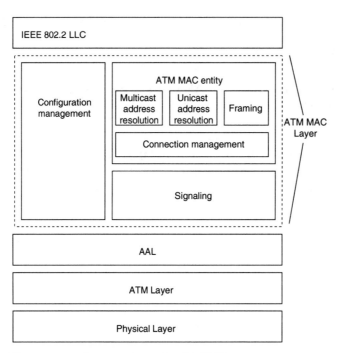

Figure 3.2   Protocol stack of LANE

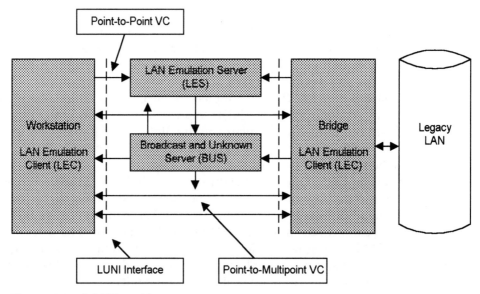

Figure 3.3   LANE architecture

tween the connectionless Ethernet/Token Ring environment and the connection-oriented ATM environment. It also allows ATM-enabled devices to communicate with LAN Emulation devices. LAN Emulation allows for logically separate emulated LANs to coexist on the same physical ATM network.

LAN Emulation does not allow users to leverage the end-to-end class of service functionality which ATM provides in end systems; however, it will provide for a higher bandwidth and a more stable network infrastructure for large building and campus backbones. It also requires that Ethernet, Token Ring, and FDDI be separate, since it does not provide transparent bridge functions between these technologies. It does not support MAC layer protocols such as FDDI SMT or Token Management.

3.5.2 Components of LAN Emulation

Traditional LANs use the 48-bit MAC address. The MAC address is globally unique. This nonhierarchical LAN address assigned by the manufacturer, identifies a network interface in the end station. The use of a MAC address is practical in a single LAN segment or in a small internet. However, large bridged networks become difficult to manage and experience large amounts of broadcast traffic in attempting to locate end stations. The address space of a large network is preferably hierarchical. This makes it easier to locate a particular point on the network; such an address, however, restricts the mobility of the network users. The E.164 address used in public ATM is hierarchical.

To emulate a LAN, the ATM network must support addressing using MAC address scheme: each ATM MAC entity must be assigned a 48-bit MAC address from the same address space, to facilitate its identification. As noted, an ATM network, whether public or private, uses a hierarchical address. The address resolution operation in LANE binds the end station MAC address to the physical address of the ATM port to which the end station is currently connected. When an end station is attached to an ATM switch port, a registration protocol exchanges the MAC address between the ATM network and the end station.

The LAN Emulation service consists of several pieces of software and hardware operating on one or more platforms. Prior to explaining the operation, some definitions are necessary:

- LAN Emulation Client (LEC). Software that resides at the edge device. The edge device is where the emulated service is rendered in terms of the conversion between protocols.

- LAN Emulation Server (LES). Provides initialization and configuration functions, address registration and address resolution. Since ATM and legacy LANs use very different addressing schemes, a way to map the two is important, particularly with a view to subnetworks, where the addressing capabilities of ATM may be lacking.

- Broadcast and Unknown Server (BUS). Provides the mechanism to send broadcasts and multicasts to all devices within the Emulated LAN.

- LAN Emulation User-Network Interface (LUNI). The protocol used by the LEC to communicate over the ATM network.

In a traditional LAN, all frames (unicast, multicast, and broadcast) are broadcast to all stations on the shared physical medium; each station selects the frames it wants to receive. A LAN segment can be emulated by connecting a set of stations on the ATM network via an ATM multicast virtual connection. The multicast virtual connection emulates the broadcast physical medium of the LAN. This connection becomes the broadcast channel of the ATM LAN segment. With this capability, any station may broadcast to all others on the ATM LAN segment by transmitting on the shared ATM multicast virtual connection.

3.5.3 *LAN Emulation Operation*

Background Considerations

Address resolution in LANE can be implemented, in principle, by either a broadcast mechanism similar to IP ARP, or by a distributed database mechanism. In both, the source sends an address resolution request containing the destination MAC address and its own MAC and ATM addresses [3].

For unicast address resolution, a broadcast mechanism requires that the source broadcast the requests to all stations on the local ATM LAN segment and to all ATM LAN segments connected via bridges. After *self-checks*, the station that owns the requested MAC address replies with its current ATM address. The reply may be sent on the broadcast channel for the ATM LAN segment, or the destination may set up an ATM connection to the source. For multicast ARP, an algorithm may be specified to convert from a group MAC address to a group ATM address; alternatively, a simple server mechanism may be implemented for multicast addresses.

In database address resolution, the method recommended by The ATM Forum, requests are received by an address server in the network. The server keeps a table containing MAC-to-ATM address mappings. The table is updated as part of the registration protocol whenever a station joins or leaves the network. The server may support both unicast and multicast address resolution. The address server must be implemented as a distributed database to protect against failure. In turn, this requires a more complex implementation than a broadcast implementation.

The situation where the destination is not directly attached to the ATM network but is attached to a LAN connected to the ATM network via bridge, is more complex. When using a broadcast ARP implementation, the bridge can reply to the address request with its own ATM address, as a proxy for the destination, on the assumption that the bridge contains the destination MAC address in its forwarding table. In the database ARP approach, the address server on the ATM network must contain entries not only for the directly attached devices but also for all stations attached on internets. To sustain this, each internet device must continually update the address server with the contents of its forwarding table; this could be demanding in large bridged networks.

The two approaches to ARP can be transparently combined. End stations can assume that a broadcast mechanism is in use. The multicast server can also act as an address server. It can intercept ARP requests submitted for broadcast to an ATM LAN segment, and respond with the required address from its database. The address resolution database can be built from the exchange of addresses in the registration protocol, and also by learning processes used by transparent bridges. If no entry is found in the database, then the server can use the broadcast address resolution mechanism.

Operation of the LAN Emulation User-Network Interface (LUNI)

The LUNI operates in five stages:

1. *Initialization*   Prior to information transfer, the LEC must perform some housekeeping operations. This begins in the initialization stage. The LEC must find the LAN Emulation Configuration Server (part of the overall LES). It first uses the Interim Local Management Interface (ILMI) to attempt to obtain the address from the switch. If that fails, it will attempt to use what's called the *well-known ATM address*. This is a predetermined address which is used on all ATM networks. If that fails, it attempts to use the PVC, with VPI/VCI=0/17. This is a well-known PVC. Finally, if that fails, it will try the LES.

2. *Configuration*   Upon initialization, the LEC must determine the type of emulated LAN and maximum frame size. It must also send its ATM address, MAC address, LAN types, and requested frame sizes. It can also optionally request to join a particular emulated LAN.

3. *Joining* Once the LEC has passed through the initialization and configuration stages, it can then *join* the emulated LAN. The LEC sends a join request to the LES. This request contains its ATM address, LAN information, MAC address, and proxy information (if appropriate). Proxy information is appropriate if the LEC is acting on behalf of additional end stations. The LES responds with a join response containing the results.

4. *Registration and BUS Initialization* Upon a successful join, the LEC must register all MAC addresses with the BUS. The MAC address 0xffffffffffff (broadcast address) will then be mapped to the BUS ATM address. The LEC establishes a point-to-point connection with the BUS. The BUS adds the LEC onto its point-to-multipoint circuit for the specific emulated LAN.

5. *Information Transfer* Once the housekeeping functions are complete, the LEC can transfer data. Data can be transferred either to a specific address, or broadcast to all devices of the emulated LAN. In a unicast, the LEC determines the destination ATM address either by checking its ARP cache, or through a LAN Emulation Address Resolution Packet (LE-ARP). It then establishes a SVC (if not established) to the destination and begins transferring information. To send a broadcast, the LEC will forward the information to the BUS to be sent out on the point-to-multipoint circuit.

A LAN segment could be emulated by directing all of the traffic for the segment on the broadcast channel. However, most LAN traffic is unicast; therefore it is more efficient to support unicast communications. Not only does this reduce traffic, but greater security is achieved because the unicast traffic appears only at the two pertinent stations. An ATM LAN segment can then support higher aggregate bandwidth than would be the case if all traffic were transmitted on the same broadcast channel. Furthermore, the use of individual virtual connections for unicast traffic allows greater control of the quality of service. To establish a point-to-point ATM virtual connection for each instance of unicast communication, the current location of the destination end station must be discovered and expressed as a destination address that the ATM signaling service can understand; this operation is called *address resolution* [3]. The ATM signaling service must then be initiated to establish a point-to-point ATM virtual connection, with the appropriate quality of service, to the destination. Within the end station, this operation must be implemented in the software of the ATM MAC Layer, to offer a transparent service to the LLC Sublayer.

3.6 Narrowband ATM Access

The ATM protocol is most efficient when operating at high speeds. As stated before, these cells are 53 bytes long, with 48 bytes of payload and 5 bytes of header information. This is almost a 10% overhead for the header information, just at the ATM Layer. (There are other inefficiencies at the AAL and Physical Layers.) The ATM-level inefficiency is not considered excessive when operating at high speeds, given ATM's ability to mix voice, video, and data.

Currently, low-speed access links are the norm for most WAN environments. ATM's overhead becomes burdensome at these speeds, typically 56 Kbps to T1 (1.544 Mbps). The ATM Forum addressed this requirement by developing a new UNI aimed at increasing the efficiency for low-speeds links. This new UNI is called the *Frame UNI* (FUNI). It operates on frames which can have payloads of up to 4,096 bytes.

Frame Relay, Data Exchange Interface (DXI), and FUNI are all frame-based standards:

1. Frame Relay defines HDLC as part of its specification, and adds a header to support DLCI (Data Link Control Identifier) addressing.

2. DXI/UNI is an evolution of the ATM DXI (e.g., see [1]) which defines router interfacing to an ATM CSU (through HSSI), though the DXI/UNI also defines V.35 and nx64,000 (via a regular CSU). For nx64,000, frames are carried all the way to the switch at the Central Office. The AAL 5 Convergence Sublayer and VPI/VCI addressing scheme is used. The ATM DXI/UNI allows a customer to access a network supporting ATM technology based on HDLC frames. The purpose of this interface is to provide HDLC access to ATM at low speeds.

3. FUNI is separate from DXI/UNI. It can be thought of as a superset of DXI/UNI. The difference between the two is that FUNI extends Q.2931 signaling for SVCs. It also carries AAL 5 Convergence Sublayer PDUs. Hence, FUNI defines an alternative HDLC-based protocol for use access to ATM.

Using ATM DXI one can support legacy DCEs by encapsulating frames and giving them to a Central Office-interworking unit, which then prepares them for ATM transport. This approach is good for PVCs, but not for SVCs. For SVCs one should use FUNI: here the same encapsulation is used for the User Plane and for the Control Plane; it entails a dual-stack interworking unit at the switch/Central Office.

Figures 3.4 and 3.5 depict the protocol stacks involved in Frame Relay, DXI, DXI/UNI, and FUNI. The FUNI supports full ATM signaling, enabling frame-

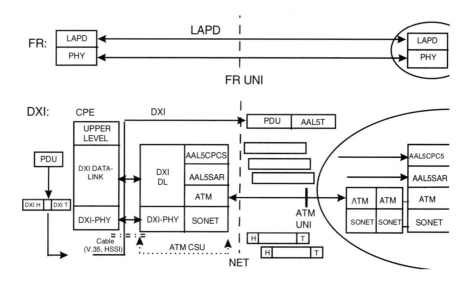

Figure 3.4   Top: Frame relay protocol stack; bottom: DXI protocol stack

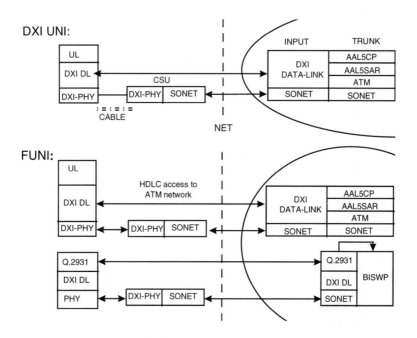

Figure 3.5   Top: DXI UNI; bottom: FUNI protocol stack

oriented devices such as bridges and routers to set up switched circuits and negotiate class of service with the network. The FUNI header contains flags to indicate standard ATM features such as cell-loss priority, congestion notification, and the presence of operations and maintenance traffic. The FUNI specification details the appropriate mapping function to go between frame headers and cell headers. It also supports Adaptation Layers 3, 4, and 5. For management, FUNI supports the ILMI. The commercial future of FUNI is uncertain.

3.7 ATM Switches

End users requiring ATM services can either secure the service from a carrier, or build their own networks. In campus situations, it may be reasonable for an organization to develop its own network. This would entail the acquisition of a number of ATM switches and ancillary support equipment (e.g., NICs for routers, PCs, and servers). For WAN applications, carriers tend to be the best option. In any event, ATM switches must be deployed.

There are two forms of ATM switch: backplane-based systems and matrix switches.

In backplane-based systems, ATM cells are transported across a high-speed bus linking ATM modules. Each ATM module receives cells according to VPI/VCI values that identify connections and their paths.

Backplane-based ATM systems are relatively simple and inexpensive to develop, but this architecture does not scale well. For example, to support 16 ports operating at OC-3 (155 Mbps), the backplane speed must be 2.480 Gbps. The same number of ports at OC-12 (622 Mbps) would require a backplane speed of 9.952 Gbps. These speeds are now out of reach for backplanes, consequently, this would be a bottleneck, preventing ATM's ability to operate at high bandwidths.

Matrix switching is the current preferred method for meeting this high-speed capability. The switching architectures for traditional PBX systems using STM (synchronous transfer mode) are well understood, but these architectures may not be suitable for ATM switching. First, an ATM switch must accommodate much higher speeds than a PBX. Moreover, the statistical behavior of the ATM streams passing through an ATM switching system differs from traffic through a PBX. Consequently, researchers are now proposing a number of ATM switching architectures.

To support ATM, a switching architecture must meet the following requirements:

- The switch must be able to support very high aggregate throughput with a small switching delay. In addition to supporting the billion-bps internal speeds required for multiple ports, the processing time to switch a single cell from one port to another must be less than 3 microseconds. Processing time must be less than 1.5 microseconds if the cell is to be switched between two switches.

- Support of broadcast and multicast is also necessary. Only point-to-point connections are allowed in classical switches. ATM systems, however, are required to broadcast or multicast information to many destinations. Applications that require this capability include the distribution of rates on financial markets to branches and individual traders, as well as e-mail.

- Nonblocking operation is another important consideration for ATM switches. In some cases, switching fabrics are unable to establish a connection even though two ports are available. This may be caused by a lack of resources within the switch, leading to inefficiency. In ATM, the concept of nonblocking is slightly different than in a traditional circuit switch; however, there is still a need to support a connection with a specified grade of service, if pertinent resources are available. Sometimes ports on a switch card have more aggregated bandwidth than the slot-to-bus speed, creating blocking.

- Resource contention. Many cells may be destined for a single output port within the ATM switch at the same time. The ATM architecture assumes a low cell-loss rate, so it is important to provide a multithreaded queuing mechanism that stores the cells competing for the same out-port. Another way of saying this is that the switch must *guarantee* the stipulated grade of service.

Buffering can be done at the input or output, or in a central portion of the switching element. Each philosophy involves a different degree of complexity and probability of cell loss. Balancing all these considerations, input queuing is gaining support as the preferred method. The end user has little control on these factors, beyond the initial selection of the switch: the architecture is a design factor which is controlled by the switch manufacturer or by the carrier (having selected a specific switch). The user may not even be technically equipped to undertake the detailed research needed to determine what the switch vendor is doing and the architecture is appropriate. It should be noted that while there is basically one switching architecture for voice switches (namely Time-Space-Time—all voice switches are the same), there is no consensus as to the ATM switching architecture, and every vendor uses a different approach or twist. The alternatives include: the crossbar network, the Batcher-Banyan network, Bianchini network, and the Buffered Benes network.

3.8 Tasks Receiving Continuing Attention

As noted at the outset of this chapter, the ITU-T definition of standards for ATM left a number of gaps and ambiguities that await final resolution. For example, LAN traffic that passes over an ATM backbone or other intermediary network initially depended upon proprietary implementations by various vendors; there is no interoperability between equipment made by different vendors. (LANE technology will address that problem.) There is interest in supporting Virtual LANs (VLANs) in a standardized fashion; this will also be possible using LANE principles.

The ATM Forum was established as a vendor group, focusing primarily on the development of ATM implementers' agreements. These agreements extend and implement ITU-T specifications. For example, The ATM Forum has published two extensions to the UNI standard. Current ATM Forum projects include traffic management in a large network, LAN Emulation version 2, and more extensive UTP (unshielded twisted-pair copper wire) support.

A large scale network, including private internets, requires a comprehensive method for end-to-end traffic management. It must be able to resolve congestion in two segments: between the user workstation and the switch, and between multiple switches. This requires flow control throughout a network, including all end devices and intermediate devices.

Resilient LAN emulation, also on the active agenda of The ATM Forum, would permit LAN traffic (typically generated by legacy technology like Ethernet or Token Ring) to be switched transparently over an ATM network as if it were passing through a bridge. This would replace current vendor-specific proprietary solutions that obstruct interoperability.

In any discussion of ATM, a clear distinction must be made between WAN ATM and LAN ATM. WAN ATM technology has been available since the late 1980s, and the service has already undergone price reductions. ATM LAN technology, including LANE and ATM to the desktop, are relatively newer; their price performance points still need to improve. By 1997 this technology should also reach commodity status.

ATM is not the most economical or practical solution in the near term for relatively low-speed (and, preferably low-cost) access directly to the desktop. Niche users having special requirements including multimedia or high traffic volumes will need to adopt hybrid solutions: ATM for their special purpose applications and legacy LANs for connections to the backbone. Products that support convergence between ATM and non-ATM hosts are not yet stable enough for large scale production network usage.

ATM's original objectives, reflected in current products, focus on high-speed fiber connections. Prices for ATM adapters are declining rapidly, but running fiber to the desktop and supporting it with ATM hardware would nevertheless be costly. In the near term, moreover, much of the bandwidth made available would be unused surplus. Most of today's workstations and servers are not likely to fill the bandwidth that ATM makes possible.

The ATM Forum and vendors are addressing solutions that would bring ATM functionality to the desktop at moderate speeds over less expensive media. The ATM Forum is devising a physical basis for ATM traffic over various categories of UTP cabling. This contrasts, for example, with the more expensive shielded or coaxial cables which were traditionally used by early deployment of LAN technologies, like Ethernet.

Two alternative proposals have been offered by AT&T-Hewlett-Packard and IBM for support of 51-Mbps (OC-1) traffic over Category 3 UTP. Support of 155-Mbps (OC-3) traffic will require Category 5 UTP.

In an effort originally separate from The ATM Forum, IBM has pursued a standard for 25 Mbps over Category 3 UTP. Now The ATM Forum has also standardized a 25-Mbps Physical Layer. Tentative support has been declared by 25 vendors. The IBM proposal departs from the SONET-type signaling advocated by the AT&T-Hewlett-Packard project for 51 Mbps. IBM remains loyal to the Manchester coding associated with Token Ring for its 25-Mbps ATM standard.

UTP error rates and carrying capacity have been increased substantially in recent years, but UTP is nevertheless limited. None of the low-speed/UTP proposals is scalable to higher bandwidths beyond 155 Mbps. However, 155 Mbps to the desktop should be adequate for a number of years. For example, one can support good-quality video at 1.544 Mbps (with MPEG-1), and can support HDTV at 21.5 Mbps.

As in the old combats between DEC/Ethernet and IBM/Token Ring, differences between solutions sponsored by different groups of vendors complicate the choice of low-speed wiring and network specifications to the desktop.

The ATM Forum has developed specifications for:

• Intercarrier interchange of information.

• A private UNI that defines the originating system to a private switch interface.

• A private NNI (Network-to-Network Interface) that defines the interface and protocols between private switches.

• Congestion control, which ensures reduction in data loss to levels from minimal to zero, even in heavily loaded networks.

CHAPTER 3: ATM ARCHITECTURE

The ATM Forum is also discussing other issues. These include:

- Interoperability. It has developed a schedule for interoperability that allows vendors to ensure that, over time and in a series of steps, customers can count on multivendor interoperability.

- Legacy support (LANE, IP, MPOA.) The ATM Forum seeks to provide a clean migration path from existing LAN architectures to ATM, without the high cost of fiber cabling or ATM implementation all the way to the desktop. This approach will provide higher bandwidth and a more stable network infrastructure for large backbones on the building or campus scales. The first version has been completed, and work was underway at press time for version 2. LANE does not, however, make it possible for users to leverage ATM's end-to-end class of service functionality.

- Network management to support networks using ATM.

- An Application Programming Interface, defining interface-to-upper (Application) Layer processes to send and receive information over ATM.

References

[1] D. Minoli and M. Vitella, *Cell Relay Service and ATM for Corporate Environments* (McGraw-Hill, 1994).

[2] D. Minoli and G. Dobrowski, *Principles of Signaling For Cell Relay and Frame Relay* (Artech House, 1995).

[3] Peter Newman, ATM Local Area Network, *IEEE Communications Magazine*, March 1994, page 86.

Part II

Management Principles of
ATM Networks

chapter 4

Fundamentals

*U*ntil recently, the telecommunications industry emphasized the transmission and switching technology required to support ATM and its protocols.

Now, however, ATM developers are also starting to give management issues the attention they deserve. This chapter covers network management functions, and protocols in the context of ATM technology. It introduces:

- *Types of management capabilities.*
- *OSI network management categories.*
- *The basics of fault management and accounting management.*
- *Configuration management, performance management, and security management.*
- *ATM services requiring network management.*

4.1 Introduction

Generally, a corporate enterprise network consists of a variety of subnetworks—for example, LANs, FDDI rings, and WANs—which may be based on a number of technologies. Additionally, these networks can be private, or they can be hybrid. Hybrid networks consist of private facilities (e.g., hubs and switches) as well as public facilities, which provide particular communication services. The network management functions discussed in this chapter apply to the entire enterprise network, as well as to particular subnetworks.

Corporations are looking for capabilities to manage local subnetworks such as LANs; local communications equipment such as channel service units, multiplexers, routers, bridges, hubs, etc.; networking applications software; and wide area communication services such as dedicated digital lines, frame relay, SMDS, and now, cell relay service (CRS). Even in well-established pre-ATM environments, there is no single network management solution that meets all of the user's needs, forcing network management personnel to utilize a variety of equipment and software to access management information and initiate appropriate actions. For example, organizations having UNIX-based systems and utilizing TCP/IP-based networks may use UNIX—as well as SNMP-based management tools. In multiprotocol networks, customers may use combinations of open (e.g., SNMP) and proprietary management tools (e.g., SNA's NetView). The introduction of ATM-based services may complicate this predicament, unless the appropriate networking infrastructure is put in place. This challenge dictates that corporate ATM planners acquire an understanding of which network management features can be expected in the context of ATM services and products.

For simplicity, this discussion assumes that the network in question is strictly ATM-based (both in the private and in the hybrid case); however, many of the principles discussed here apply equally well to multitechnology/multigeneration networks.

Figure 4.1 depicts the realms of network management in an ATM environment. Carriers need to manage the infrastructure which they use to provide ATM services to users (including cell relay, SMDS, frame relay, and circuit emulation); this is labeled 1 in the figure. When users install their own ATM-based network from "scratch," namely, when they install their own ATM switches, these users need to support many (but not necessarily all) of the network management functions that a carrier supports through the use of a Network Management System (NMS); this is labeled 3 in the figure. Many users will simply obtain ATM services from a carrier. In this case, the users need (only) a mechanism to manage certain aspects of their service. This functionality is referred to as *Customer Network Management* (CNM) and is labeled 2 in the figure. CNM service supported by carriers (e.g., LECs and ICs) facilitates planning, operation, maintenance, administration, reconfiguration, etc. of the carrier's portion of the customer's hybrid ATM network, and of the services provided.

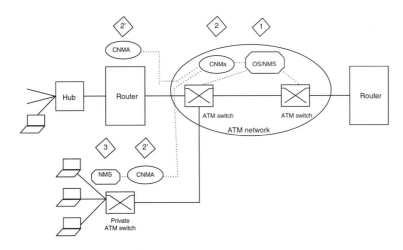

OS/NMS: An operations system/network management system;
CNMa: A customer network management agent;
CNMA: A customer network management application.

Figure 4.1   Realms of network management

The emphasis in this book, and in the chapters that follow, is on the functions labeled 2, (2'), and 3 in this figure. Typical network management functions required by corporations include equipment reconfiguration, service reconfiguration, fault isolation (including sectionalization of faults between different carriers or geographical areas), detection of service degradation, and notification and assessment of relevant network or equipment events. The ATM CNM information provided by ATM carriers is expected to be similar to management information typically collected now over LANs and LAN interconnection equipment (e.g., routers and bridges) [1]. Such an approach minimizes the need for new software, new protocols, and new applications to be added to the existing management systems that will be used, perhaps with minor modifications, by early adopters of ATM.

As implied in Figure 4.1, effective network management depends on communications among network elements (such as ATM switches and supporting administrative software systems—that is, Operations Systems, OSs) and user's network management systems. Typically, private networks employ network management systems based on the use of the Simple Network Management Protocol (SNMP), while public networks have moved toward the use of OSI network management protocols to manage their switches, namely the Common Management Information Protocol (CMIP).[1]

From the user's point of view, a workstation (or other system) implementing the NMS for a user-owned ATM switch, or the CNM Application (CNMA) for a carrier-provided service, will be the visible window into the ATM network. This workstation will be used to examine faults, collect performance monitoring information, collect usage and traffic measurements, and provision or modify the ATM service (i.e., add users or change the characteristics of the service, e.g., assigned peak bandwidth). For fault events, the information must be available immediately to the appropriate corporate individuals, including telecommunication and data communications managers, departmental data network managers and their staff, and certain (sophisticated) end users. Responses to inquiries for other information (e.g., performance or usage statistics) must be available in a timely but not necessarily instantaneous manner.

The following list illustrates the type of capabilities that are needed to manage large corporate networks, as well as to maximize employee productivity, which is the ultimate goal of any corporation. The features shown in this list are typically found in commercially available pre-ATM LAN/WAN network management systems. ATM-based CNMAs and NMSs will need similar features:

---

[1] In theory, CMIP can also be used in private networks; however, in practice, SNMP is the norm.

- NMSs encompass mechanisms for the collection of, access to, and modification of relevant management information, and the presentation of management information to the corporate network management personnel in a friendly, useful, data-reduced, yet detailed manner.

- NMSs encompass mechanisms for determining the status of network resources, generating alarms, reconfiguring network resources, and collecting statistics used to detect, isolate, and correct failures.

- NMSs afford the manager the ability to examine and manipulate management information on physical transmission facilities, operational aspects of the organization's software and hardware, and the organization's use of carrier transmission and higher layer network services.

Table 4.1 depicts, at a general granular level, the functional scope of ATM network management functions in public switch, private switch, and Customer Network Management environments. (Hybrid environments use a mix of all three; however, the corporate manager will tend to see the world from a CNM point-of-view.) Network management occurs at the physical level (for example, handling equipment failures, transmission link failures, etc.), at the logical level connectivity (e.g., looking at VPC/VCC status), and at the service level (e.g., looking at QoS issues, assigned bandwidth, etc.), as discussed in the next section.

It should be noted that until recently, the major emphasis of ATM planning was in support of *fastpacket* data services; hence, the emphasis of this treatment is on data services. Also, a significant level of penetration has occurred in the context of routed enterprise networks and intranets. More recently, however, there has been interest expressed in supporting voice and video over ATM. The rationale for this shift in focus is that there already are several services supporting traditional data services, particularly LAN interconnection, e.g., switched T1, dedicated T1, and Fractional T1, packet services, SVC and PVC frame relay, and SMDS. Also, data applications do not at this time generally require the full bandwidth afforded by ATM (e.g., 622 Mbps), except in case of first-tier backbones carrying highly concentrated traffic. Video applications, on the other hand (e.g., video on demand, video conferencing, video distribution, image-based communication, etc.), can readily make use of these bandwidths. Although this book focuses on fastpacket data services, some, if not all, of the (network-supported) ATM management capabilities can also be used in the video context.

	Public switch	Private switch	CNM
Typical protocol	CMIP	CMIP (less common) or SNMP (more common)	SNMP
Fault measurements	Alarms (AIS[a], RDI[b] VPC/VCC status) Connectivity (end-to-end and/or segment loopback, activation/ deactivation)	Alarms (AIS, RDI VPC/VCC status) Connectivity (end-to-end and/or segment loopback, activation/ deactivation)	Alarms (e.g., VPC/VCC status) Connectivity (end-to-end and/or segment loopback, activation/ deactivation)
Performance monitoring	Physical Layer ATM Layer Service Layer	Physical Layer ATM Layer Service Layer	Physical Layer ATM Layer Service Layer
Network data collection	Port information Virtual channel/ Virtual path information	Port information Virtual channel/ Virtual path information	Virtual channel/ Virtual path information
Usage measurements	Ingress traffic Egress traffic QoS information Billing	Ingress traffic Egress traffic QoS information Billing	Billing
Traffic measurements	QoS Cell loss Cell delay Cell delay variation Service priorities (based on particular ATM service)	QoS Cell loss Cell delay Cell delay variation Service priorities (based on particular ATM service)	QoS Cell loss Cell delay Cell delay variation Service priorities (based on particular ATM service)
Service provisioning and modifying	Ports,VPI/VCI,QoS PVC/SVC, peak or sustainable band-width, interworking options, etc.	Ports,VPI/VCI,QoS PVC/SVC, peak or sustainable band-width, interworking options, etc.	VPI/VCI, QoS PVC/SVC, peak or sustainable band-width, interworking options, etc.

[a] AIS denotes an alarm indication signal.
[b] RDI denotes a remote defect indicator (formerly called FERF, for far end receive failure).

Table 4.1   Typical network management tasks and corresponding data in an ATM context (examples)

4.2 Types of Management Capabilities

One encounters *noninterlocking* jargon in discussing network management. This arises from the fact that the terminology originates from several sources, as follows:

- M-plane (Management Plane). ITU-T nomenclature in discussing the B-ISDN model.

- Layer Management and Layer Management Entities (LMEs). ISO and ITU-T Network Management standards.

- Broadband Local Management Interface (B-LMI—see below). The ATM Forum.

- Customer Network Management and SNMP. IETF (Internet Engineering Task Force) and carriers.

- Telecommunication Management Network (TMN—Chapter 10). ITU-T (Recommendation M.3010).

Within the context of B-ISDN, which is the ATM management plane defined by the B-ISDN protocol architecture (Chapter 3), management capabilities exist in the form of what are called Layer Management capabilities and Systems Management capabilities. In this description, Layer Management correlates to logical level, [2] while Systems Management correlates to the service level as well as other end system-specific functions (e.g., self diagnosis). Layer management usually works in conjunction with the protocol at the given layer; it uses protocol error events and accumulation of such events, to undertake management functions (e.g., alert somebody—specifically, Systems Management—that something may be occurring). Systems Management performs interlayer coordination. Hence, Systems Management supervises overall end systems communications functions, and coordinates the behavior of the individual subsystems (e.g., the layers) within a single communicating system. It follows that Systems Management software interacts with the Layer Management software, to collect values of attributes, counters, timers, etc., to control and operate the communication aspects of the end system in question.

Figure 4.2 depicts a high-level map of the various proposed ATM network management functions visible to the end user; these will be discussed below in greater detail.

---

[2] One can view physical level functions, such as link failure, as Layer Management at the Physical Layer of the protocol stack.

For any layer of the underlying network architecture, both protocol-specific network management information (protocol data units, counters, timer values, timer expiration occurrences, attributes, protocol error occurrences, and other capabilities listed in Table 4.1) and nonprotocol-specific network management information needs to be collected. Layer Management (specifically, ATM Layer) functionality includes capabilities such as loopback, performance monitoring, alarm surveillance, etc. Two types of connections have been defined at the ATM Layer: Virtual Path Connections (VPCs) and Virtual Channel Connections (VCCs). Users are interested in management information about both types of connections. Layer Management capabilities are usually implemented via in-band flows, using specialized cells. As seen in Figure 4.2, these flows can be on a segment-basis or end to end.

Figure 4.2 also shows an out-of-band process known as *Broadband Local Management Interface* (B-LMI). This capability has also been called *Interim LMI* (ILMI), under the assumption that some of its functions will migrate to the CNM—we use B-LMI to distinguish this capability from the Frame Relay ILMI. The issue of the need for a B-LMI when a feature-rich CNM protocol is implemented, was still being debated at press time.

More sophisticated, service-related functions and capabilities are implemented at a higher level. These functions deal with service aspects such as changing subscription parameters, obtaining billing information, reconfiguring VPCs and VCCs, etc. These capabilities are supported via a separate CNM structure and underlying protocol, such as SNMP or, possibly, CMIP. One can consider CNM to encompass Systems Management. Figure 4.3 depicts the CNM environment in the cell relay service context, providing some additional detail, compared with Figure 4.1.

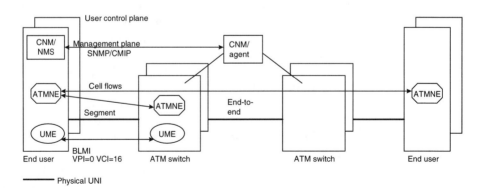

UME: A UNI management entity
ATMME: A ATM (Layer) management entity
B-LMI: A broadband local management interface

Figure 4.2   Simplified view of various ATM management mechanisms

4.3 OSI Network Management Categories

The Open Systems Interconnection Network Management (OSINM) standards have defined five functional areas pertinent to management of communication networks [2–7] (See Table 4.2). The description of the functional areas is independent of how they are implemented. The functional areas apply to all three realms shown in Figure 4.1; namely, they apply to private, public, and hybrid networks. This widely accepted nomenclature is used in the rest of this book. The functional areas defined in OSINM are discussed next.

4.3.1 Fault Management

Fault management encompasses fault detection, isolation, and the correction of abnormal operation. Fault management is the discipline of detecting, diagnosing, bypassing, repairing and reporting on network equipment and service failures.

Faults (persistent or transient) cause communication systems to fall short of their operational objectives. Faults manifest themselves in terms of a variety

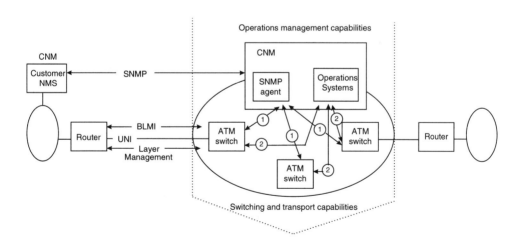

1 A switch/SNMP agent interaction (CMIP-based)
2 A switch/CMISE interaction (CMIP-based)

Figure 4.3   Positioning of layer management, B-LMI, SNMP (CNM), and CMIP (carrier operations) in public networks

IEC/ISO	ITU-T	Title
10040		Information Technology—Open Systems Interconnection—Systems Management Overview
10164	Part 1 X.730	Information Technology—Open Systems Interconnection—Systems Management Overview Amendment 1: Management Knowledge Management Architecture
10164	Part 2 X.731	Information Technology—Open Systems Interconnection—Systems Management: State Management Function
10164	Part 3 X.732	Information Technology—Open Systems Interconnection—Systems Management: Attributes For Representing Relationships
10164	Part 4 X.732	Information Technology—Open Systems Interconnection—Systems Management: Alarm Reporting Function
10164	Part 5 X.734	Information Technology—Open Systems Interconnection—Systems Management: Event Report Management Function
10164	Part 6 X.735	Information Technology—Open Systems Interconnection Systems Management: Log Control Function.
10164	Part 7 X.736	Information Technology—Open Systems Interconnection—Systems Management: Security Alarm Reporting Function
10164	Part 8 X.740	Information Technology—Open Systems Interconnection—Systems Management: Security Audit Trail Function
10164	Part 9 X.741	Information Technology—Open Systems Interconnection—Systems Management: Object and Attributes for Access Control
10164	Part 10 X.742	Information Technology—Open Systems Interconnection—Systems Management: Accounting Metering Function
10164	Part 11 X.739	Information Technology—Open Systems Interconnection—Systems Management: Workload Monitoring Function
10164	Part 12 X.745	Information Technology—Open Systems Interconnection—Systems Management: Test Management Function
10164	Part 13 X.738	Information Technology—Open Systems Interconnection—Systems Management: Summarization Function
10164	Part 14 X.737	Information Technology—Open Systems Interconnection—Systems Management: Confidence and Diagnostic Test Categories

Table 4.2   IEC/ISO network management recommendations [2]

IEC/ISO	ITU-T	Title
10164	Part 15 X.xxx	Information Technology—Open Systems Interconnection—Systems Management: Summarization Function: Scheduling Function
10165	Part 1 X.720	Information Technology—Open Systems Interconnection—Structure of Management Information: Information Model
10165	Part 2 X.721	Information Technology—Open Systems Interconnection—Structure of Management Information: Definition of Management Information
10165	Part 4 X.722	Information Technology—Open Systems Interconnection—Structure of Management Information: Guidelines for the Definition of Managed Objects
10165	Part 5 X.723	Information Technology—Open Systems Interconnection—Structure of Management Information: Generic Management Information
10165	Part 6 X.724	Information Technology—Open Systems Interconnection—Structure of Management Information: Requirements and Guidelines for Implementation Conformance Statement Proformas associated with Management Information
12060	Part 1	Information Technology—International Standardized Profiles—OSI Management—Management Functions Part 1: General Management Capabilities.
12060	Part 2	Information Technology—International Standardized Profiles—OSI Management—Management Functions Part 2: Alarm Reporting and State Management Capabilities.
12060	Part 3	Information Technology—International Standardized Profiles—OSI Management—Management Functions Part 3: Alarm Reporting Capabilities.
12060	Part 4	Information Technology—International Standardized Profiles—OSI Management—Management Functions Part 4: General Event Report Management.
12060	Part 5	Information Technology—International Standardized Profiles—OSI Management—Management Functions Part 5: General Log Control.

Note: A managed object is an abstraction of a real resource being managed; it contains information required for effective management.

Table 4.2 *Continued*

of events; error event detection provides a capability to recognize them. Steps included in fault management are:

1. Trace and identify faults.

2. Accept and act upon error detection notifications.

3. Carry out sequences of diagnostic tests.

4. Correct faults.

5. Maintain and examine error logs.

4.3.2 Accounting Management

Accounting management enables charges to be established for the use of communications resources, and for costs to be identified for the use of such resources. Accounting management functions include:

1. Inform users of costs incurred or resources consumed.

2. Enable accounting limits to be set and tariff schedules to be associated with the use of resources.

3. Enable costs to be combined where multiple resources are used to achieve a specified communications objective.

4.3.3 Configuration Management

Configuration management identifies, exercises control over, collects data from, and provides data to communications systems for the purpose of initiating and providing continuous reliable connectivity. Configuration management supports provisioning and status & control (status & control functions entail monitoring and controlling certain aspects of the ATM switch done as routine/scheduled maintenance or done as corrective maintenance in case of failure conditions.) Configuration management steps include:

1. Set the parameters that control the routine operation of the communications system.

2. Associate names with managed objects and sets of managed objects.

3. Initialize and terminate managed objects.

4. Collect information (on demand) about the current condition of the communications system.

5. Obtain announcements of significant changes in the condition of the communication system.

6. Change the configuration of the system.

Configuration management is concerned with maintaining an accurate inventory of hardware, software, and circuits, and with the ability to change that inventory in a smooth and reliable manner in response to changing service requirements. Configuration and name management insures consistency and validity of operating parameters, naming and addressing tables, software images and hardware configurations of managed systems.

4.3.4 Performance Management

Performance management enables one to evaluate the behavior and effectiveness of resources and related communications activities. Performance management steps include:

1. Gather statistics about the system.

2. Maintain and examine logs of the system's history.

3. Determine system performance under natural and degraded conditions (real or self-induced).

4. Alter modes of operation of the system for the purpose of conducting performance management activities.

Performance management is concerned with the utilization of network resources and the ability to meet user service level objectives.

4.3.5 Security Management

Security management supports the application of security policies. Security is an important issue: unauthorized or accidental access to network control functions must be eliminated or minimized. Security management steps include:

1. The creation, deletion, and control of security services and mechanisms.

2. The distribution of security-relevant information.

3. The reporting of security-relevant events.

Security management controls access to both the network and the network management systems.

4.3.6 *Other Aspects*

While at the functional level these functions are generally the same for all types of networks, the specific realization of these capabilities in an ATM context, as well as some inevitable peculiarities, are intimately related to ATM constructs (e.g., cells, treatment of cells in the case of congestion, service categories, QoS, etc.). Table 4.3 provides a summary of these five functional areas (applicable to all three ATM management realms of Figure 4.1). Chapters 7, 8, and 9 provide ATM-specific descriptions of these functions in support of corporate ATM networks.

Some people have proposed explicitly adding the following functions to the OSINM functions: capacity management, provisioning management, and administration management. Capacity management includes demand forecasting, network design, and network engineering. In network planning, the network manager consolidates usage trends and performance data to develop options and models for potential network changes. Capacity planning is the on-going fine-tuning of a network, such as adding or rearranging trunks. Planning also must accommodate periodic events such as seasonal rearrangements and periodic reoptimization of the network, as well as scheduled moves and changes.

Provisioning management includes service ordering, installation, and preservice testing. Its functions support bringing equipment into service, initializing the equipment, and controlling the state and other appropriate parameters of the equipment.

Administration management includes equipment inventory, corporate directory functions, database administration, and generation of management reports. In practical terms, these functions can be subsumed in the five functional classes described above; however, because of historical precedent, these terms continue to be used in distinct form.

Some, particularly in the carrier environment, also continue to use other terminology that has been employed in the past. Traditionally, network management consisted of the following areas:

1. Maintenance and fault isolation.

2. Capacity planning.

3. Network traffic management.

Accounting management functions:

> Aggregation of usage measurements
>
> Format and transmit usage measurements

Configuration management functions:

> Backup data for purposes of future restoral
>
> Managing assignable inventory
>
> Schedule and sequence the activation/deactivation of an assignment
>
> Selecting and assigning resources
>
> Updating and querying data

Fault management functions:

> Analysis of alarms and report findings
>
> Analysis of test/diagnostic results and report findings
>
> Correlation of multiple alarms
>
> Maintaining log of alarms
>
> Select, run, and abort generic testing routines and diagnostics

Performance management functions:

> Accumulation of performance monitoring and traffic management data
>
> Analysis of performance management data and report notable findings
>
> Correlation of alerts/alarms and report findings
>
> Update or query performance management data and control information

Security management functions:

> Authentication
>
> Control access
>
> Monitoring data and system integrity
>
> Provide and manage audit trials
>
> Recovering from intrusions
>
> Reporting security alarms

Table 4.3   Summary of ATM network management functions

4. Network data collection.[3]

5. Switch memory administration.

6. Accounting and billing.

Table 4.4 depicts some relationships between the new terminology and the traditional terminology. Taken as a group, all of these functions, particularly in a carrier's context, have been called Operations, Administration, and Maintenance (OAM).

	Traditional carrier terms					
OSI category	Maintenance	Network Traffic Management	Network Data	(Switch) Memory Administration	Accounting and billing	Capacity Planning
Performance Management	X	X				X
Fault Management	X	X				
Configuration Management	X	X		X	X	X
Security Management				X		
Accounting Management					X	

Table 4.4   Mapping of traditional network management functions to OSI functions

---

[3]Network Data Collection (NDC) deals with collection of network traffic information to provide detailed insight into traffic flows and concomitant impacts to the (ATM) network. NDC does not itself perform management functions; it provides data to downstream processes that perform management functions. This information, collected every few minutes or hours, is used to support a variety of functions, including network utilization, network capacity management, network design, service surveillance, interswitch facilities servicing and forecasting, and other analysis. Also see Chapter 8.

4.4 ATM Services Requiring Network Management

ATM is being viewed as a platform capability that supports native cell relay service (PVC and SVC), frame relay service (PVC and SVC), SMDS, and circuit-emulation services. There is also work underway to support TCP/IP, video, interworking of cell relay and frame relay, and interworking of ISDN (voice, and clear-channel nx64 kbps) and ATM. Figure 4.4 depicts this set of services from a Protocol Layer point-of-view. The wide variety of services possible with ATM makes network management more challenging. Initial carrier thrust is likely to be in the simple cell relay service arena.

As noted in Section 4.1, a typical corporate "network" often consists of a complex mix of multiple networks, each often administered and operated by a distinct entity. For example, routers are common in an ATM context. For efficient and complete network management, it is essential that management information be exchanged among these entities. Even when considering cell relay service by itself, the issue of integrated network management is important. In the LAN environment, both locally and in internetworking arrangements, a growing supply of products already provide network management capabili-

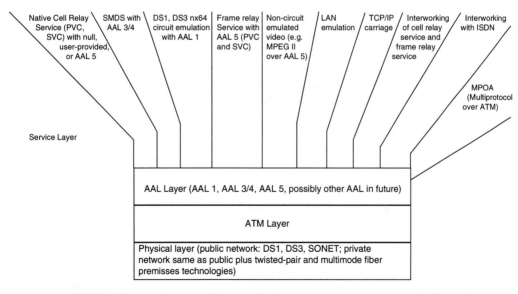

(Typical protocol peer in CPE or network node.)

Figure 4.4   Services supported by ATM

ties, supporting tasks such as network operation, isolation, diagnosis, and resolution of communications-related problems. Since initially CRS is expected to be used for data applications already deployed on LANs, it is important to organizations that evolving ATM network management systems operate synergistically with existing LAN-based network management systems. The corporate manager does not want to use several terminals (or even unintegrated windows on a windowing workstation) to manage various aspects of the organization's enterprise network.

Three network management alternatives or roles have been proposed by carriers for situations where organizations use public ATM services and/or have hybrid networks [8]:

- Carrier support of a CPE-based network management application. Two alternatives are possible:
  1. The carrier network provides information relevant to a customer's use of the CRS as a whole. (SNMP is required for the access to this service.)
  2. The carrier network provides information related to a customer's UNI to the local serving ATM switch only. (The ATM Forum's B-LMI is required for the access to this service).

- Carrier network support of monitoring and surveillance layer management protocols.

- Carrier network support of CRS CNM applications.

The exchange of information to accomplish the network management tasks discussed above and in the previous sections, can take place via a number of interfaces and procedures. In the treatment that follows we examine:

1. Layer Management.

2. B-LMI.

3. CNM/SNMP.

4. Carrier Operations/CMIP (Chapter 10).

References

[1] D. Minoli, *First, Second, and Next Generation LANs* (McGraw-Hill, 1993).

[2] ISO/IEC 10040; 10164 Parts 1–11; 10165 Parts 1–6; 12060 Parts 1–5.

[3] D. Minoli, "Network Management Functions: Telecommunications Hardware," *Datapro Report NM20-100-101*, June 1989.

[4] D. Minoli, "Managing Local Area Networks: Fault and Configuration Management," *Datapro Report NM50-300-401*, August 1989.

[5] D. Minoli, "Managing Local Area Networks: Accounting, Performance, and Security Management," *Datapro Report NM50-300-501*, June 1989.

[6] D. Minoli, "Network Monitoring and Control," *Datapro Report NM20- 200-101*, June 1989.

[7] D. Minoli, "Evolving Security Management Standards," *Datapro Report NM20-500-101*, June 1989.

[8] Bellcore Technical Advisory TA-NWT-001248, *Generic Requirements for Operations of Broadband Switching Systems*, October 1993.

chapter 5

Fundamentals: Managing the Physical and ATM Layers

Layer management occurs at the Physical Layer, the ATM Layer, and the AAL Layer.[1] Network management functions in general, and operations and maintenance procedures in particular, require the exchange of operations information among various nodes in the network.

At the Physical Layer, endpoints of each facility exchange operations information via overhead fields built into the signal framing structure of the underlying transmission medium.

When operations information is associated with the stream of user data across a physical or logical connection, as is the case with error detection codes, or when timing is critical (e.g., in reporting failure/congestion indications), a direct embedding technique (i.e., one that uses a bit-oriented protocol) is employed.

This chapter identifies mechanisms required at the Physical and ATM Layers to support the flow of bit-oriented operations information between peer-to-peer Physical and ATM Layer termination points. It also discusses the Broadband Local Management Interface.

5.1   Introduction

ATM services may rely on DS1, DS3, and Synchronous Optical Network (SONET) physical facilities. Therefore, one needs to identify mechanisms to communicate operations information across DS1, DS3, SONET, and Physical Layer Convergence Procedure (PLCP) paths; additionally, ATM Virtual Path and Virtual Channel connections are of interest.[2]

ATM Layer management, as seen in Figure 5.1, provides a supporting role for systems management functions. These management functions include fault, performance, configuration, and metasignaling management functions. (Security and resource management functions may be added in the future.) However, the ATM Layer management performs only the ATM Layer aspects of those functions. (ATM Layer management also provides a supporting role for the signaling functions of the Control plane, including *metasignaling*.) See Table 5.1.

Functions performed by the ATM Layer management entity may be applied to ATM Peer-Peer connections when they are needed. To perform its func-

---

[1] The AAL Layer is terminated in the network only when there is network or service internetworking. For simple CRS, the network does not get involved with the AAL Layer.
[2] Portions of this chapter are based on [6]

Function	Activity
Connection (configuration) management	The ATM Layer Management Entity performs the establishment/removal processes of ATM Peer-Peer connections
Fault management	The ATM Layer Management Entity performs the alarm surveillance, loopback, and continuity check processes of ATM Peer-Peer connections
Metasignaling	The ATM Layer Management Entity manages different types of signaling channels (when needed)[a]
Performance management	The ATM Layer Management Entity performs the activation/deactivation of performance monitoring and reporting processes of ATM Peer-Peer connections

[a] Q.2931-based signaling, when there is a single signaling entity across the UNI, does not require metasignaling, which is a set of *device power-up* procedures to obtain a signaling channel, before the actual signaling session can take place. Metasignaling is needed when there are multiple signaling entities on a UNI, or when the Service Profile capability is employed. Initial ATM implementations do not require metasignaling.

Table 5.1 ATM layer management functions

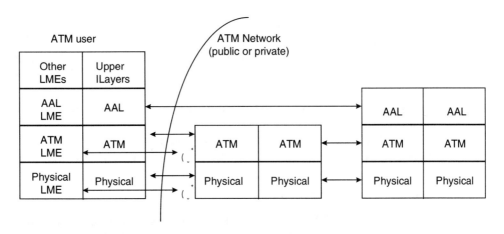

Figure 5.1 ATM LMEs (Layer Management Entities)

tions, the ATM Layer management entity uses two types of interactions with the ATM-entity [1]:

1. Exchange of local information between the ATM-entity and the ATM Layer management entity (called *ATMM-entity*). To support this interaction, an ATM node has local associations between the ATM-entity and the ATMM-entity.

2. Peer-to-peer communication between ATMM-entities. To support this interaction, ATM Layer management information is transported between two or more ATMM-entities, and conveyed by bidirectional communication methods called *Type A* and *Type B*. (See Figure 5.2.)

The Type A communication method uses a separate ATM User-User connection (which cannot be used for any other purpose) and a user data cell indication in the Payload Type Identifier (PTI) field within this connection. ATM Layer management information is placed in the cell payload. The link identifier (VPI/VCI) of this ATM User-User connection is assigned by standardization, provisioning, or signaling. Metasignaling and VPC OAM flows (F4) use this method. Their VPI values are the same as those used for Control or User Plane communications, and their VCI values are standardized. There are two cases of OAM F4 flows:

- Segment OAM flow is used for ATM Layer management communications among the ATMM-entities at the endpoints of a VPC segment.

- End-to-end OAM flow is used for ATM Layer management communications among the ATMM-entities at end systems.

All intermediate systems of the given VPC can copy the information received on these OAM flows, as well as send information on them. The information received on either segment OAM flow or end-to-end OAM flow can be removed only at the endpoints of the OAM flow (segment endpoint or connection endpoint, respectively).

The Type B communication method uses a Layer management indication for the PTI field. ATM Layer management information is placed in the cell payload. The link identifier (VPI/VCI) of the associated ATM User-User connection is used in both directions. There are two cases of OAM F5 flows:

- Segment OAM flow is used for ATM Layer management communications among the ATMM-entities at the endpoints of a VCC.

- End-to-end OAM flow is used for ATM Layer management communications among the ATMM-entities at end systems of a VCC.

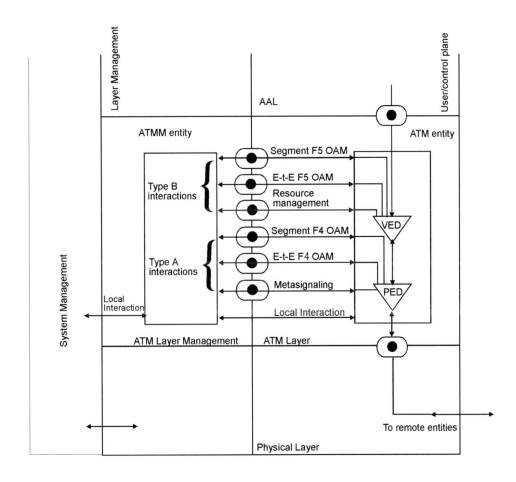

VED denotes VPI/VCI encoding/PED denotes PTI encoding/decoding. ● denotes Service Access Point (SAP)

Figure 5.2 ATM entities, ATMM entities, and management interactions

All intermediate systems of the given VCC can copy the information received on OAM flows, as well as send information on them. The information received on either segment OAM flow or end-to-end OAM flow can be removed only at the endpoints of the OAM flow (segment endpoint or connection endpoint, respectively).

Figure 5.2 shows the two types of interactions at an end system of an ATM Peer-Peer connection; Type A and Type B communication methods are also shown. (This figure provides a more detailed view of the peer interactions in Figure 5.1.)

5.2 Physical Layer Operations Flows

In support of Physical Layer operations, bit-oriented operations flows are used for each of the following [2—4]:

- DS1 Transport Systems.
- DS3 Transport Systems.
- PLCP Paths.
- SONET Transport Systems.

The mechanisms for such communications are discussed in the sections that follow.

5.3 DS1 Level Operations Flows

DS1 rate facilities that support ATM use the Extended Superframe Format (ESF) [5]. Bit-oriented operations information is communicated between the entities terminating a DS1 path via a 4-kbps data link channel, and a 2-kbps Cyclic Redundancy Check (CRC) channel. The Extended Superframe Format makes these overhead channels available by making efficient use of the DS1 framing bits. Specifically, 18 of the 24 DS1 framing bits in the ESF are used for bit-oriented operations communications: 6 for error detection (CRC-6) and 12 for a 4-kbps data link channel; see Figure 5.3 [5]. The 4-kbps data link channel is used to report far-end performance monitoring results, to activate and deactivate a line-level loopback, and to notify downstream equipment about failures that have occurred upstream.

5.4 DS3 Level Operations Flows

A DS3 M-frame consists of seven subframes, each consisting of eight blocks of 85 bits each; see Figure 5.4. The first bit of each block is a DS3 overhead bit, thus making available a total of 7×8 = 56 overhead bits in a DS3 M-frame. The overhead bits are categorized into five classes: F-bits, M-bits, P-bits, X-bits, and C-bits. The F-bits and M-bits are used for M-subframe and M-frame align-

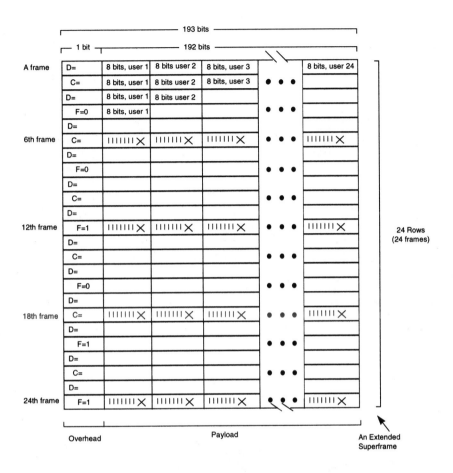

Figure 5.3 Bit layout in DSI ESF format (from top left to bottom right)

ment, respectively. The P-bits, X-bits, and C-bits are used for the communication of operations information between peer DS3 termination entities. The P-bits are used for parity checking and to collect performance monitoring data. The X-bits are used by terminating equipment to signal a failure condition (yellow alarm) to the other end of the DS3 facility. The C-bits have application-specific uses by DS3 transport systems [2].

5.5 PLCP Level Operations Flows

The ATM Physical Layer Convergence Protocol defines the mapping of ATM cells onto the existing DS3 and DS1 facilities. PLCP overhead consists of the

Time length of M-Frame:
8x7x85/44,736,000=
106.402 microseconds

680 bit (8 blocks of 84+1 bus)

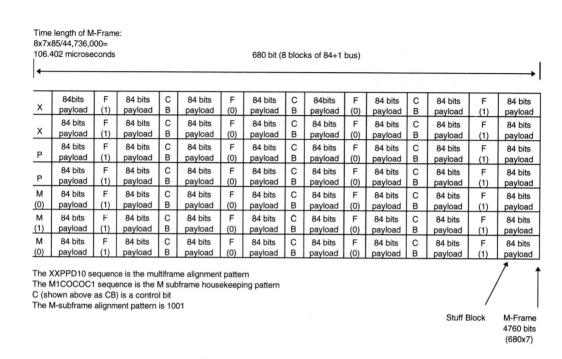

The XXPPD10 sequence is the multiframe alignment pattern
The M1COCOC1 sequence is the M subframe housekeeping pattern
C (shown above as CB) is a control bit
The M-subframe alignment pattern is 1001

Stuff Block   M-Frame
4760 bits
(680x7)

Stuff Block

8th block of 84 payload bits

		F (1)	Stuff Bit 1	Info Bit 2	Info Bit 3	Info Bit 4	Info Bit 5	Info Bit 6	Info Bit 7	Info Bit 8				
X		F (1)	Stuff Bit 1	Info Bit 2	Info Bit 3	Info Bit 4	Info Bit 5	Info Bit 6	Info Bit 7	Info Bit 8				
X		F (1)	Info Bit 1	Stuff Bit 2	Info Bit 3	Info Bit 4	Info Bit 5	Info Bit 6	Info Bit 7	Info Bit 8				
P		F (1)	Info Bit 1	Info Bit 2	Stuff Bit 3	Info Bit 4	Info Bit 5	Info Bit 6	Info Bit 7	Info Bit 8				
P		F (1)	Info Bit 1	Info Bit 2	Info Bit 3	Stuff Bit 4	Info Bit 5	Info Bit 6	Info Bit 7	Info Bit 8				
M (0)		F (1)	Info Bit 1	Info Bit 2	Info Bit 3	Info Bit 4	Stuff Bit 5	Info Bit 6	Info Bit 7	Info Bit 8				
M (1)		F (1)	Info Bit 1	Info Bit 2	Info Bit 3	Info Bit 4	Info Bit 5	Stuff Bit 6	Info Bit 7	Info Bit 8				
M (0)		F (1)	Info Bit 1	Info Bit 2	Info Bit 3	Info Bit 4	Info Bit 5	Info Bit 6	Stuff Bit 7	Stuff Bit 8				

Stuffing for the Jth DS2 channel occurs in the M-subframe J, in the Jth information bit of the
last block (the CB bits are set to 111 for that M-subframe if stuffing occurs - otherwise they are 000)

Figure 5.4   DS3 frame

following: framing octets (A1 and A2), path overhead identifier octets (Z6-Z1), Bit Interleaved Parity (BIP) - 8 octet (B1), PLCP path status octet (G1), and the cycle/stuff counter octet (C1). See Figure 5.5 [6]. Of these overhead fields, the B1 and G1 octets of each PLCP frame are used to communicate operations information between peer PLCP level management entities. The BIP-8 error detection code in the B1 field supports PLCP path error monitoring and the collection of PLCP path level performance data. The first four bits of the G1 byte are used to report far-end performance information to the near end (e.g., a Far End Bit Error (FEBE) indication). The fifth bit in the G1 byte is used to convey (to the downstream PLCP path terminating entity) the detection of a

PLCP (1 Octet)	Framing (1 Octet)	POI (1 Octet)	POH (1 Octet)	PLCP Payload (53 Octets)	
A1	A2	P11	Z6	First ATM cell	
A1	A2	P10	Z5	Second ATM cell	
A1	A2	P09	Z4		
A1	A2	P08	Z3		
A1	A2	P07	Z2		
A1	A2	P06	Z1		
A1	A2	P05	X		
A1	A2	P04	B1		
A1	A2	P03	G1		
A1	A2	P02	X		(13 or 14
A1	A2	P01	X	Eleventh ATM cell	nibbles)
A1	A2	P00	C1	Twelfth ATM cell	Trailer

POI = Path Overhead Indicator
POH = Path Overhead
BIP-8 = Bit Interleaved Parity-8
X = Unassigned - Receiver to ignore

Order and transmission of all PLCP bits and octets are from left to right and top to bottom. The figure shows the most significant bit (MSB) on the left and the least significant bit (LSB) on the right.

Figure 5.5 Mapping of ATM cells into DS3 frames using PLCP

yellow alarm condition upstream.The remaining three bits in the G1 byte are not used for ATM PLCP-based interfaces.

5.6   SONET Level Operations Flows

SONET overhead fields exist at three distinct levels: Section Level, Line Level, and Path Level; see Figures 5.6 and 5.7 [5]. ATM switching systems terminate all three of these levels and process the three corresponding overhead fields. The bit-oriented operations information encoded in the SONET Section, Line and Path overhead fields is used to 1) report SONET level alarm, failure, status, and error indications (such as FEBE, indication) and 2) provide forward error detection information (e.g., BIP-8 error detection codes) for the detection of transmission errors and the collection of SONET level performance data.

5.7   ATM Layer Operations Flows

For VPs, end-to-end OAM capabilities are supported via specially-marked ATM cells, which are transmitted over VCs with specific VCI values (these are known as F4 Flows). For VCs, operation functions are supported via cells marked with an appropriate codepoint in the Payload Type Indicator field (these are known as F5 Flows). Some of the functions supported are shown in Table 5.2.

Fault management functions	Alarm surveillance: AIS (Alarm Indication Signal) Alarm surveillance: RDI (Remote Defect Indicator) Connectivity verification: Cell Loopback Continuity check
Activation/deactivation	Performance monitoring Continuity check
Performance management functions	Forward monitoring Backward reporting Monitoring/reporting

Table 5.2   Layer management functions included in ATM/cell relay

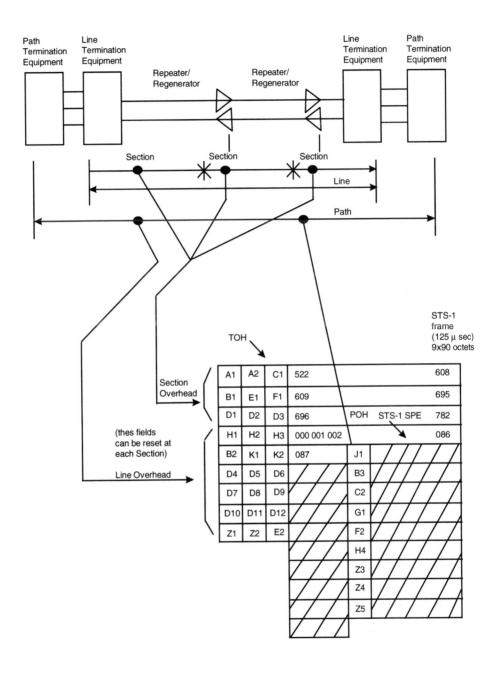

Figure 5.6   SONET frame

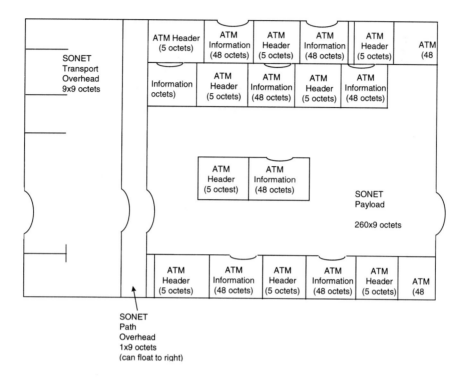

Figure 5.7 Mapping of ATM cells into SONET frame

For some VPCs or VCCs, in-band connection-specific operations information are communicated between the various VPC or VCC nodes (defined as any node accessing or terminating a VPC or VCC). Examples include failure indication, performance monitoring data, and test requests. The required mechanisms for transmitting such information at the VP and VC levels are discussed below.

5.7.1 VPC Operations Flows (F4 FLows)

VPC operations flows are made possible via specially marked ATM cells. These cells are referred to as Operations and Maintenance (OAM) cells, and are distinguished from user data cells by an indicator in the ATM cell header. Specifically, VPC OAM cells are identified by a unique set of VCI values. There are two kinds of F4 flows which can simultaneously exist in a VPC:

- *End-to-End F4 flow*   This flow is used for communicating end-to-end VPC operations information. VCI value 4 is used for identifying OAM cells that comprise F4 flows.

- *Segment F4 flow*   VCI value 3 is used for identifying OAM cells communicated within the bounds of a single VPL or group of interconnected VPLs in the purview of a single provider's network. A VPL or group of VPLs that is independently managed using such OAM cells is referred to in I.610 as a VPC Segment.

5.7.2 VCC Operations Flows (F5 Flows)

VCC operations (F5) flows also make use of OAM cells. These OAM cells have the same VCI/VPI values as the user cells of the VCC and are distinguished from other cells transported over a particular connection by the Payload Type Indicator (PTI) value. There are two types of F5 flows which can simultaneously exist in a VCC:

- *End-to-End F5 flow*   PTI value 5 (101) is used to identify OAM cells used for communicating end-to-end VCC operations information.

- *Segment F5 flow*   PTI value 4 (100) is used to identify OAM cells communicated within the bounds of a single VCC link or group of interconnected VCC links in the purview of a single provider's network. A VCC link or group of VCC links that is managed using such OAM cells is referred to in I.610 as a VCC Segment.

Endpoints of a connection or connection segment, including user equipment, terminate and process all incoming OAM cells that belong to the connection. Such endpoints may also generate and insert OAM cells for downstream processing. Intermediate points along a connection or connection segment may monitor OAM cells passing through them and insert new OAM cells, but they do not terminate the OAM flow.

A number of VPC/VCC management functions exist. To accommodate these functions, three OAM cell types have been defined:

- *Fault Management OAM Cells*   These OAM cells are transmitted to indicate failure conditions, such as a failed facility or discontinuity at the virtual path or channel level. These cells may also be used to perform various test functions on a virtual connection or connection segment (e.g., as part of a reactive trouble isolation procedure).

- *Activation/Deactivation OAM Cells*   This cell type is used for activating and deactivating the OAM cell generation, and processing functions associated with certain VPC/VCC management capabilities.

- *Performance Management OAM Cells*   These OAM cells are transmitted regularly between endpoints of selected virtual connections or connection segments, and are used to monitor parameters, such as errored cell block ratio, cell loss ratio, and misinserted cells, for performance monitoring.

Although the OAM cell payload format for each OAM cell type is different, there are some fields that are common:

- *OAM Cell Type*   This 4-bit field indicates the type of management function performed by the OAM cell (e.g., performance management, fault management, or activation/deactivation). Valid values for this field are shown in Table 5.3.

- *OAM Function Type*   This 4-bit field indicates the actual function performed by the OAM cell. Standardized values of this field per OAM Cell Type value are shown in Table 5.3.

- *Reserved Field*   This 6-bit field has been reserved for future specification. This field is encoded with a default value of all zeroes.

- *CRC-10 Error Detection Code*   This field carries a CRC-10 error detection code that is calculated over the entire OAM cell payload. This field is used by

OAM Cell Type	Value	OAM Function Type	Value
Fault management	0001	AIS	0000
		RDI (FERF)	0001
		OAM cell loopback (LB)	0010
		Continuity check (CC)	0100
Performance management	0010	Forward monitoring	0000
		Backward reporting	0001
		Monitoring/reporting	0010
Activation/deactivation	1000	Performance monitoring	0000
		Continuity check	0001

Table 5.3   OAM type/function identifiers

CHAPTER 5: FUNDAMENTALS: MANAGING THE PHYSICAL AND ATM LAYERS

ATM Layer entities to detect errored OAM cells and thus avoid processing any corrupted operations information.

The manner in which unused octets and unused bits (i.e., incomplete octets) are coded is also common across all OAM cell types. The term *unused* refers to part of a cell either not assigned to any field, or any field that is not used in a particular application. All unused OAM cell information octets are coded as binary 01101010. All unused OAM cell information field bits are coded as all zeros. The common part of the OAM cell is illustrated in Figure 5.8.

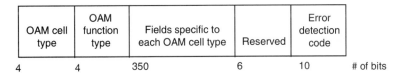

OAM cell type	OAM function type	Fields specific to each OAM cell type	Reserved	Error detection code	
4	4	350	6	10	# of bits

Figure 5.8   OAM cell common part

As of press time, not all switch manufacturers support OAM flows. In particular, manufacturers high-end central-office type switches (e.g., AT&T, Alcatel, DSC, Fujistu, Nortel, and Siemens) tend to support these flows, while manufacturers of smaller ATM switches tend not to support the flows. Some support the ATM Forum defined Fault Management flows (LB, AIS, RDI/FERF), but not the Bellcore-defined Performance Management and Activation/Deactivation flows [8].

5.8   *Broadband Local Management Interface*

CRS must be properly configured and monitored to ensure satisfactory end-to-end performance. The Broadband Local Management Interface (also known as Interim Local Management Interface) provides bidirectional exchange of management information across a UNI, between two adjacent UNI management entities (UMEs).

A standard B-LMI Management Information Base (MIB) has also been defined. This MIB contains configuration and status information related to the physical link and associated VPC/VCCs.

A UME can access the MIB information associated with its adjacent UME via the B-LMI communication protocol. Figure 5.9 illustrates the B-LMI communications protocol stack. Adjacent UMEs supporting B-LMI act as peers, and each UME contains both an agent application and a management applica-

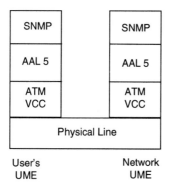

Figure 5.9   B-LMI Protocol Stack

tion. The adjacent UMEs contain the same MIB; however, semantics of some MIB objects may be interpreted differently. Table 5.4 depicts some of the key functions that can be supported.

Management information related to the operation of the ATM UNI is hierarchically organized into a MIB as follows:

- Physical Layer management information.

- ATM Cell Layer management information.

- VPC level management information.

- VCC level management information.

The UNI management information corresponds to configuration and status information. In addition, optionally, the ATM cell layer performance and traffic statistics may be provided. The tree structure of the MIB is shown in Figure 5.10.

MIB objects are defined using a subset of Abstract Syntax Notation One (ASN.1) following the conventions specified in [8]. All MIB objects are, by default, read only across the B-LMI, unless otherwise specified as readable and writable across the B-LMI for a specific UNI MIB object. Tables 5.5 and 5.6 list the objects contained in the Physical Port and Virtual Path object groups, respectively.

Physical Layer	Interface index
	Interface address
	Transmission type
	Media type
	Operational status
ATM Layer	Maximum number of VPCs
	Maximum number of VCCs
	VPI/VCI address width
	Number of configured VPCs
	Number of configured VCCs
	Port type
ATM Layer statistics	ATM cells received
	ATM cells dropped on receive side
	ATM cells transmitted
VP connection	VPI value
	Shaping traffic descriptor
	Policing traffic descriptor
	Operational status
	QoS category
VC connection	VPI/VCI value
	Shaping traffic descriptor
	Policing traffic descriptor
	Operational status
	QoS category

Table 5.4   B-LMI functions associated with ATM/cell relay

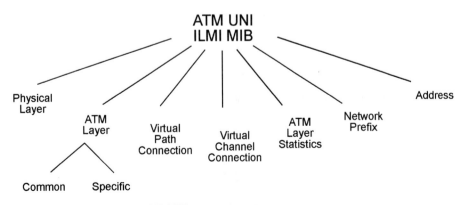

Figure 5.10   ATM B-LMI MIB tree structure

Objects	Type	Definition	Remarks
Interface index	Integer	Implicitly defines the physical interface over which the ILMI messages are received	Provides the UME with the identifier to retreive UNI management information from its adjacent UME
Interface address	Integer	Public UNI address	Encoding is based upon ITU-T E.164 address and is currently defined as a number or a number plus subaddress
Transmission type	Object ID	Identifies the physical interface which is currently defined as either STS-3c or DS3	Uniquely determines the transmission speed of the physical interface
Media type	Object ID	Defines the physical media type supported at a UNI	Currently public UNI types are coaxial cable, single-mode fiber, and multimode fiber
Operational status	Integer	Identifies the operational state of the physical interface (in-service, out-of-service, or loopback)	Out-of-service and loopback indicate that the UNI is unavailable for cell transmission
Transmission type-specific Information	Object ID	Points to additional transmission and/or media specific information about a UNI	Points to other Physical Layer MIBs

Table 5.5   Physical Port object group [5]

Objects	Type	Definition	Remarks
Interface index	Integer	Implicitly defines the physical interface over which the ILMI messages are received	
VPI	Integer	Assigned VPI value for a VPC	
Operational status	Integer	Specifies the current operational state of the VPC (up, down, or unknown)	This information may be provided for the end-to-end VPC
Shaping traffic descriptor	Object ID	Points to the shaping parameters for cells transmitted on a VPC across a public UNI	
Policing traffic descriptor	Object ID	Points to the UPC parameters for policing cells received on this VPC	
QoS category	Integer	Defines the QoS category of the VPC	

Table 5.6   Virtual Path objects

References

[1] Bellcore Technical Advisory TA-NWT-001113, *Asynchronous Transfer Mode (ATM) and ATM Adaptation Layer* (AAL) Protocol Generic *Requirements*, Issue 2, July 1993.

[2] Bellcore Technical Advisory TA-NWT-001112, *Broadband ISDN User to Network and Network Node Interface Physical Layer Generic Criteria*, August 1992.

[3] T1 LB/91-05, *Broadband ISDN User-Network Interfaces: Rates and Formats Specifications.*

[4] ITU-T Recommendation I.610, *B-ISDN Operations and Maintenance Principles and Functions,* June 1992.

[5] D. Minoli, *Enterprise Networking—Fractional T1 to SONET, Frame Relay to BISDN* (Artech House, 1993).

[6] D. Minoli, M. Vitella, *Cell Relay Service and ATM in Corporate Environments* (McGraw-Hill, 1994).

[7] *ATM User-Network Interface Specification,* Version 3.0, ATM Forum, August 1993.

[8] Bellcore Technical Advisory TA-NWT-001248, *Generic Requirements for Operations of Broadband Switching Systems,* October 1993.

[9] RFC 1155, *Structure and Identification of Management Information for TCP/IP-based Internets,* SRI International, March 1993.

chapter 6

Fundamentals: Customer Network Management

*C*ustomer Network Management (CNM) refers to a set of activities supported by public networks to facilitate planning, operations, administration, reconfiguration, and maintenance of an end user's service view.

ATM-based CNM service provides corporate managers with capabilities to manage their access to and the use of the public ATM transport network and services. The initial CNM service supported by carriers provides Cell Relay Service customers with capabilities to manage their access to and the use of exchange PVC CRS and ATM UNIs.

CNM customers can use CNM-provided information to determine if the UNIs are properly configurated, to detect, isolate, and correct error conditions associated with the customer's use of the CRS, to analyze performance, and to reconfigure some service subscription parameters, i.e., PVCs.[1]

This chapter discusses key aspects of CNM services. As of press time, however, few if any carriers were ready to offer users CNM features. The hope is that such services will be available in the future.

6.1   The Manager-Agent Model

The basic OS/NM and SNMP network management model, implicit in Figure 4.1, is called the *Manager-Agent model*. In this model, Figure 6.1, a system in the ATM network or in the ATM switch acts as the Agent for resources to be managed by the management system, which is the Manager (or Network Manager). Figure 4.1 distinguished between a CNM application (CNMA) used in the context of managing a public network service, and an NMS used to manage a physical switch (public or private); such a distinction is not always necessary, and the term *NMS* can be employed to refer to both.

In the realm of network management, the various elements of the enterprise network—the transmission facilities, the communications equipment (multiplexers, routers, bridges, and hubs), the public networks, etc.—are viewed as managed (or manageable) resources.

Managed resources which are capable of information processing, e.g., servers, computers, routers, bridges, hubs, and public networks execute software supporting network management processes. These processes support functions such as event detection and event notification, traffic measurement, and logging of occurrences of significant events. The processor supporting such pro-

---

[1]PVC CRS became widely available in 1995; SVC CRS was expected to become available in 1996 or 1997.

cesses is known as a *network management agent*. For each relevant function performed by a network management agent, there is an associated set of related information; such information characterizes the status, performance, and behavior of the managed resource.

To support the required network management capabilities, network management agents must exchange network management information with one another, or with the Network Manager. (The Network Manager resides on a processor referred to as *The Network Management System*.) Data exchange between network management agents, or between network management agents and the Network Manager is achieved through a management-specific protocol. Management information protocols related to Layer Management (Chapter 5) are called *Layer Management Protocols*. Management information protocols that operate between network management agents and Network Managers (with corresponding entities residing at the application layer of the protocol architecture) are called *Management Application Protocols* (MAPs).

Examples of managed ATM resources are switch line termination cards (physical resources) and routing tables (logical resources). The resources are managed using Manager-to-Agent and Agent-to-Manager interactions. For example, the manager can send requests to the agent to perform an operation such as setting the entries of a routing table; the agent can report events such as an alarm indicating a power supply or line card failure. CRS CNM information is accessed with two primitive operations, Read and Write;[2] complex NMS operations and functions can be performed by retrieving simple counter and integer data for further processing.

The *NMS/CNMA* needs to support and physically interface with many distinct types of managed systems, whether from a single or from multiple vendors. New systems are added on an ongoing basis to the private or public network, as technology evolves and new services are introduced. Also, it is

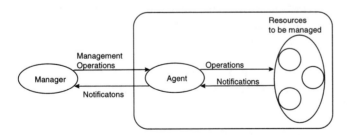

Figure 6.1 OSI Network Management Model

---

[2] In early version of the CNM service offered by carriers, read-only access is expected to be provided.

often the case that one wants to enhance the NMS itself with new functions and new algorithms (e.g., artificial intelligence) [1]. The NMS/CNMA interface needs to be designed to facilitate such evolution to proceed in an unhindered manner. This is accomplished using open standards. To make a CNM service effective, the designers of such capability in the public network must identify a set of management information specific to CRS that complements the database of management information about the enterprise network already available to the corporation in the pre-ATM context, that is viewed by the datacom manager as essential to maintaining an optimally operational network. Table 6.1 identifies possible CNM features supported by cell relay service.

Administer trouble reports

Initiate tests

Receive unsolicited event notifications

Request event notification

Request network intervention

Retrieve "network configuration",
   e.g., who is in the multipoint call

Retrieve performance information

Retrieve UNI configuration information

Retrieve usage information

Retrieve VPC/VCC configuration information

Support security policies

Table 6.1   Typical CNM features for ATM networks

Because of the heterogeneity of corporate enterprise networks, the CRS CNM features must work synergistically with the CNM features of other wide areas data services, such as SMDS and Frame Relay service. The advantages of this approach include the following:

1. The user can follow the same procedures in managing that component of the enterprise network as for other components: the same kind of information is available.

2. Developers of NMS can more readily develop applications if they have already built applications for the other services.

3. Carriers can use the same network support architectures. (However, a carrier may choose to offer ATM CNM services through separate CNM servers, or may choose to offer the service through integrated CNM servers.)

CNM service capabilities are based on CRS and ATM network requirements described in the documents shown in Table 6.2 [2] (also see Figure 6.2). The PVC CNM service capabilities are planned to be offered by LECs and AAPs (Alternate Access Providers) in two phases which are correlated to the CRS service phases: Phase 1 PVC CRS CNM service capabilities were scheduled to begin in 1995; Phase 2 capabilities are scheduled to begin in 1996 [3].

6.2   SNMP Constructs

Carrier-provided CNM capabilities (consisting of an agent in the network) along with a customer-owned NMS/CNMA, provide users of public Cell Relay Service with the capability of managing their access to the network and certain aspects of the Carrier-provided CRS service. To specify a CRS CNM service (namely, capabilities in the network and features in the user's NMS) one must define the following:

• Service objectives for the CNM service.

• Set of CRS CNM information for managing the service and ATM network.

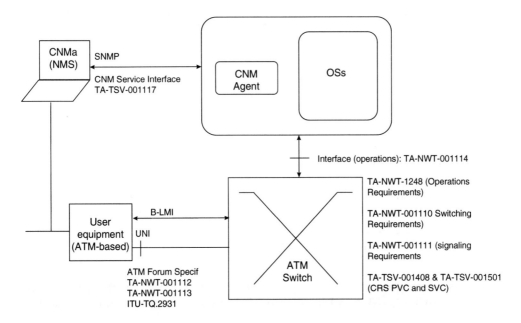

Figure 6.2   Key specifications pertaining to ATM and ATM management

ITU-T	I.113: B-ISDN Vocabulary of Terms
	I.121R: Broadband Aspects of ISDNI.150: B-ISDN ATM Functional Characteristics
	I.211: B-ISDN Service Aspects
	I.311: B-ISDN General Network Aspects
	I.321: B-ISDN Protocol Reference Model and its Applications
	I.327: B-ISDN Functional Architecture Aspects
	I.361: B-ISDN ATM Layer Specification
	I.362: B-ISDN ATM Adaptation Layer Functional Description
	I.363: B-ISDN ATM Adaptation Layer Specification
	I.371: B-ISDN Traffic Control and Congestion Control
	I.413: B-ISDN UserNetwork Interface
	I.432: B-ISDN UserNetwork Interface Physical Layer
	I.610: B-ISDN UNI Operations and Maintenance Principles
Bellcore	TA-NWT001110: Broadband ISDN Switching System Generic Requirements
	TA-NWT001111: Broadband ISDN Access Signaling Generic Requirements
	TA-NWT001112: Broadband ISDN User to Network Interface and Network Node Interface Physical Layer Generic Requirements
	TA-NWT001113: Asynchronous Transfer Mode (ATM) and ATM Adaptation Layer (AAL) Protocols Generic Requirements
	TA-TSV001408: Generic Requirements for Exchange PVC Cell Relay Service
	TA-TSV001409: Generic Requirements for Exchange Access PVC Cell Relay Service
	TA-TSV001501: Generic Requirements for Exchange SVC Cell Relay Service

Table 6.2   Key B-ISDN documents

- CRS CNM service capabilities that can be supported by the CNM information.

- Procedural means to provide subscriber access for obtaining CRS information. For the user to obtain access to the CNM information, a Management Application Protocol between the carrier's CNM Agent and the NMS/ CNMA must be defined. The string-based Simple Network Management Protocol (also known as SNMPv1) can be used initially as the MAP for access to CNM information. See Figure 6.3.

Six SNMP modules must be supported to accomplish the task at hand, as documented in Table 6.3. In addition, retrieval of CNM information and reception of event notifications must be specified. Capabilities to allow a subscriber to modify CRS information (e.g., addition of a PVC) may become available soon. Integrated CNM capabilities to manage multiple services provided on an ATM platform, such as PVC CRS, SVC CRS, SMDS over ATM, and frame relay service over ATM, are also contemplated by carriers for 1996 and beyond. B-LMI access and the support of the B-LMI MIB, as well as layer management tools, can be considered part of the CNM definition [3].

6.3 CNM Functionality in the ATM Context

At the functional level, users need capabilities to monitor, measure, and analyze the end-to-end network performance, as well as to detect, isolate, and rectify failures in communication equipment and transmission facilities.

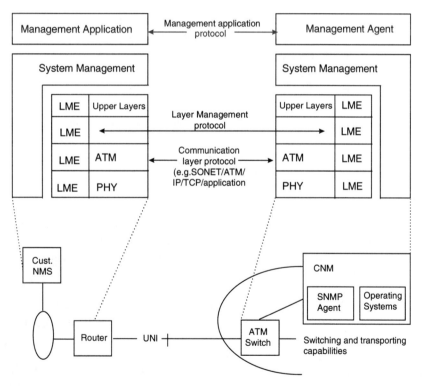

Note: Both layer and systems management functionality can be supported or provided by the CRS carrier.

Figure 6.3 Protocols in support of network management

MIB II System and Interfaces groups (RFC1213)
> Management Information Base for Network Management of TCP/IP-based Internets, RFC 1213, M. T. Rose, March 1991

Interfaces Evolution Group
> Internet Draft, K. McCloghrie, F. Kastenholtz, August 1993

ATM MIB
> Definition of Managed Objects for ATM Management, Internet Draft, M. Ahmed, K. Tesink, August 1993

DS1 MIB (RFC 1406)
> Definition of Managed Objects for the DS1 and E1 Interfaces Type, RFC 1406, F. Baker, J. Watt, January 1993.

DS3 MIB (RFC 1407)
> Definition of Managed Objects for the DS3 and E3 Interfaces Type, RFC 1407, T. A. Cox, K. Tesink, January 1993.

SONET MIB
> Definition of Managed Objects for the SONET Interface Type, Version 2, Internet Draft, T. A. Cox, K. Tesink, August 1993.

(PVC) CRS Subscription MIB
> Definition of Managed Objects for Exchange PVC CRS Subscription, Enterprise-specific MIB Internet Draft, M. Ahmed, K. Tesink, August 1993

Note: All documents are available from Network Information Center, SRI International, Menlo Park, CA.

Table 6.3   Structures required for Customer Network Management of cell relay service

Certain CNM queries will result in only small amounts of information being sent to the manager (i.e., notices of event indications), while invocation of other CNM capabilities may result in the generation of long reports. This section describes CNM service capabilities that are planned to be supported for ATM end users.

The Simple Network Management Protocol (SNMP) already is in wide use in IP networks, and is a plausible candidate for ATM-based enterprise networks.

Initially, published specifications covered only PVC cell relay service; other capabilities are expected to follow [4]. Preferably, the CRS CNM capabilities offered by carriers are consistent and synergistic with the CNM features of other WAN data services (SMDS and Frame Relay service) that could be employed by corporations, perhaps as a transitional step, in support of their overall enterprise networks.

To perform CNM functions, a public network CNM agent communicates with the end user's network management system. By accessing and controlling the CNM information, the end user's network management system manages the public network portion of the end user's communications network. SNMP is employed as the management protocol for communications between the NMS and the ATM PVC CNM agent. Alternative access configurations supporting SNMP exchange could be supported (see the next section). UNI-specific CNM information to support ATM capabilities can be categorized as follows:

- Physical level CNM information.

- ATM cell level CNM information.

- VPC level CNM information.

- VCC level CNM information.

The types of information that may be supported for each level listed above are configuration information, status information and performance and traffic statistics. At the physical level, configuration information provides information such as transmission types (e.g., DS3 or SONET transmission) and media types (e.g., fiber optic or coaxial cable). Status information provides information on the availability status of the physical link (e.g., DS3 alarm state), and performance and traffic statistics provide counts such as DS3 or SONET Path severely errored seconds and unavailable seconds. At the ATM cell level, configuration information provides information such as the number of configured VPCs, the maximum number of VPCs, the maximum number of active VPI bits, and the amount of unused bandwidth available at a UNI. Performance and traffic statistics provide counts of ATM cells transmitted or received across a UNI, counts of errored cells, and counts of cells having unrecognized VPI and VPI/VCI values.

At the VPC or VCC level, configuration information provides information such as the VPI value or VPI/VCI values and Usage Parameter Control (UPC) traffic parameters (e.g., the VPC peak rate and QoS parameter). Status information provides information such as the operational state of a VPC or a VCC at a UNI (e.g., up, down, or testing the state of a VPC or a VCC).

Performance and traffic statistics provide counts such as the number of cells transmitted or received across a VPC or a VCC, the number of discarded cells due to UPC peak rate violation, and the number of times the cell rate exceeds the traffic peak rate on a VPC or a VCC [4].

Organizations may use a gamut of equipment and software to access the CNM service, ranging from simple terminals to high end workstations running sophisticated network management SNMP-based applications. The corporate manager can connect the network management equipment (e.g., UNIX workstation with appropriate software) to access the CRS CNM service in three ways:

1. Directly on the CRS access path.

2. Through some other transmission/network service (e.g., dedicated digital or analog line).

3. On a LAN on the customer's premises, with indirect access to the CRS and the CRS CNM service through other equipment, such as a router attached to an ATM UNI.

Information collection varies, based on the NMS/CNMA design. Some applications are written so that CRS CNM information can be requested or is posted upon the occurrence of faults or other significant events; other applications periodically collect CRS CNM information and take appropriate actions based on the results of that polling procedure. ATM PVC CNM service capabilities enable end users to [3, 5]:

- Initiate tests.
- Retrieve UNI configuration profile information.
- Modify UNI configuration profile information.
- Retrieve VPC/VCC subscription profile information.
- Modify VPC/VCC subscription profile information.
- Request event notifications.
- Request network intervention.
- Retrieve general CNM information.
- Modify general CNM information.
- Retrieve performance information.
- Retrieve usage information.
- Request trouble reports.

These are described briefly on the following pages.

6.3.1 *Initiate Tests*

This capability allows end users to initiate tests in isolating problems in their networks which span across the public ATM network and services. For example, end users can activate an ATM level loopback (e.g., activating OAM cell loopback capability using CNM service) which could help in fault isolation. Similarly, end users can activate VCC or VPC performance monitoring using this service.

6.3.2 *Retrieve UNI Configuration Profile Information*

This capability allows end users to retrieve UNI configuration information such as descriptions of how a UNI is currently provisioned or configured (e.g., number of VPCs configured at a UNI, transmission speed of a UNI, number of higher level services supported at a UNI). In addition, this service capability also provides end users with the ability to retrieve information on the amount of unused bandwidth available at a UNI.

6.3.3 *Modify UNI Configuration Profile Information*

This capability allows end users to modify UNI configuration information, such as the amount of unused bandwidth available at a UNI.

6.3.4 *Retrieve VPC/VCC Subscription Profile Information*

This capability allows end users to retrieve subscription-related information, such as descriptions of how a VPC is currently provisioned or configured.

6.3.5 *Modify VPC/VCC Subscription Profile Information*

This capability allows end users to modify VPC/VCC configuration such as how a VPC or VCC is to be provisioned or configured.

6.3.6 Receive Event Notifications

This CNM service capability allows an end user to receive unsolicited event notifications upon the occurrence of events that can affect the end user's use of ATM network and services. An example of an unsolicited event notification could be the indication of a failure condition generated on occurrence of a VP-AIS (Alarm Indication Signal). Event notifications can help end users isolate problems in their networks. Examples of events that could trigger event notifications are given below [4, 3]:

- Restart/reset CNM service.
- Failure/restoration of a UNI.
- Failure/restoration of a PVC connection.
- Failure/restoration of a specific higher layer network service.
- Changes to UNI configuration information.
- Changes to ATM cell level configuration information.
- Changes to VPC or VCC subscription information.
- Changes to SVC service subscription information.
- Authentication failure and authentication failure threshold exceeded.

6.3.7 Request Event Notifications

This capability allows the end user to request notification of predefined and possibly end user-defined events. An example is the ability to activate notification when there is a change in the end user's PVC configuration information (e.g., UPC parameters of a VPC).

6.3.8 Request Network Intervention

This capability allows end users to request network intervention on their behalf. There could be situations when the end user may not have immediate access to the malfunctioning equipment and thus cannot take care of the problem immediately (e.g., to reset or turn-off the equipment). Therefore, the end user could request temporary suspension of a specific UNI or a PVC until the problem is fixed.

6.3.9 Retrieve General CNM Information

This capability allows end users to retrieve information related to the general characterization and status of a given UNI and the ATM PVC CNM system. Examples could include UNI operational status, CNM contact, and CNM system uptime.

6.3.10 Modify General CNM Information

This capability allows end users to modify information related to the general administrative status of a given UNI. For example, this service might be used by an end user to turn off a UNI or to indicate that the UNI be subjected to a test by the network.

6.3.11 Retrieve Performance Information

This capability allows end users to retrieve information that will assist in the characterization of the performance of the network, as well as network and service utilization. For example, an end user may want to determine the number of cells submitted and delivered over a VPC by the network, counts of errored cells or other performance information, such as Loss of Cell Delineation events per access link.

6.3.12 Retrieve Usage Information

This capability allows end users to retrieve usage information related to UNI. This information may be used by end users in determining how to allocate costs associated with the use Cell Relay Service within the end user's organization, and may also be used to support traffic analysis.

6.3.13 Request Trouble Reports

This capability allows end users to create a new trouble report (e.g., on detection of a problem) related to a UNI. In addition, end users can use this service capability to request the status of an existing trouble report (e.g., open or closed status), to remove an existing trouble report (e.g., cases where the end user made an error in reporting the trouble), to add more information to an existing trouble report, and to retrieve information related to repair activity on reported troubles.

6.4 The Simple Network Management Protocol

SNMP is widely used in IP networks, therefore it makes sense for ATM-based enterprise networks. SNMP messages are typically carried via the UDP/IP protocol stack [1]. SNMP (RFC 1157, May 1990) is a specification of a protocol for the management of interconnected networks. SNMP allows transfer of data pertaining to fault, performance, and configuration management of TCP/IP-based systems in general, and ATM in particular.

SNMP was declared a draft standard by the Internet Activities Board in March 1988. It was elevated to Recommended Standard status in April 1989, with the release of the Common Management Protocol Over TCP/IP (CMOT) specification. As of May 1990, SNMP became a full Internet standard, known as RFC 1157. Work led to the definition, in the ASN.1 (Abstract Syntax Notation One) language, of a Structure of Management Information (SMI—RFC 1155, May 1990, and earlier RFC 1065) and Management Information Base (MIB —RFC 1156, May 1990, and earlier RFC 1066). A new MIB, known as MIB II, was defined in RFC 1213 (March 1991). (In what follows, the term *MIB* refers specifically to MIB II.)

RFC 1157 (a re-release of RFC 1098) defines a simple protocol by which management information for a network element may be inspected or altered by logically remote users. In particular, together with its companion RFCs which describe the structure of management information along with the management information base, the protocol provides a simple, workable architecture and system for managing TCP/IP-based interconnected networks. SMI describes how managed objects contained in the MIB are defined. The MIB is a virtual information store. Table 6.4 enumerates the key RFC specifications in support of SNMP.

The SNMP protocol uses five types of operations which are used to obtain and manipulate management information:

- *GetRequest* is employed by the SNMP manager to retrieve specific management information.

- *GetNextRequest* is employed by the SNMP manager to retrieve management information via traversal of the MIB.

- *Set* is employed by the SNMP manager to modify specific management information.

- *Trap* is employed by the SNMP agent for unsolicited event notification.[3]

- *GetResponse* is employed by the SNMP agent to respond to GetRequest, GetNextRequest, and Set messages.

Hundreds of vendors have developed products based on SNMP. In the absence of interoperating and fielded OSI-based network management systems, SNMP has become a de facto standard for management of multivendor TCP/IP-based networks. For example, SNMP agents support about 75% of the available bridge products and 80% of the routers. About 40 vendors (including HP, Sun, Novell, Bay Networks, DEC, and Cisco) offer what is known as a *generic SNMP Manager*. Such a generic agent can query any SNMP agent (for all MIB II objects), and can import a legitimate draft-status or private MIB.

Many of the vendors of ATM equipment also have announced support for SNMP. Such equipment covers the following areas:

Protocol	Document
SNMP	RFC 1157[a]
SMI	RFC 1155[b]
MIB II	RFC 1213[c]
SNMP over IPX suites	RFC 1298
SNMP security protocols	RFC 1352
SNMP administrative model	RFC 1351
A convention for describing SNMP-based agents	RFC 1303
SNMP over OSI suites	RFC 1283
SNMP communication services	RFC 1270
SNMP MUX protocol and MIB	RFC 1227
SNMP over Ethernet	RFC 1089

[a] Earlier document: RFC 1098.
[b] Earlier document: RFC 1065.
[c] Earlier documents: RFC 1066 and RFC 1156.

Table 6.4   Key SNMP specifications

[3]Traps track events such as Cold Start, Warm Start, Link Down, Link Up, Authentication Failure, Neighbor Loss, as well as vendor-specific events.

- Switching systems for public networks.

- Enterprise network switches, for high end private networks.

- LAN hubs (switches) for high end client-server users.

- LAN hubs (switches) for use as campus backbones.

- Digital Service Units (DSUs) which allow existing internetworking equipment (e.g., routers) to access ATM networks.

- Network interface cards (NICs) which allow high end workstations to access ATM LAN.

- Routers with ATM-based WAN cards

Table 6.5 lists some key early entrants in the ATM products arena; this list is expected to grow substantially over time.

SMI is a policy statement describing how the managed objects (hosts, terminals, routers, bridges, gateways, etc.) are defined. Such definitions basically involve agreement on a standard language for management; the notation employed is the ASN.1, mentioned above. One of the basic definitions in the SMI pertains to the representation of data elements.

Each object has a name, a syntax, and an encoding. The name also specifies the object type. The object type, together with an object instance, is employed to uniquely identify a specific instantiation of the object. The syntax defines the abstract data structure corresponding to the given object type. The encoding of the object type specifies how that object type is represented, using the object's syntax. An example of an object is shown in Figure 6.4. (Figure 6.4 also shows a vendor-specific trap.)

The MIB represents the database of management information and parameters. The management parameters are stored in a tree-structured database. All mandatory variables listed there must be supported, either statically (with null or default value), or dynamically (i.e., actually employed by the device in question) [5].

MIB II (RFC 1213) contains about two hundred objects, and as of September 1991, rendered obsolete the previous MIB definition (RFC 1156). There are "Draft", "Proposed Standard" and "Experimental" MIBs for about five dozen network/device types, including T1 networks, Ethernet, Token Ring, Bridge, FDDI network, SMDS network, Frame Relay network, and T3 network. There are also private or vendor-specific MIBs (numbering over 500 at press time).

SNMP provides a means of communicating information between the management station and the managed devices. An SNMP user/manager issues instructions (set, get, etc.) to managed objects; the SNMP agent executes the instructions and responds.

Company	Products
3Com Corporation Santa Clara, CA	ATM LAN, Hub, Router, or DSU Product
Adaptive Corporation Redwood City, CA	ATM LAN, Hub, Router, or DSU Product
ADC Telecommunications Minneapolis, MN	Network and WAN Equipment
ADC Fibermux Corporation Chatsworth, CA	ATM LAN, Hub, Router, or DSU Product
ADC Kentrox Portland, Oregon	ATM LAN, Hub, Router, or DSU Product
Alcatel Network Systems Raleigh, NC	Network and WAN Equipment
Ascom Timeplex Woodcliff Lake, NJ	Network and WAN Equipment
Bay Networks Santa Clara, CA	ATM LAN, Hub, Router, or DSU Product
BBN Communications Cambridge, MA	Network and WAN Equipment
Cabletron Systems Rochester, NH	ATM LAN, Hub, Router, or DSU Product
Cascade Communications Westford, MA	Network and WAN Equipment
Cisco Systems/Stratacom Menlo Park, CA	ATM LAN, Hub, Routers
Digital Link Corporation Sunnyvale, CA	ATM LAN, Hub, Router, or DSU Product
DSC Communications Plano, TX	Network and WAN Equipment
FiberCom, Inc. Roanoke, VA	ATM LAN, Hub, Router, or DSU Product
FORE Systems Pittsburgh, PA	ATM LAN, Hub, Switches
Fujitsu Network Switching Raleigh, NC	Network and WAN Equipment

Table 6.5   Early vendors of ATM products—partial list

Company	Products
General DataComm Middlebury, CT	Network and WAN Equipment
GTE Government Systems Communications Needham Heights, MA	ATM LAN, Hub, Router, or DSU Product
Hitachi Norcross, GA	Network and WAN Equipment
Hughes LAN Systems Mountain View, CA	ATM LAN, Hub, Router, or DSU Product
IBM New York, NY	ATM LAN, Hub, Router, or DSU Product
Lucent Technologies Lincroft, NJ	Network and WAN Equipment
NEC America Irving, TX	Network and WAN Equipment
Newbridge Networks Kanata, Ontario Canada	Network and WAN Equipment
Nortel Research Triangle Park, NC	Network and WAN Equipment
Retix	ATM LAN, Hub, Router, or DSU Product
Siemens Stromberg-Carlson Boca Raton, FL	Network and WAN Equipment
Synernetics North Billerica, MA	ATM LAN, Hub, Router, or DSU Product
Telco Systems, Inc.	Network and WAN Equipment
Thomson CSF Boulogne-Billancourt, France	Network and WAN Equipment
TRW Space Communications Division Redondo Beach, CA	ATM LAN, Hub, Router, or DSU Product
TRW Space Communications Redondo Beach, CA	Network and WAN Equipment
Ungermann Bass Santa Clara, CA	ATM LAN, Hub, Router, or DSU Product

Table 6.5 *Continued*

Object:

```
logicalToExplicitHub OBJECT-TYPE
SYNTAX INTEGER (1..65335)
ACCESS read-write
STATUS optional
DESCRIPTION
    "The value of this object identifies the hub for which
    this entry contains management information"

:: = {logicalToExplicitEntry 2}
```

Trap:

```
perselectedVCChange TRAP-TYPE
ENTERPRISE minoliinc
VARIABLES { ifIndex }
DESCRIPTION
    "A preselected VCChange trap signifies that the
    preselection of the signaling Virtual Channel has been
    change."
:: = 7
```

Figure 6.4   Example of an Object and a Trap

Although SNMP uses a subset of ASN.1, and ISO CMIP (Common Management Information Protocol) uses ASN.1, it does not follow that the SNMP protocol is a subset of the CMIP protocol. SNMP is not upward-compatible with CMIP. A two-stage approach for network management of TCP/IP-based interconnected networks was initially planned.

In the short term, SNMP was to be used to manage nodes in the Internet community. In the long term, the use of the OSI network management framework was to be examined. RFC 1065 and RFC 1066 were designed so as to be compatible with the SNMP and OSI network management frameworks. RFC 1109 notes that the requirements of the SNMP and the OSI network management frameworks were more different than anticipated. As such, the requirement for compatibility between the SMI/MIB and both frameworks was suspended. This action permitted the operational network management framework, SNMP, to respond to new operational needs in the Internet community by producing documents defining new MIB items. Table 6.6 summarizes some of these key concepts.

6.4.1 Protocol Specification

The network management protocol is one by which the variables of an agent's MIB may be inspected or altered. Communication among protocol entities is accomplished by the exchange of messages, each of which is entirely represented within a single UDP datagram using the Basic Encoding Rules (BER) of ASN.1.

A message consists of a version identifier, an SNMP community name, and a PDU. A protocol entity receives messages at UDP port 161 on the host with which it is associated, for all messages except for those which report traps. (Messages which report traps are received on UDP port 162.) An implementation of this protocol need not accept messages whose length exceeds 484 octets.

It is mandatory that all implementations of the SNMP support the five PDUs identified earlier: GetRequest-PDU, GetNextRequest-PDU, GetResponse-PDU, SetRequest-PDU, and Trap-PDU.

The top-level actions of a protocol entity which generates a message are as follows:

1. It first constructs the appropriate PDU as an ASN.1 object.

2. It then passes this ASN.1 object, along with a community name, its source transport address, and the destination transport address, to the service which implements the desired authentication scheme. This authentication service returns another ASN.1 object.

3. The protocol entity constructs an ASN.1 Message object, using the community name and the resulting ASN.1 object.

4. This new ASN.1 object is serialized, using BER/ASN.1, and sent using a transport service to the peer protocol entity.

The top-level actions of a protocol entity which receives a message are as follows:

1. It performs a rudimentary parse of the incoming datagram to build an ASN.1 object corresponding to an ASN.1 Message object. If the parse fails, it discards the datagram and performs no further actions.

Agent	Software capability built into an SNMP-managed device. Key features: contains an IP address entity; knows the address of a manager to which traps are issued; supports a set of SNMP objects (from a few to several hundred types); and uses UDP/IP to transmit messages between managers and agents).
Community name	A security mechanism (password/alphanumeric character string) included in each SNMP message. Features: predefined to the managed device; provides "weak" security; tiered hierarchical structure of managed objects is possible. Secure SNMP supports stronger security mechanisms.
MIB	A collection of objects (up to 200 types), structured as specified in RFC 1213. Private MIBs contain objects that only the agent software from a specified vendor supports.
Object	Formal description of an element of management information. Objects comprised of parameters such as: Object ID, Object Type, Values (integer, counter, or string), and Access (read-write, read-only, etc.)
Get message	The GetRequest Message is issued by an SNMP management station to an agent. The GetResponse message contains response information from the device/agent back to the station. Either single objects or multiple objects can be queried/responded by a single Get message.
Set message	Message that enables operator at an SNMP management station to change the value of an object contained at an SNMP agent (as long as the object is defined as read-write). Used to control managed devices.
Trap message	Message issued unilaterally by a managed device upon recognition that a certain predefined condition/threshold has been met. Six trap conditions are defined in SNMP, but vendors have added vendor defined traps. Of the specified SNMP traps, the Cold Start (power supply interruption) and the Authentication Failure (unauthorized attempt to access the device's agent) are the two most commonly implemented.

Table 6.6   Key SNMP concepts

2. It verifies the version number of the SNMP message. If there is a mismatch, it discards the datagram and performs no further actions.

3. The protocol entity passes the community name and user data found in the ASN.1 Message object, along with the datagram's source and destination transport addresses to the service which implements the desired authentication scheme. This entity returns another ASN.1 object, or signals an authentication failure. In the latter case, the protocol entity notes this failure, (possibly) generates a trap, discards the datagram, and performs no further actions.

4. The protocol entity performs a rudimentary parse on the ASN.1 object returned from the authentication service to build an ASN.1 object corresponding to an ASN.1 PDU's object. If the parse fails, it discards the datagram and performs no further actions. Otherwise, using the named SNMP community, the appropriate profile is selected, and the PDU is processed accordingly. If as a result of this processing, a message is returned, then the source transport address that the response message is sent from will be identical to the destination transport address to which the original request message was sent.

For detailed operation of the protocol the reader is referred to RFC 1157.

6.4.2 *Common Management Information Protocol*

For completeness, this section provides a short synopsis of CMIP features. As noted, CMIP tends to be used by public ATM switches, as well as by some high end private ATM switches.

The CMIP primitives are as follows:

- M-GET   Retrieve values of attributes of one or more managed objects in the confirmed mode.

- M-SET   Modify the attribute values of one or more managed object in the confirmed or nonconfirmed mode.

- M-CREATE   Create an instance of a managed object; always done in a confirmed mode.

- M-DELETE   Delete one or more managed objects all contained in a subtree in the confirmed or nonconfirmed mode.

- M-ACTION   Perform an action specific to one or more managed objects in the confirmed or nonconfirmed mode.

- M-EVENT-REPORT   Report the occurrence of a notification from a managed object in the confirmed or nonconfirmed mode.

- M-CANCEL-GET   Cancel a previously issued Get request in the confirmed mode.

Note: The confirmed/unconfirmed feature corresponds to the Open Systems Interconnection Basic Reference Model primitive treatment. In the confirmed mode a response to the service (primitive) is expected (required); in the unconfirmed mode, no response is provided.

The protocol stack for CMIP-based operations is as follows:

- *Application Layer*   CMISE (ISO 9595 and 9596),
     ASCE (ITU-T X.217 and X.227),
     ROSE (ITU-T X.219 and X.229).

- *Presentation Layer*   ITU-T X.216, X.226, and X.208,
     ASN.1 (ITU-T X.209).

- *Session Layer*   ITU-T X.215 and X.225.

- *Transport Layer*   ISO 8073.

- *Network Layer*   ISO 8473, 9577, ITU-T X.25.

- *Data Link Layer*   LAPB or AAL5 over ATM.

- *Physical Layer*   V.35 or DS1/DS3/SONET.

6.5 *Carriers' CNM Roles*

This section[4] describes potential CNM roles on the part of carriers (Local Exchange Companies, in particular), based on the layer, B-LMI, and CNM capabilities discussed thus far. As noted at the beginning of this chapter, carriers have not yet offered CNM services. The hope remains that they will do so in the future.

---

[4]This section was written by Mr. Minoli while at Bellcore. It is based on the public-domain information published in reference [3].

6.5.1 Carrier Network Support of Users' NM Applications

In this case, the carrier's network role is to support the users' network management applications with information about the CRS service. The subscriber uses a customer-based network management application to retrieve and process network management information from a number of resources, including retrieval, from the network, of CRS CNM information. The user's network management application collects network management information from other equipment through a Management Application Protocol (SNMP in particular, but perhaps also CMIP; in addition, the B-LMI may be used in conjunction with the exchange CRS UNI), and uses this network management information to support management of the organization's ATM network. The organization's equipment participating in the network management information exchange may have a client/server relationship, or may act as peers. In this setup, the organization's network management application provides a network management service, and the network supports the application by providing access to network management information relevant to managing ATM UNIs.

6.5.2 CRS CNM Service Access through SNMP

In this case, the carrier's network providing CRS offers access to CRS CNM information it maintains through the SNMP between the customer's SNMP NMS/CNMA and the carrier-provided SNMP "agent" application, called a *CRS CNM Agent*. See Figure 6.5. SNMP Protocol Data Units are transported between the NMS and the agent using the connectionless User Datagram Protocol (UDP) and the Internet Protocol (IP) operating over CRS. (SNMP could also be provided operating UDP/IP over leased or dialup—here the CNMA signal path would clearly have to be outside of the ATM UNI.) The CNMA provides the network management capabilities for the user, as well as the human interface. (These capabilities and the human interface are determined by the vendor, which develops the customer's SNMP-based CNMA—a typical organization would buy the CNMA from a vendor, as covered briefly in Section 6.6.)

Note: For initial CNM carrier offerings, SNMP Version 1 is slated to be used, given its dominant position among customer base. SNMP Version 2 offers improved security features, which may be important for later phases 4 CRS CNM service, to support read-write access to certain CRS CNM capabilities. (The SNMP community has a specific migration coexistence strategy for the two versions of the protocol; thus, when SNMP Version 2 has established a larger

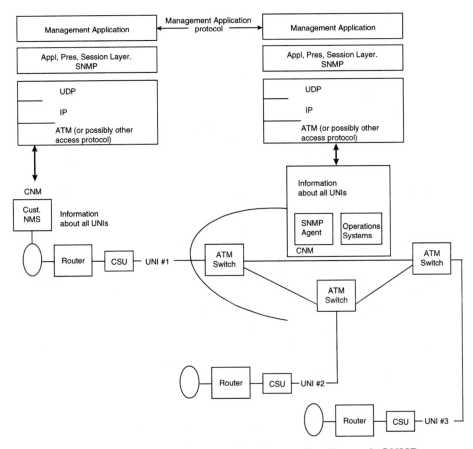

Figure 6.5   CRS CNM service provided by carrier through SNMP

user base, smooth transition will be possible for the support of CRS CNM service.) The role of the CRS CNM Agent can be twofold:

1. Provide access to CRS CNM information. The CNMA provides further network management capabilities using this information to tailor it to particular organizational use, or to integrate it with network management information obtained from other resources within the organization's network.

2. Aggregate CRS CNM information, or generate event notifications for further processing by the CNMA.

6.5.3 CRS Service Access through B-LMI

Another, similar, but more limited role that the carrier network may play is to support the organization's network management applications by providing information about a customer's use of the local ATM switch only, through a protocol called here B-LMI (also known as *ILMI*—see Section 5.8). This approach differs from the role described above, where the carrier network supplies information about the customer's use of the service as a whole, through a SNMP CRS CNM Agent representing the service provided by the carrier's network. In the B-LMI case, the information is made available by the ATM switch, and not to the service as a whole. (The CNM Agent approach discussed above is more powerful, since the information that can be accessed via SNMP is a superset of the information accessible via B-LMI.) See Figure 6.6. The carrier network providing CRS offers access to CRS CNM information it maintains through the exchange of B-LMI protocol data units between the organization's B-LMI application and a carrier-provided B-LMI application at the local interface. Protocol data units are transported between the customer and the ATM switch using the B-LMI protocol operating over a permanent VC; since the B-LMI is operated directly over a VC without support of a network-layer internetwork protocol such as IP, B-LMI requests and responses must be generated and retrieved at the equipment that terminates that particular VC—the router in the figure.

6.5.4 Monitoring and Surveillance of Layer Management Protocols

In this case, the carrier's network role is to support monitoring and surveillance of layer management protocols. In this approach, the organization and the network cooperatively provide a monitoring and surveillance capability that assists both parties in detecting and isolating failures in the network. This is done by supporting peer layer management entities (see Figure 6.7, which builds on Figure 5.1); both user equipment and network equipment exchange information relating to events related to the service. The organization accesses CRS CNM information through the use of a hardware module that provides information on the status and performance of a specific interface.

For example, at the Physical Layer, a channel service unit (CSU) monitors the DS1, DS3, or SONET signals described in Section 5.5. The ATM OAM cells described in Section 5.5 are also viewed as a layer management protocol. The information may be displayed as an indicator light, an alphanumeric LCD, or

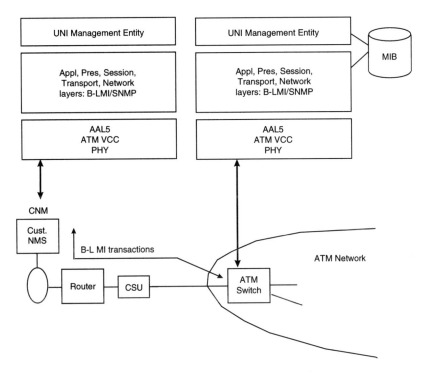

Figure 6.6   B-LMI network management arrangement

through a local protocol analyzer port at the CSU/DSU itself. Also, the hardware usually sends these signals back to other user's equipment to a line-monitoring application on a workstation, or to an NMS through SNMP; the signals are then processed and made available to the organization's personnel in a workstation window.

6.5.5 LEC Network Support of CRS CNM Applications

The carrier's network role in this case is to provide multifeatured CRS CNM applications. Here the CNMA reside in the carrier's network, not in the user's equipment. In this approach, the CRS CNM applications enable a user's network management personnel to access CRS CNM information specific to the customer's use of the CRS through a display-only terminal. See Figure 6.8.

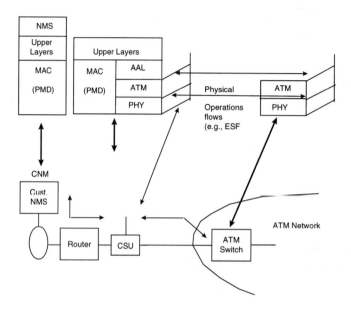

Figure 6.7   Joint monitoring of operations flows

6.6 Network Management Systems ATM Products

Commercially available NMSs fall into three major categories:

1. NMS platforms, supporting a run-time environment as well as an applications development environment, along with testing capabilities.

2. Stand-alone management systems.

3. (Passive) monitoring systems.

Although some NMS are monolithic (e.g., the stand-alone NMSs), more often they consist of several software modules, possibly assembled from different vendors. (See Figure 6.9; Figure 6.10 provides more details.) These modules are as follows:

1. A platform that supports runtime functionality, such as executing the communications stacks discussed in the previous sections, managing the user interface, and maintaining a database management system (e.g., SQL) to physically implement the information models.

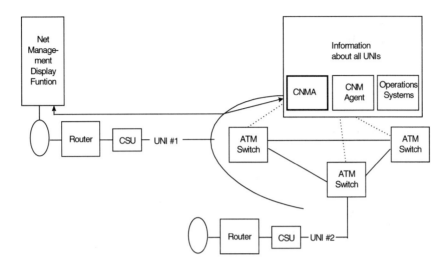

Figure 6.8   Carrier provides CNMA; user only provides basic display function

2. Development tools for building new applications. Often an NMS platform offers a (quasi) open Application Programming Interface (API) (see below) that allows programmers to easily use the platform to develop and support tailored applications.

As implied in Figure 6.9, the programming interface to the application layer of the communication stack (TCP/IP family or OSI family) is not standardized.[5] This implies that developers of communication-based applications, including network management applications, must utilize either an interface developed on the fly, or develop and promulgate as a de facto standard their own brand of APIs. The net result is that different implementations realize different interfaces, even for the same platform or programming language, limiting portability among workstations and among other processors. A de facto API achieves greater value if it is defined by groups of companies.

Consortia such as Open Software Foundation, X/Open, and IEEE have defined APIs to various application-layer protocols. For network management, a number of the platforms support an API conformant to that defined in X/Open (promulgated by X/Open Company Limited), also known as X/Open

---

[5] One example is the Windows Telephony API [5.21]; however, this API is not applicable to the network management environment.

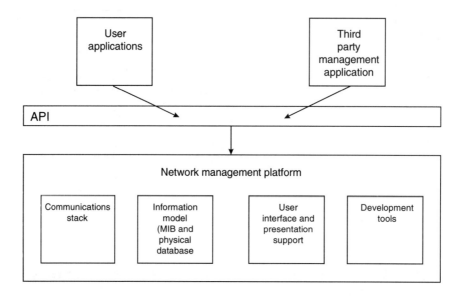

Figure 6.9 NMS modules

Management Protocol API (XMP API). See Figure 6.11. This facilitates the development of the specific (ATM) management applications needed by organizations, since the developer can utilize the power of the underlying platform, and invoke its features over a well-defined API. In particular, XMP API supports both CMIP and SNMP, enabling developers to rapidly create applications that, in addition to relying on the platform tools (and hence are easier to develop), are independent of the underlying communication protocols.

This means, for example, that the same platform could be used by an organization that has purchased a number of ATM premises switches that had a CMIP interface (usually the high-end switches), and at the same time is using carrier-provided CRS, for some portion of the enterprise network. The parameters used for management (as well as other functions) can be viewed in terms of a local representation called OSI-Abstract-Data Manipulation Objects. X/Open OSI-Abstract-Data Manipulation (XOM) API is the interface that can be used by NMS/CNMA for manipulating the objects [6] (see Figure 6.10). In this

---

[6] In the context of network management, objects represent abstractions of physical and logical resources such as network elements (including ATM switches), transmission lines, termination cards, computing systems, etc.

(1) Run-time tools

(1.1) Intrinsic platform services

(1.1.1) User interface services

Provide support for presentation of management information (Graphical User Interfaces and command line approaches) along with support for interaction between datacom/telecom managers and the management application. Typically provide topological displays of networks and computing systems based on icons and windows; display of database-resident network information (e.g., inventories) is supported, as is support for physical interfaces for applications development.

(1.1.2) Management operations support services

Provide utility services to the management platform intrinsic functions, and to the management applications executing above the platform (e.g., event management service for collection, filtering, logging, conversion, and internal routing of management events.)

(1.1.3) Communications services

Provide support, through APIs, for communications interfaces (message-based or object-based) to management and communications protocols stacks used to convey/receive management information [e.g., SNMP, CMIP, and CMIP over TCP/IP (CMOT)].

(1.1.4) Object manipulation services

Provide support for the MIB; for the information exchanges between objects and management applications and services, in conjunction with location transparency; and for object-oriented applications development. Often support Object Management Group's (OMG) constructs such as Common Object Request Broker Architecture (COBRA) and Interface Definition Language (IDL).

(1.1.5) Database services

Provide support for "standardized" management data storage and retrieval via a Data Base Management System (DBMS). These services provide data base access and retrieval mechanisms (typically, Structured Query Language—SQL), database integrity, and database backup.

(1.2) Management applications

(1.2.1) Core applications

Applications to manage Specific Management Functional Areas discussed in Section 5.3, as well as applications that provide cross-are capabilities.

(1.2.2) Resource specific applications

Applications to manage particular network elements or computing systems components.

(2) Management applications development toolkits

Development tools to support development of tailored applications, which make use of intrinsic platform services (user interfaces, communications, object manipulation, and database services). The tools typically also include debugging and testing utilities.

(3) Management implementation tools

Mechanisms for global acceptance-testing of management platforms, to support testing based on test criteria, to support test procedures, and to support trouble shooting of complex distributed management platforms.

Figure 6.10   NMS environment

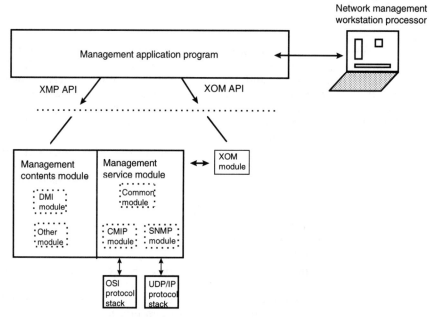

DMI: Definition of Management Information (ISO 10165 Part 2)

Figure 6.11   XMP API for network management platforms

environment, the NMS applications can be developed using the encode and decode functions provided by the XOM API, instead of direct ASN.1 encoding rules.

6.7 *Key Vendors of ATM NMSs*

Table 6.7 lists some key vendors of NMS systems that may be used (or extended) to support ATM.

Company	Products
Bay Networks San Jose, CA.	Optivity (SunConnect's SunNet Manager and IBM's NetView/6000)
Cabletron Systems Inc. Rochester, New Hampshire	Spectrum for Open Systems; supports SNMP (CMIP and SNMPv2 later)
Cisco San Jose CA	Ciscoworks/Cisco View; ATM, router, and LAN switches network management
Digital Equipment Corp. Maynard, MA	PolyCenter NetView Platform
HewlettPackard Corp. Fort Collings, CO	Network Node Manager (based on HP's Open View); supports SNMP and CMIP
IBM Corp. White Plains, NY	NetView/6000
Lucent Technologies Bedminster, N.J.	Total Network Management (based on the BaseWorX platform)
NetLabs Inc., Los Altos, CA	Overlord
Network Equipment Technologies Redwood City, CA	NMS with gateway to CMIP
Objective Systems Integrators, Folsom, CA	NetExpert. NMS product based on expert systems for multi-protocol multi-vendor environments
Open Software Foundation, Cambridge, MA	Distributed Management Environment
SunConnect Mountain View, CA	SunNet Manager

Table 6.7 Key Vendors of NMS Systems ATM Grade—partial list

References

[1] E. Ericson, L. Ericson, D. Minoli, *Expert Systems Applications to Integrated Network Management*, Artech House, 1989.

[2] D. Minoli, G. Dobrowski, *Understanding Signaling: The Road to Switched Frame Relay and Cell Relay Services*, Artech House, Norwood, Mass. 1994.

[3] Bellcore Technical Advisory TA-TSV-001117, *Generic Requirements for Exchange PVC CRS Customer Network Management Service*, September 1993.

[4] Bellcore Technical Advisory TA-NWT-001248, *Generic Requirements for Operations for Boradband Switching Systems,* October, 1993.

[5] T. A. Cox, et al, "SNMP Agent Support for SMDS," *IEEE Network Magazine,* September 1991, page 33 ff.

Part III

Operational Management of
ATM Networks

 *chapter 7*

Managing ATM Networks: Fault and Configuration Management

*F*ault management is a fundamental determinant of a network's availability and reliability. Managers must have tools to track, resolve, and even anticipate or prevent outages and service impairments.

Configuration management is also crucial. Managers must be able to reconfigure an ATM network quickly and easily to meet changing needs and respond to emergencies that may range from demand peaks to physical disasters.

These two critical Network Management Specific Management Functional Areas (SMFAs) are examined in the context of a hybrid network, where the organization obtains CRS (defined in Chapter 4) from a carrier, as well as from a private ATM network/switch perspective. All of these issues also apply to public ATM switches and to CNM.

Specific topics include:

- Fault management.
- Alarm surveillance.
- Fault localization and testing.
- Managing multiple ATM switches.
- Configuration management.
- General capabilities.
- Configuration of multiple ATM switches.

7.1 Fault Management

This section addresses the fault management functions used to detect and isolate trouble in an ATM network [1]. Table 7.1 enumerates some of the functions that must be supported to deal with faults at the general level; Table 7.2 depicts the set of specific functionality that has been proposed for ATM (switches) [2].

As seen in Table 7.2, the fault management functions may be grouped into two general categories: alarm surveillance functions, which include failure monitoring and failure notification capabilities; and failure localization and testing functions, which include capabilities that enable an NMS to sectionalize a fault, analyze circuit and equipment characteristics, and enable an ATM Network Element, such as a switch, to diagnose its own internal status. These are discussed below, followed by a description of the Fault Management cell.

Allow, inhibit, and change the conditions for alarm reports.

Allow, inhibit, and define the logging of alarms.

Allow, inhibit, and reset audible or visual alarm indications.[a]

Assign and request alarm event criteria.

Build, maintain, and examine error logs.

Initiate and control tests.

Input, edit, review, and cancel trouble reports.[a]

Receive alarm reports.

Receive and react to error detection notifications.

Receive automatic restoration reports.

Receive test result reports.

Rectify faults of communication system.

Request and receive fault localization diagnostic reports.

Request, receive, and schedule alarm summary reports.

Set up test access.

Trace and identify faults.

Undertake sequences of tests.

[a] More typical in an ATM switch than in a CRS NMS environment

Table 7.1   Fault management functions relevant to ATM

7.1.1 Alarm Surveillance

Alarm[1] surveillance functions are designed to facilitate in the detection and notification of network faults. For ATM switches, alarm surveillance measures are performed on a continuous basis by features within NEs and Management Systems. Alarm surveillance is concerned with monitoring for anomalies, defects, and failures [3]:

- *Anomaly*   A discrepancy between the actual and desired characteristics of an item. The desired characteristic may be expressed in the form of a specification. An anomaly may or may not affect the ability of an item to perform a required function. Framing bit errors and frame format code violations such as CRC and BIP are examples of anomalies.

- *Defect*   A limited interruption in the ability of an item to perform a required function. A defect may or may not lead to maintenance action, depending

---

[1] Portions of this material are expanded from Reference [1].

Alarm surveillance	Physical Layer defect and failure detection with inband maintenance signals
	Alarm surveillance for ATM over DSn
	Fault detection when Physical Layer Convergence Protocol is used
	Fault detection when Physical Layer Convergence Protocol is not used
	DSn inband maintenance signals
	Alarm surveillance for ATM over SONET
	Loss of cell delineation
	ATM Layer defect and failure detection with inband maintenance signals
	VP Alarms
	VC Alarms
	Alarm indication signal (AIS)/remote defect indicator (RDI)[a]
	Continuity check capability
	Alarm propagation on circuit-emulation connections
Failure reporting	Failure reporting when failure is detected locally
	Failure reporting when failure is inferred from alarm signals
Fault local-ization and testing	Internal diagnostics
	VPC/VCC testing capabilities
	Loopback

[a] Formerly, this was known as FERF.

Table 7.2   ATM-specific fault management capabilities

on the results of additional analysis. Successive anomalies causing a decrease in the ability of an element to perform a required function are considered a defect. Short intervals of Loss of Signal, Alarm Indication Signal, Loss of Pointer, and Loss of Frame are examples of defects.

- *Failure*   The termination of the ability of an item to perform a required function. A failure is declared when a defect has been detected and that defect persists for some specified length of time. Both local and remote failures can be observed by NEs using maintenance signaling functions in transport overhead (e.g., Alarm Indication Signals for upstream failures).

Anomalies are the first indication that there is trouble in the network. If there is a sufficient occurrence of anomalies during a short period (usually a small fraction of a second), a defect is declared. The network element notifies other network elements using inband alarms such as an Alarm Indication Signal (AIS). Automatic actions are initiated within the network element to correct the problem. If the defect continues to persist (e.g., a few seconds), a failure is declared, and the appropriate management system is notified.

There are three major aspects of the alarm surveillance process (see Table 7.2). The first involves the detection of faults in the Physical and ATM Layers respectively, and the declaration of defect and failure states in the network element. The second major aspect involves the transmission of inband alarm indications such as AIS and Remote Defect Indicators (RDIs) among NEs affected by the defect. The third aspect of alarm surveillance involves failure reporting.

Physical Layer Defect and Failure Detection

DSn and SONET interfaces, although similar, have some important differences in their failure states. Each is discussed separately below.

Alarm Surveillance for ATM over DS1 and DS3

At the Physical Layer, the following faults exist for DS3 transmission systems that use the PLCP to carry ATM cell streams:

- Loss of Signal (LOS).

- Loss of Frame (LOF).

- PLCP LOF.

The PLCP LOF state is defined as the persistence of a PLCP Out of Frame (OOF) for 1 ms [4]. The PLCP OOF is declared when an error occurs in both the A1 and A2 PLCP framing octets (see Figure 5.5), or in two consecutive invalid Path Overhead Identifier (POI) octets.

The following faults exist for DS1 and DS3 systems that use direct cell mapping instead of the PLCP:

- LOS.

- LOF.

- Loss of Cell Delineation (LCD).

DS1 and DS3 Inband Alarms

DS1 and DS3 downstream alarms include the AIS as defined in reference [5]. Upstream alarms include the DS3 RDI and (when PLCP is used) the PLCP yellow alarm [4].

Alarm Surveillance for ATM over SONET

At the Physical Layer, the following faults exist for SONET transmission systems carrying ATM cell streams:

- LOS.

- LOF.

- Loss of Pointer (LOP).

- LCD.

The LCD state is an ATM-specific state. It applies to all transmission systems that do not use PLCP. In normal operation, cells are delineated (i.e., extracted) from a transmission payload after the starting position of the first cell is located. However, if seven consecutive cells have HEC (Header Error Control) violations,[2] an Out-of-Cell-Deliniation (OCD) anomaly will occur. The OCD anomaly will continue until either cell delineation is reestablished or a transition is made into the LCD defect state.

ATM Layer Defect and Failure Detection

Faults can be detected at the ATM Layer from notification of Physical Layer faults. This section describes the communication of VP/VC alarms at the ATM Layer.

VP/VC Alarm Indications

At the ATM level, two alarm indications have been defined:

- *Alarm indication signals* VP-AIS and VC-AIS alarms are generated by the node detecting a defect to alert the downstream nodes that a defect has been detected upstream. These alarms are communicated by using Fault Management OAM cells with the AIS function type.

- *Remote defect indications* VP-RDI and VC-RDI alarms are generated by the node terminating a defective connection to alert the upstream nodes that a defect has been detected downstream. These alarms are communicated by using Fault Management OAM cells with the RDI function type.

See Figure 7.1 for an illustration of the flow of VP/VC AIS and RDI alarms.

---

[2]The HEC mechanism allows the receiving entity to detect errors, and if the appropriate mechanism is implemented, to correct a single bit error in the header. (Not all switches, though, implement this capability.)

The Fault Management cell contains fields to note the failure type and failure location. Encodings of these fields are to be standardized.

VP Alarms

A VPC fault can be detected at the ATM Layer either by receiving an indication from the Physical Layer or by receiving an indication from an ATM entity. The procedure for generating alarms varies slightly, depending on whether the fault is detected at a connecting point, originating point, or terminating point of the VPC:

1. *Fault at connecting point*   When a defect is declared at the ATM Layer of a connecting point, AIS cells are generated and periodically sent downstream for each VPC affected by the failure. The first cell is sent between 50 and 500 ms after the defect indication. The lower bound of 50 ms was chosen to allow for protection switching before generation of AIS cells. The upper bound of 500 ms is required to support signaling channels to provide defect detection times for signaling channels that are comparable to those obtained today. AIS cells continue to be generated until the defect state is exited [2].

   At the terminating endpoint, when one AIS cell is received on a VPC, the AIS defect state is declared, and the endpoint sends RDI cells upstream to alert those nodes that a defect has been detected downstream. This contin-

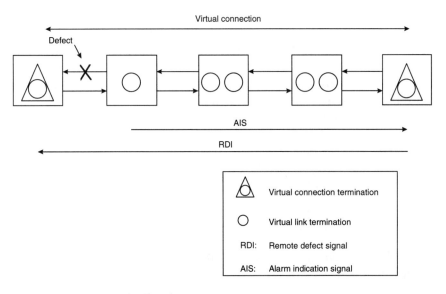

Figure 7.1   Alarm indications

ues until either a valid cell is received, or no AIS cell is received within a specified time period.

At the originating point, the RDI state is declared when one RDI is received. The RDI state is exited when no RDI cell has been received for a specified period of time.

2. *Fault at the originating point* When the defect is detected at the originating endpoint, the procedure is the same, except that RDIs received at the originating endpoint are ignored (as well as the RDI state).

3. *Fault at terminating point* When the defect is detected at the terminating end, the procedure is the same as the connecting point case, except that no VP AIS cells are generated.

VC Alarms

VCC faults can be detected at the ATM Layer either by indications from the Physical Layer, or by indications from a VPC terminating point. Unlike VP alarms, VC alarms are not generated for all VCCs, but only for preselected connections. This allows all VCCs to be alarmed if desired, but allows suppression of alarms where they are not desired. If a VC-AIS is generated, then the endpoint also generates a VC-RDI. The interaction between VP and VC alarms is shown in Figure 7.2.

The state transitions, flow of VC-AIS and VC-RDI cells, and timings for a VCC with a fault are the same as for VPCs, except that the generation of alarms for a VCC is optional.

Physical (DSn/SONET) level alarm indications may result in the generation of VPC alarm indications, which in turn may result in the generation of VCC alarm indications. This interaction of SONET and ATM level alarms is illustrated in Figure 7.3. This propagation of alarms points to the need for alarm correlation functions in a network management system to identify cause-and-effect relationships and simplify rectification processes.

AIS/RDI Cell Payload Structure

The AIS/RDI cell payload structure is shown in Figure 7.4. Currently both ITU and T1 have standardized the size of the Failure Type field as 8 bits. As of writing time, ITU had not yet agreed on the size of the Failure Location field. Each field is described below:

- *OAM Function Type* This field identifies the functions of the Fault Management cell as being AIS (0000) or RDI (0001).

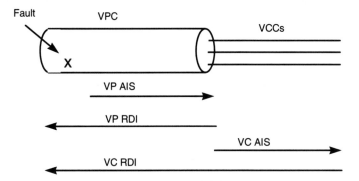

Figure 7.2   VP alarms and VC alarms

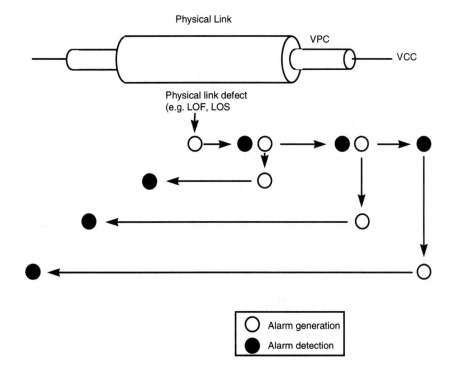

Figure 7.3   Alarm propagation

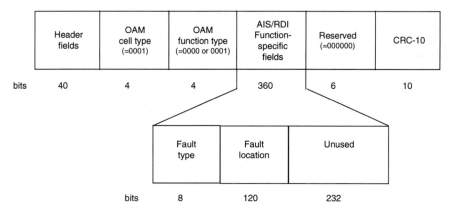

Figure 7.4 AIS/RDI Fault Management OAM cell format

- *Failure Type*   This field is used to identify the type of failure that has occurred.

- *Failure Location*   This field is used to identify the location of a failure.

Failure Reporting When Failure is Detected Locally

An entity may automatically recover from a defect in a short period of time. Thus, a transition into a defect state should not result in the generation of a report to a Management System or the removal of the entity from service. To ensure this, a delay timing mechanism is used.

ATM-specific failures are declared only after the defect persists for a specified interval. Once a failure is declared, a failure indication is set in the NE. When a NE detects a failure, it is reported to an appropriate Management System as an alarm, and thus requires immediate attention by the appropriate Management System [6].

A low level fault, such as a transmission system LOF, could cause multiple higher level fault indications. When an entity detects a failure, it reports only the lowest level failure. The relevant lower level defects and failures for each interface type are:

- *SONET*   LOS, LOF, LOP, LCD, VP AIS/RDI, and VC AIS/RDI.

- *DS3 using PLCP*   LOS, LOF, PLCP LOF, VP AIS/RDI, and VC AIS/RDI.

- *DS1*   LOS, LOF, LCD, VP AIS/RDI, and VC AIS/RDI.

Failure Reporting when Failure is Inferred from Alarm Signals

If the NE has been informed of defects detected by other NEs, through VP/VC AISs or RDIs, it first enters the AIS or RDI defect state, and if the defect persists, then enters the AIS or RDI failure state. The AIS or RDI failure state may or may not be automatically reported by the NE to the Management System. Indications that are not automatically reported will, however, be made available to and retrievable by the management system.

In any network, it is desirable that a Management System not receive redundant AIS and RDI defect notifications. This can be achieved by reporting AIS and RDI failures only at ingress to the network, i.e., at UNIs in the incoming direction.

7.1.2 Fault Localization and Testing

This section identifies testing functions that may be used to isolate internal network element failures down to the "smallest" repairable/replaceable unit of hardware/software. In addition, it identifies capabilities that enable a network provider to perform tests on individual VPCs and VCCs. Internal diagnostics relate to vendor-specific aspects of a NE, while VPC/VCC testing capabilities are generic.

OAM Loopback Capability

Indications of trouble on a particular VPC/VCC may come in the form of performance monitoring data or alarm surveillance procedures, or customer trouble reports may indicate that a particular VPC/VCC is experiencing trouble. Upon receipt of a trouble report, tests may be initiated to verify the existence of the reported trouble, identify the nature of the trouble, and isolate its cause.

The OAM loopback capability [2] can be used to

- Verify connectivity.

- Isolate faults.

- Perform preservice acceptance tests.

OAM cell loopbacks are performed by inserting Fault Management Loopback cells at one point along a connection, with instructions in the cell payload for the cell to be looped back at another point along the connection. See Figure 7.5 for a graphical view of the functionality.

The format of the Loopback Fault Management cell is shown in Figure 7.6. Each field is described below:

- *OAM Function Type*   This field identifies the Fault Management cell as being a Loopback cell (and therefore identifies the format of the function-specific fields).

- *Loopback Indication*   The last bit of this field provides a Boolean indication of whether the cell has been looped back. When the loopback point receives a Loopback cell with the bit set to 1, it changes the Loopback Indication to 0, and initiates a Loopback cell in the opposite direction, containing the same information in the remaining Loopback fields. When this indication is 0, the Loopback cell is not looped back.

- *Correlation Tag*   At any given time, multiple Loopback cells could be inserted in the same connection. This field provides a means of correlating transmitted OAM cells with received OAM cells.

---

a) *End-to-end loopback*   A VP end-to-end loopback cell is inserted by a VP end-point, and looped back by the corresponding VP end-point.

b) *Access line loopback*   A VP segment loopback cell is inserted by the customer or the network, and looped back by the first ATM node in the network or customer equipment, respectively. For this application, the segment is defined by mutual agreement.

c) *Inter-domain loopback*   A VP segment loopback cell is inserted by one network operator, and looped back by the first ATM node in an adjacent network operator domain. For this application, the segment is defined by mutual agreement.

d) *Network-to-endpoint loopback*   A VP end-to-end loopback cell is inserted by one network operator, and looped back by the VP end-point in another domain.

e) *Intra-domain loopback*   A VP segment loopback is inserted by a VP connection/segment end-point or a VP connecting point, and looped back by a VP segment or a VP connecting point. For this application, the use of the Loopback Location Identifier is a network operator option.

Loopback Operation—refer to Figure 7.5

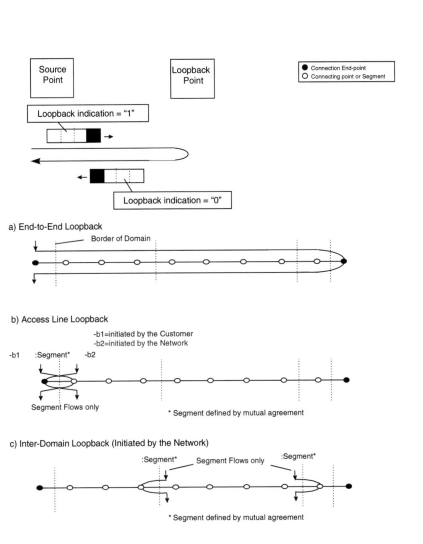

a) End-to-End Loopback

b) Access Line Loopback

c) Inter-Domain Loopback (Initiated by the Network)

d) Network-to-endpoint Loopback

e) Intra-Domain Loopback (initiated by the Network)

Figure 7.5 Loopback operation

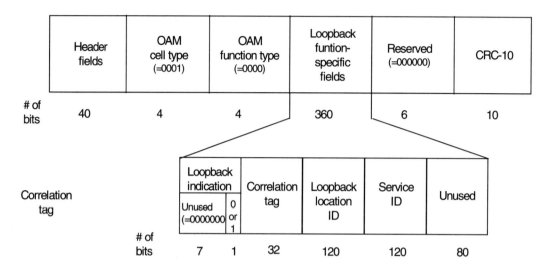

Figure 7.6   Loopback Fault Management OAM cell format

- *Loopback Location ID (optional field)*   This field identifies the point along the virtual connection or segment where the loopback is to occur. The default coding is all 1s, and represents the endpoint of the connection or segment.

- *Source ID (optional field)*   This field identifies the source originating the loopback cell. The default coding is all 1s.

Whenever an entity receives any Loopback cell, it must determine the appropriate action. It must decide whether to:

- Loopback the cell.

- Copy the cell, if the entity initiated the cell, which has completed its loopback.

- Pass the cell without further action.

7.1.3 *Managing Multiple ATM Switches*

The issue of network management becomes more complex when one needs to manage multiple switches.

Such situations arise in the context of a public carrier, as well as in corporate environments that have deployed more than one private ATM switch.

There has been interest in distributing management/operations support functions in a more efficient manner. This is done by defining Network Element Management Layer functions,[3] which are meant to be carried out on a group of switches. Some such functions are particular to a single switch (as defined above: accumulation of switch-specific performance information, detection of faults at a switch, etc.); other such functions are used across a network of switches. Examples of aggregated fault management functions include

- *Correlate multiple alarms*   As the transport and switching network grows (e.g., high-speed SONET interfaces which may carry hundreds of thousands of Virtual Path Connections and Virtual Channel Connections), the number of alarms generated by the individual fault events increases. While the ATM switches themselves will be required to keep from generating redundant alarms, there may be redundant alarms generated across ATM switches. This Network Element Management Layer capability correlates multiple alarms and eliminates obvious redundancy and duplication.

- *Analyze alarms and report findings*   After redundant alarms have been eliminated, Network Element Management Layer capabilities analyze the alarms that remain to determine the systemic or fundamental cause for the detected trouble, and the responsible hardware. The results of such analysis is communicated to the appropriate network management personnel.

- *Log alarms*   This Network Element Management Layer capability involves logging alarms reported by the individual ATM switches in the subnetwork.

- *Initiate/run testing*   This Network Element Management Layer capability involves selecting, running, and terminating diagnostic routines on individual switches as well as on the set of switches.

- *Analyze test results and report the information*   This function supports the analysis of all test results across the collection of ATM switches, to sectionalize the problem and determine the systemic cause of the fault.

---

[3] Do not confuse this concept with the Layer Management entities defined in the previous chapter. The Network Element Management Layer (which is part of TNM discussed in the next chapter) contains functions that may be used to manage resources individually and in aggregation as a subnetwork. The Element Layer's view of the network is fairly detailed. The Network Element Layer has visibility of the vendor-specific intricacies (if any) of the various elements in the network. This topic is revisited in Chapter 10.

7.1.4 Customer Network Management

Table 7.3 provides a summary of the CNM features discussed in the previous chapter, along with some potential future capabilities. Fault management aspects are indicated.

Function	FM
Receive event notifications (over SNMP)	X
Retrieve ATM UNI and CRS configuration information (over SNMP)	
Retrieve ATM UNI performance information (over SNMP)	
Retrieve connection (PVC) configuration information (over SNMP)	
Retrieve general CRS CNM information (over SNMP)	X
Receive event notifications (over B-LMI)	X
Retrieve ATM UNI configuration information (over B-LMI)	
Retrieve ATM UNI performance information (over B-LMI)	
Initiate tests (future)	X
Modify general CRS CNM information (over SNMPv2) (future)	
Modify UNI and CRS configuration information (over SNMPv2) (future)	
Reconfigure PVCs (over SNMPv2) (future)	X
Request event notifications (over SNMPv2) (future)	X
Retrieve usage information (over SNMPv2) (future)	
Support trouble report administration (over SNMPv2) (future)	X

Table 7.3   CNM Functions, fault management

7.2   Configuration Management

7.2.1 General Capabilities

Configuration management refers to functions that identify, collect data from, exercise control over, and provide data to network elements.

It can be either management system-driven or Network Element (e.g., switch)-driven. An example of management system-driven configuration management is a system communicating a cross-connection request to a switch.

An example of NE-driven configuration management is an NE reporting to a management system upon the physical installation of an interface card. The main configuration management functions, at the ATM switch level, (private or public) are summarized in Tables 7.4 and 7.5.

ITU-T Recommendation M.3010 identifies the following configuration management functions for ATM switches:

- *External Update support*   This relates to the switch's ability to report configuration changes that are transparent to the management system environment. These updates are perceived to be external to the (traditional) process of updating a switch's database.

- *Memory update support*   This relates to a switch's ability to support database updates initiated by a management system.

- *Memory query support*   This relates to a switch's ability to support database queries initiated by a management system.

- *Memory backup and restoration support*   This relates to a switch's ability to backup its database and restore RAM whenever switch data is lost or compromised.

- *Software download support*   This relates to a switch's ability to support local/remote downloads of new software.

7.2.2   *Managing Multiple ATM Switches*

Examples of Aggregated Configuration Management functions include:

- *Manage assignable inventory*   This Network Element Management Layer function involves maintaining data that describe the current state of the network. Systems responsible for this function maintain data representing the NEs, the facilities that terminate on the NEs, and the VPI/VCI translations.

- *Assign resources*   This Network Element Management Layer function refers to the ability to select and assign previously installed network resources in response to requests initiated by higher layer management application entities. For example, this would entail determining and ultimately assigning the most appropriate physical and logical resources to use in configuring a Permanent Virtual Connection.

- *Activation/deactivation of an assignment*   Associated with every assignable resource is a service state indicating whether the resource is in service (activated) or out of service (deactivated). The activation or deactivation of a

Automatic restoration in an ATM switch through backup

Handle notifications of an ATM switch's components presence, disconnection, etc.

Initialize, update, and query the ATM switch's database

Insert, remove, interconnect, and disconnect channels

Installation of equipment in the network

Request and receive ATM switch configuration status reports

Request and receive ATM switch current status information

Request and receive reports on storage status

Request and receive status of VPLs and VCIs

Request and receive switching activities and status of automatic transmission restoration

Schedule ATM switch status information reporting

Table 7.4   Key configuration management functions

External update support

    Operational state changes
    Automatic node configuration and change reporting

Memory update support

    Configuration of UNIs, B-ICIs, and B-ISSIs
    Configuration of VPLs and VCLs
    Configuration of Point-To-Point and Point-to-Multipoint ATM connections
    Activating and deactivating switch functions
    Suppression and duplication of autonomous messages

Database query support

Database backup and restoration

Software download support

Table 7.5   ATM-specific configuration management capabilities for ATM switches [2]

resource may be based on pending/future activity or may involve multiple entities where sequencing of state changes is required.

- *Backup data*   This Network Element Management Layer function refers to the ability to maintain memory backups and restoring memory upon recovery from a memory affecting outage.

7.2.3 Customer Network Management

Table 7.6 provides a summary of the CNM features discussed in the previous chapter, along with some potential future capabilities. Configuration management aspects are indicated.

Function	Configuration management
Receive event notifications (over SNMP)	
Retrieve ATM UNI and CRS configuration information (over SNMP)	X
Retrieve ATM UNI performance information (over SNMP)	
Retrieve connection (PVC) configuration information (over SNMP)	X
Retrieve general CRS CNM information (over SNMP)	X
Receive event notifications (over B-LMI)	
Retrieve ATM UNI configuration information (over B-LMI)	X
Retrieve ATM UNI performance information (over B-LMI)	
Initiate tests (future)	
Modify general CRS CNM information (over SNMPv2) (future)	X
Modify UNI and CRS configuration information (over SNMPv2) (future)	X
Reconfigure PVCs (over SNMPv2) (future)	X
Request event notifications (over SNMPv2) (future)	
Retrieve usage information (over SNMPv2) (future)	
Support trouble report administration (over SNMPv2) (future)	

Table 7.6   CNM functions, configuration management

7.3 ATM-based Services Other than CRS

It was indicated in Chapters 2 and 4 that ATM technology can be used as a platform to support a variety of (fastpacket) services (Figure 7.7). Although the switch management features apply to the entire platform, the CNM features discussed above and in Chapter 6 are principally in support of CRS. Other services have their own intrinsic management capabilities. (See, for example [7, 8], as well as [9—11].) A user obtaining multiple services from the ATM platform would have, most likely, to establish separate CNMAs to support these services; however, the intrinsic management of a (private) switch would use the mechanisms discussed here.

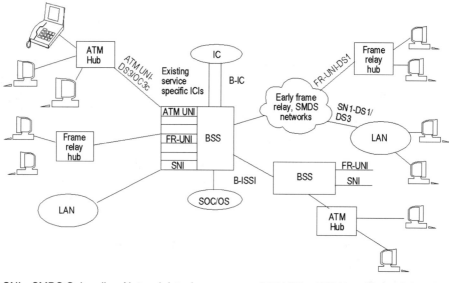

SNI—SMDS Subscriber Network Interface
FR-UNI—Frame Relay User Network Interface
B-ISSI—BISDN Inter-Switching System
    Interface
B-ICI—BISDN Inter-LATA Carrier Interface

ATM UNI—ATM User Network Interface
ICI—Inter-LATA Carrier Interface
SOC—Subnetwork Operations Control
OS—Operations System
BSS—Broadband Switching System
    (ATM Switch)

Figure 7.7   Early ATM/broadband network

References

[1] D. Minoli, M. Vitella, *Cell Relay Service and ATM in Corporate Environments* (McGraw-Hill, 1994).

[2] Bellcore Technical Advisory TA-NWT-001248, *Generic Requirements for Operations of Broadband Switching Systems,* October, 1993, Livingston, NJ.

[3] T1M1.3 Standard on Performance Monitoring for DS1, DS3, SONET.

[4] Bellcore Technical Reference TR-TSV-000773, *Local Access System Generic Requirements, Objectives and Interfaces in Support of Switched Multi-Megabit Data Service,* June 1991, Livingston, NJ.

[5] Bellcore Technical Reference TR-NWT-000191, *Alarm Indication Signal Requirements and Objectives,* May 1986, Livingston, NJ.

[6] Bellcore Technical Reference TR-TSy-000474, OTGR: *Network Maintenance: Network Element,* July 1991, Livingston, NJ.

[7] Bellcore Technical Reference TR-TSV-001062, Generic *Requirements for SMDS Customer Network Management Services,* Issue 1, March 1992, Livingston, NJ.

[8] Bellcore Technical Reference TA-TSV-001371, *Frame Relay (PVC) Customer Network Management Service,* September 1993, Livingston, NJ.

[9] Bellcore Technical Reference TR-TSV-001064, *SMDS Phase 1 Operations Information Model,* December 1993, Livingston, NJ.

[10] Bellcore Technical Reference TA-TSV-001235, *Exchange Access SMDS Operations Interface Model,* Issue 1, April 1993, Livingston, NJ.

[11] Bellcore Technical Reference TA-TSV-001379, *Frame Relay Network Operations Using OSI,* July 1993, Livingston, NJ.

chapter 8

Managing ATM Networks: Performance Management

*A*ll *ATM platforms, whether customer-owned or in the public network, are likely to serve many customers having a variety of widely differing traffic profiles (e.g., constant bit rate traffic, compressed but buffered digital video, compressed but unbuffered digital video, uncompressed digital video, video distribution, video conferencing, high-capacity bursty data, and voice).*

These circumstances are conducive to congestion, which can lead to service degradations or outright breakdowns. Performance management is of crucial importance. Performance management consists of network management functions designed to monitor and assess a system's ability to carry out its assigned functions through the collection and analysis of selected performance data.

Basic functions discussed in this chapter include:

- *Performance monitoring, including protocol monitoring, VP/VC performance monitoring, and protocol test access.*

- *Network traffic access functions, including measures of congestion, thresholding capabilities, network traffic management surveillance measures, and network traffic management controls.*

8.1   Performance Monitoring

Performance monitoring[1] refers to the periodic assessment of a system's ability to carry out its assigned function through the collection and analysis of appropriate performance data. The intent of performance monitoring procedures is to capture intermittent error conditions and trouble resulting from any gradual deterioration of network equipment. Performance monitoring is useful because it enables network providers to detect troubles early enough to be corrected before they become more severe. Performance management (PM) functions are listed in more detail in Table 8.1.

At the user level, Quality of Service (QoS) is one of the key measures. The ATM switch needs to guarantee that the QoS is met. QoS is service specific; SMDS has its QoS objectives; Frame Relay Service has its QoS objectives; and Cell Relay Service has its QoS objectives.

For CRS, a QoS class can be defined via explicitly specified performance parameters (Specified QoS class) or with no specified performance parameters (Unspecified QoS class, also known as a *best effort class*). A Specified QoS class

---

[1] Portions of this material are expanded from reference [1].

Performance monitoring functions

Monitoring of physical transmission facilities (facility monitoring)

ATM over DS1/DS3
ATM over SONET

Protocol monitoring

Protocol monitoring with respect to ATM Cell Header
Protocol monitoring of OAM cells
Protocol monitoring of AAL 1, AAL 3/4 (SAR and CS), and AAL 5

VP/VC performance monitoring

VC/VP PM cell generation
Data collection to support VP/VC performance monitoring
Activation/Deactivation procedures for VP/VC performance monitoring

Protocol test access

Network traffic access functions

Support needed for all congestionable modules
Measures of congestions
Thresholding capabilities
Network Traffic Management surveillance measurements
Network Traffic Management Controls

Note: Refer to Reference [2] for a complete treatment of these topics.

Table 8.1   Key Performance Management Functions in ATM

specifies a set of performance parameters and the objective values for each performance parameter identified. Examples of performance parameters that could be in a QoS class are cell transfer delay, cell delay variation, and cell loss ratio. Within a specified QoS class, up to two cell loss ratio parameters may be specified.

If a specified QoS class contains two cell loss ratio parameters, then one parameter is for all CLP=0 cells, and the other parameter is for all CLP=1 cells of the ATM connection. A QoS class could contain, for example, the following performance parameters: mean cell transfer delay, a cell delay variation, a cell loss ratio on CLP=0 cells, and a cell loss ratio on CLP=1 cells. The two actual QoS classes under consideration by (some) carriers are as follows:

- Class 1. CLR $\leq 1.7 \times 10^{-10}$; CTD (99th percentile) = 150 μsec; CDV (10^{-10} quantile) = 250 μsec.

- Class 2. CLR $\leq 10^{-7}$; CTD (99th percentile) = 150 msec; CDV (10^{-10} quantile) = 250 msec.

To support the desired functionality, an ATM switch (public or private) should support as many as possible of the performance measurements and related network management in the traffic measurement and service measurement areas shown in Table 8.2. As seen in Table 8.1, within the context of ATM networks, performance monitoring supports the following capabilities:

- Monitoring of Physical Transport Facilities.

- Monitoring of Virtual Path Connections and Virtual Channel Connections.

- Protocol Monitoring.

8.2 Monitoring Details

8.2.1 Physical Transport Facility Performance Monitoring

For public ATM facilities, DS1, DS3, and SONET transport systems may be used. These systems have a well-defined set of performance management functions [3], and are not described here.

8.2.2 VPC/VCC Performance Monitoring

VPCs and VCCs may extend across a number of independently monitored transport facilities to connect service entities in ATM switching systems or to provide semipermanent logical connections for end-to-end customer services or customer-to-network signaling.

In either case, it is expected that the network provider or users will, at times, want to monitor the performance of their semipermanent connections. A VPC/VCC performance monitoring function has been defined to meet this need. This function applies to VP/VC segments as well.

VPC/VCC performance monitoring is accomplished using OAM cells. Issues include:

- The mechanism for VPC/VCC PM cell generation.

- The VPC/VCC performance monitoring parameters.

- The activation/deactivation procedure for VPC/VCC monitoring.

- The ATM switch should gather and threshold the following congestion measurements for each congestionable ATM module:

  1. Percent utilization of the ATM module.

  2. Counts of ATM cells discarded by the ATM module.

- The ATM switch should include automatic network traffic management controls to improve performance during ATM module and switch-wide congestion events.

- The ATM switch should be able to report the maximum sustained throughput on a per-interface basis. It must able to report the buffer and processor occupancy measurements for all traffic-sensitive resources in the switch.

- The ATM switch should provide the service monitoring measurements as follows:

  1. The switch should support all ESF DS1 performance monitoring requirements specified in TA-TSY-000820, for all interfaces where ATM cells are mapped to a DS1 signal.

  2. The switch should support all the standards DS3 performance monitoring requirements specified in TA-TSY-000820, for all interfaces where ATM cells are mapped to a DS1 signal.

  3. The switch should support the PLCP performance monitoring requirements specified in TA-TSY-000773 and TA-NWT-001112.

  4. The switch should support all the standards SONET performance monitoring requirements specified in TA-NWT-000253, for all interfaces where ATM cells are mapped to a SONET signal.

  5. The switch should count and threshold the following performance parameters on a per UNI, B-ISSI, or B-ICI basis:

     - Number of cells discarded due to HEC violations.

     - Out-of-Cell delineation.

     - Cells discarded due to ATM Layer header errors.

  6. The switch should use Threshold Crossing Alerts when counts for these parameters are exceeded during a measurement interval. The alerts must contain the following information: specific interface involved, condition code identifying the measurement type, value of the parameter, and date and time of occurrence of the event.

Table 8.2   Typical ATM performance functions and measurements

7. The switch should maintain error logs; the information in the logs must be retrievable.

8. The switch should count and threshold the following:

    • Number of OAM cells discarded due to failed CRC-10 tests.

    • Number of OAM cells discarded due to invalid values of the OAM Cell Type, OAM Function Type, or function-specific fields.

9. The switch should count and threshold Convergence Sublayer errors at interworking points.

10. The switch should count and threshold Segmentation and Reassembly errors for AAL Type 3/4.

11. The switch should count and threshold protocol errors for AAL Type 1 and AAL Type 5.

12. The switch should be able to communicate with the Management System about congestionable ATM modules within itself.

• The ATM switch should support appropriate service reliability/availability, service accuracy (e.g., misrouted cells and misdelivered cells), QOS (e.g., cell delay variation), and depend ability objectives:

1. The ATM switch should meet the Frame Relay service requirements listed in TR-TSV-001369, and TR-TSV-001370, if Frame Relay Service is supported.

2. The switch should count and threshold on the number of frames that do not meet Frame Relay service requirements on a per-service parameter basis, if Frame Relay Service is supported.

3. The ATM switch should meet the SMDS service requirements listed in TR-TSV-000772, and TR-TSV-001060, if SMDS is supported.

    • The switch should count and threshold on the number of SMDS PDUs that do not meet SMDS service requirements on a per-service parameter basis, if SMDS is supported.

4. The ATM switch should meet the Cell Relay service requirements listed in TR-TSV-001408, TR-TSV-001409, TR-TSV-001501, if Cell Relay Service is supported.

    • The switch should count and threshold on the number of cells that do not meet the cell relay service requirements on a per-service parameter basis, if Cell Relay Service is supported.

Note: Although this table applies directly to public-network ATM switches, a high end private ATM switch should support many of these functions.

Table 8.2 *Continued*

ATM Layer performance monitoring has two distinct aspects. The first is the generation of Performance Management cells that communicate forward monitoring and backward reporting information among nodes of a connection. The second concerns the storage of data for each parameter, and thresholding of selected parameters.

Performance Management cells (PM cells) send forward monitoring information and backward report information. Both types of information may be sent in the same cell.

Mechanism for VP/VC PM Cell Generation

There are two classes of VP/VC monitored entities; end-to-end VPC/VCCs and VPC/VCC segments. *End-to-end monitoring* refers to monitoring the entire connection, which may span multiple networks. A *VPC/VCC segment* is a part of the connection, and is generally limited to one administration's network.

A Performance Management cell contains information about a block of user-information cells of one connection: Performance Management and other OAM cells such as Fault Management cells are not part of the block. Figure 8.1 illustrates the concept of a block. The allowable nominal block sizes [2] are 128, 256, 512, and 1024 cells. Note that the larger the block, the lower the transmission capacity overhead used for performance monitoring.

End-to-End VPC/VCC Monitoring

The steps for generating PM cells when performing end-to-end VPC/VCC performance monitoring are:

1. The originating VPC/VCC endpoint generates a BIP-16 (Bit Inverted Parity) error detection code over the payloads of the user information cells in the block. Then the endpoint will place the following information in the payload of a Performance Management OAM cell: the monitoring sequence number of the PM cell, the total user cell count (modulo 65,536), the BIP-16, and an optional timestamp. This OAM cell is the next cell transmitted on that VPC/VCC; i.e., it is transmitted before the next user-information cell of the VPC/VCC. Although the block size for a connection has a nominal

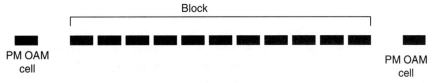

Figure 8.1   Performance monitoring block

value, the actual size of any given block may vary by as much as 50% from that nominal value. This variation allows PM cells to be inserted without delaying the flow of user cells in most cases.

2. The far end VPC/VCC endpoint compares the number of the cells received in the block with the difference between the total user cell counts of the last two PM cells it received. A mismatch in this comparison indicates lost or misinserted cells. The endpoint compares the BIP-16 in the forward monitoring cell with the result of an identical BIP-16 calculation it has performed over the same number of user-information cells. A mismatch in this comparison indicates bit errors in the block. The results from this block count of lost/misinserted cells and the number of errored parity bits in the BIP-16 code are stored until the backward reporting cell is sent.

3. The far end VPC/VCC endpoint reports the results (number of lost/ misinserted cells and number of errored parity bits) back to the originating VPC/VCC endpoint using a Performance Management OAM cell to send a backward report. This procedure is performed symmetrically for both directions of VPC/VCC transmission if bidirectional PM has been activated. Figure 8.2 shows a connection, composed of connection segments, in which PM is active in both directions. Each VPC/VCC node has the capability to monitor the bidirectional VPC/VCC by accessing the backward reporting information.

In end-to-end performance monitoring, the insertion and extraction of OAM cells is performed by the VPC/VCC endpoints, while the VPC/VCC monitor points need only to monitor incoming OAM cells.

8.2.3 VP/VC Segment PM Cell Generation

Even if a VPC/VCC is already being monitored end-to-end, VPC/VCC segment monitoring can provide more accurate measures of the network provider's part of the connection. With VPC/VCC segment monitoring, performance problems outside the segment will not affect the results of segment monitoring.

The procedure for VPC/VCC segment performance monitoring is the same as the end-to-end procedure described earlier, except that PM OAM cells are inserted and extracted at the endpoints of the segment, instead of the endpoints of the connection. Another difference is that PM cells are not forced when the block size is exceeded by 50%, so there is no maximum block size. However, it is desirable to enforce an average block size, because it improves the quality of the performance measures that are stored.

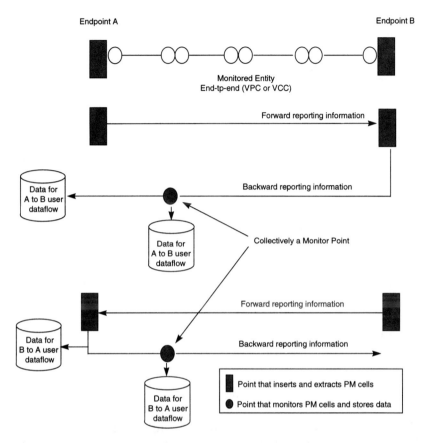

Figure 8.2 Bidirectional performance monitoring

An additional difference between end-to-end and segment monitoring is that the backward reporting flow is not always required.

PM Cell Payload Structure

The PM cell payload structure is shown in Figure 8.3. The fields are:

- *OAM Type* The OAM Type is *Performance Management*, encoded as 0010.

- *Function Type* The Function Type field specifies whether the cell is to be used for Forward Monitoring (0000), Backward Reporting (0001), or Monitoring & Reporting (0010). Note that although there are three function types, there are only two distinct functions of the PM cell: forward monitoring and backward reporting. Figure 8.3 shows which fields are used only for

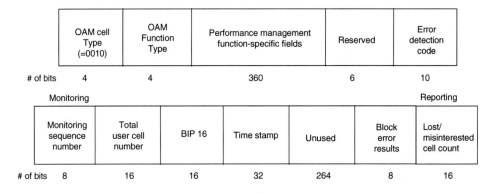

OAM cell Type (=0010)	OAM Function Type	Performance management function-specific fields	Reserved	Error detection code

# of bits   4   4   360   6   10

Monitoring   Reporting

Monitoring sequence number	Total user cell number	BIP 16	Time stamp	Unused	Block error results	Lost/ misinterested cell count

# of bits   8   16   16   32   264   8   16

Figure 8.3   Performance management OAM cell format

the forward monitoring function, and which are used only for the backward reporting function. For connections on which bidirectional performance monitoring is active, there exists the option of using all fields in a Monitoring & Reporting cell. In a Monitoring & Reporting cell, one PM cell is used to carry the forward reporting information for one direction and the backward reporting information for the other.

- *Monitoring Cell Sequence Number (MSN)*   For PM cells containing forward monitoring information, this field contains the sequence number, modulo 256. PM cells containing backward reporting information only (i.e., Reporting cells) are not included in this sequence. This field allows for the detection of a lost or misinserted Performance Management OAM cell with forward monitoring information. For Reporting cells, the MSN is encoded as 6A hexadecimal.

- *Total User Cell (TUC) Number*   This field indicates the total number (modulo 65,536) of user cells transmitted just before a monitoring cell is inserted.

- *Block Error Detection Code*   This field contains the even parity BIP-16 error detection code computed over the information fields of the block of user-data cells transmitted after the last monitoring cell.

- *Time Stamp*   This optional field may be used to represent the time at which the OAM cell was inserted. If the field is not used, it is set to all 1s.

- *Unused*   Octets in this field are encoded as 6A hexadecimal (01101010).

- *Block Error Result*   This field carries the number of errored parity bits in the BIP-16 code of a received monitoring cell. The field is used for backward reporting.

- *Lost/Misinserted Cells*   This field carries the count of lost or misinserted cells computed over the received block. The value is calculated at the receiving ATM endpoint as the number of cells received minus the number of cells expected (i.e., actual–expected). This field is used for backward reporting.

When fields are not used (e.g., the Monitoring fields are not used in the Reporting PM cell), the fields are treated as unused fields, and encoded accordingly. Note, however, when a PM cell uses the monitoring fields but does not encode a time stamp into the Time Stamp field, it is not considered "unused." In this case the Time Stamp field is encoded to its default value of all 1s.

VP/VC Performance Monitoring Parameters

As of writing time there were no international standards agreements on specific parameters for performance monitoring using OAM cells. However, there are international agreements on fundamental principles of ATM Layer cell transfer performance as defined in I.356 [4]. It is expected that performance monitoring parameters will be defined to be consistent with those agreements, on a per-VP or per-VC basis [1] [2]:

- Errored blocks.

- Severely errored blocks.

- Lost user information cells.

- Misinserted user information cells.

- Excessive cell transfer delay occurrences.

The Block Error Result can be used to distinguish between errored and severely errored blocks. The BIP-16 error code was chosen for performance monitoring, because when using this type of error detection code, it is

- Unlikely that a moderate level of background errors will result in more than four BIP columns being in error.

- Probable that a burst error event will affect greater than 4 of the BIP columns.

Thus, the number of BIP columns in error can be used to distinguish between errored blocks and severely errored blocks. The performance monitoring parameters are:

- *Errored Blocks* While acute failure conditions are generally detected by alarm surveillance methods, low-rate or intermittent error conditions in multiple equipment units may interact in an aggregate manner over a connection, resulting in poor service quality. The Errored Block parameter is designed to measure the overall quality of the connection to detect such deterioration. It may also be possible to detect characteristic patterns indicating an impending serious degradation before signal quality has dropped below an acceptable level.

- *Severely Errored Blocks* Whenever the number of errored columns is greater than a prespecified threshold, a block is counted as a severely errored block. When this threshold is set to a uniform value in a network, it allows a single interpretation of Severely Errored Block measurements by network managers. Thus, it may be desirable for all networks to adopt a uniform value.

- *Lost User Information Cells* This parameter measures cell loss, but cannot distinguish between cells lost because of header bit errors, ATM-level header errors, cell policing, or buffer overflows.

- *Misinserted User Information Cells* It is possible that a cell can be misrouted to an active VP/VC that is being monitored. This parameter is used to measure these occurrences.

- *Excessive Cell Transfer Delay Occurrences* PM OAM cells, each containing a timestamp, could be used to obtain an estimate of excessive cell transfer delay occurrences at the ATM switch that receives the timestamp information in the forward report. This count can only be made and stored at the connection/segment endpoint that receives the forward monitoring cell, as there is no field in the PM cell that allows backward reporting of excessive cell transfer delay occurrences.

Activation/Deactivation Procedure for VP/VC Monitoring

The activation/deactivation of VP/VC performance monitoring is a system management function, initiated by the appropriate management system or by the end user. Activation/deactivation cells are used in the network to provide handshaking between the two ends of the monitored entity. The performance monitoring activation/deactivation handshaking procedure serves the following purposes:

- To coordinate and synchronize the beginning or end of the transmission and downstream reception of PM OAM cells.

- To establish agreement, based on the system management activation/deactivation request, on the Block Size and the directions of transmission to start or stop monitoring.

The activation/deactivation cell format is shown in Figure 8.4, and each field is briefly described.

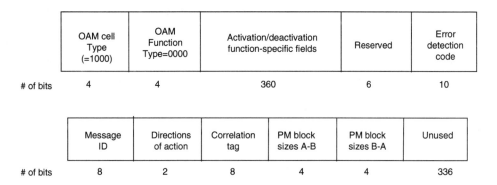

	OAM cell Type (=1000)	OAM Function Type=0000	Activation/deactivation function-specific fields	Reserved	Error detection code
# of bits	4	4	360	6	10

	Message ID	Directions of action	Correlation tag	PM block sizes A-B	PM block sizes B-A	Unused
# of bits	8	2	8	4	4	336

Figure 8.4   Activation/deactivation OAM cell format

- *Message ID (6 bits)*   This field indicates the message ID for activating or deactivating VP/VC functions. Code values are shown in Table 8.3.

Message	Value
Activate	000001
Activation Confirmed	000010
Activation Request Denied	000011
Deactivate	000100
Deactivation Confirmed	000101
Deactivation Denied	000110

Table 8.3   Message ID codings

- *Directions of Action (2 bits)*   This field identifies the directions of transmission to activate or deactivate the OAM function. The A-B and B-A notation is used to differentiate between the direction of user data transmission—away from or toward the activator/deactivator, respectively. This field value is used as a parameter for the Activate and Deactivate messages. It is encoded as 01 for B-A, 10 for A-B, 11 for two-way action, and 00 (default value) when not applicable.

- *Correlation Tag (8 bits)*   A correlation tag is generated for each message so nodes can correlate commands with responses.

- *PM Block Sizes A-B (4 bits)*   This field specifies the A-to-B PM block size or block size choices supplied by the activator for Performance Monitoring. The four bit positions in this field, from the most significant bit to the least significant bit, if set, indicates block sizes of 128, 256, 512, or 1024, respectively. For example, a value of 1010 would mean that block size 128 or 512 may be used, but not 256 or 1024. This field value is used as a parameter for the Activate and Activation Confirmed messages. The default value for this field is 0000.

- *PM Block Sizes B-A (4 bits)*   This field specifies the B-A block size or block size choices supplied by the activator. It is encoded and used in the same manner as the PM Block Sizes A-B field.

The procedure for activating performance monitoring (PM) is as follows:

1. *Request for PM Activation*   An end user or management system initiates a request at one end of the monitored entity. By definition, this endpoint is *A*, and the other endpoint is *B*. The initiation includes a specification of the directions of PM to activate, and the requested block sizes in the A-B direction (if appropriate) and the B-A direction (if appropriate). Endpoint A first determines whether it can support monitoring an additional monitored entity, and checks to make sure that PM cells are not already being generated in the requested directions. Then it determines which subset of the requested block size values in each direction it supports. If none of the values are supported by endpoint A, the request is denied, and the PM activation requester is informed.

2. *Send Activate Message*   If endpoint A can support the requested PM, it sends an Activate message, including the block size values and monitored directions, to endpoint B.

3. *Send Activation Confirmed Message* or *Activation Request Denied Message*   Endpoint B determines which of the requested block size values it can support.

If it can support multiple block sizes for a direction, it picks one. If there is at least one valid block size (one in each direction, in the case of a two-way monitoring request), then it sends an Activation Confirmed message to endpoint A. Each point along the segment/connection capable of monitoring the connection notes that PM is active.

If endpoint B does not support at least one block size in each direction of monitoring, if PM cells are already being generated in the requested directions, or if endpoint B is unable to support monitoring on any more monitored entities, then the request cannot be honored. In this case, endpoint B sends an Activation Request Denied message back to endpoint A. Endpoint A informs the PM activation requester of the denial.

4. *Beginning of PM at Endpoint B*   If endpoint B honors the PM activation request and sends an Activation Confirmed message, it begins the following processes: it generates PM cells, if PM was activated in the B-A direction; and it waits to receive PM cells, if PM was requested in the A-B direction. The first PM cell received is used only for initialization.

5. *Beginning of PM at Endpoint A*   When endpoint A receives the confirmation, or if it receives a PM cell before the timer expires when PM was activated in the B-A direction, it begins the same two activities that endpoint B did, where appropriate, and notifies its management system that performance monitoring activities have begun.

The performance monitoring deactivation handshaking procedure is:

1. *Request for PM Deactivation*   An end user or management system initiates a request at one end of the monitored entity. By definition, this endpoint is *A*, and the other endpoint is *B*. There is no correlation between the point that activated PM and the point that deactivates PM; either end can request deactivation. The initiation includes a specification of the directions of PM to deactivate. The two PM block sizes fields are not used, and hence are coded as 0000. Endpoint A first determines whether PM cells are being generated in the requested direction. If not, the request is denied, and the PM deactivation requester is informed.

It is possible that endpoint B is unable to respond (e.g., because of a power outage), and deactivation at A cannot use this handshaking procedure. Thus, the management system may deactivate its end only, but only after unsuccessfully trying deactivation with this procedure (i.e., by sending a Deactivate message).

It is possible that an endpoint will recover from a problem (e.g., power outage) and find that the other endpoint is no longer active because it deactivated PM unilaterally during the problem. In such a case, the endpoint should initiate deactivation, and reactivate if desired.

2. *Send Deactivate Message*   If endpoint A has no reason to deny the deactivation request, it relays a Deactivate message to endpoint B via an activation/ deactivation cell.

3. *Send Deactivation Confirmed Message* or *Deactivation Request Denied Message*   If endpoint B can honor the deactivation request, it sends a Deactivation Confirmed message to endpoint A.

   If endpoint B has been set to ignore deactivation OAM cells, then the request cannot be honored. An endpoint may be set to ignore deactivation messages to prevent the other endpoint from deactivating PM. In this case, endpoint B sends a Deactivation Request Denied message back to endpoint A, and informs its management system that a deactivation request was received and rejected. Endpoint A informs the PM deactivation requester of the denial.

   If PM is not active in the requested directions, the request is considered to be honored.

4. *Deactivation of PM at Endpoint B*   If endpoint B honors the PM deactivation request and sends a Deactivation Confirmed message, it makes sure that PM cells are not being generated for the appropriate directions, if the deactivation request includes the B-A direction. Endpoint B notifies the management system that performance monitoring has ended. Any point along the connection that is storing data stops that activity and notifies its management system. No processing is preformed on PM cells received after the deactivation request has been honored.

5. *Deactivation of PM at Endpoint A*   When endpoint A receives the confirmation, it ends the same two activities that endpoint B did, where appropriate, and notifies the appropriate management system that performance monitoring activities have ended. If a Deactivation Confirmed message is not received before the timer expires, the request is denied, and the PM deactivation requester is informed. If the confirmation is received after endpoint A's timer expires, endpoint A notifies the appropriate management system. The management system should then reinitiate a deactivation procedure.

An intermediate point that may wish to store PM history data needs to know when PM has been activated on a connection. It may do this by looking for Activation Confirmed messages, and notifying the appropriate management system.

8.2.4 Protocol Monitoring

Protocol monitoring is associated with every layer of the ATM protocol stack. Principal functions include:

- ATM cell header processing (discarded cells and detection of bit errors), which relates to the Physical and ATM Layers.

- Monitoring the ATM Adaption Layer, including AAL 3/4 and AAL5.

Protocol Monitoring of ATM Cell Header Processing

ATM cells are processed at various levels internal to an ATM entity. For example, at the Transmission Convergence sublayer of the Physical Layer, ATM cells are delineated from the SONET payload envelope, and the ATM cell header is examined for bit errors as part of a Header Error Control algorithm. At the ATM Layer, the cell header is processed to support functions such as cell routing and generic flow control. Deterioration or defects in ATM cell header processing equipment, software bugs, and corrupted VPI/VCI translation tables could compromise the ability of an ATM entity to perform these functions, resulting in discarding cells and the degradation of end-to-end service. By monitoring the ATM entity's ability to successfully process ATM cells, network operators can quickly detect ATM cell header processing malfunctions and initiate corrective actions. This will serve to minimize the overall impact on the network, as well as the end users supported by it.

To facilitate protocol monitoring, the ATM entity maintains counts of the following performance parameters:

- *Cells Discarded Due to Header Bit Errors*   A count is kept of the number of cells discarded due to header bit errors. Counting is suppressed when a Physical Layer problem is detected. This measure gives an implicit indication of intermittent errors in the Physical Layer, because Physical Layer problems will generally result in the corruption of multiple cell headers.

- *Cells with Detected Header Bit Errors*   A count of the number of cell headers in which one or more bit errors are detected provides an indication of the effect of bit errors on the ATM cells. The counting of cells with detected header bit errors is suspended when a Physical Layer problem occurs.

- *Cells Discarded Due to ATM Layer Header Errors*   At the Physical Layer, cells are checked for header bit errors and discarded if necessary, and Unassigned Cells and Invalid Cells are extracted. The remaining cells are submitted to the ATM Layer, where a series of checks are performed on the contents of the headers. Cells having preassigned traffic type indications that do not conform to the allowed combinations of VPI/VCI, PTI, and CLP are discarded. For example, a cell used for point-to-point signaling cannot have a 1 in the first bit of the PTI. Cells without preassigned traffic type indications may also be discarded; for example, the VPI/VCI value might not conform to an active address. Another source of errors is receipt of OAM cells that cannot be processed; for example, PM cells being received on a connection for which Performance Monitoring is not active. If a cell has ATM Layer errors, then the cell will not be processed further. The number of discarded cells due to ATM Layer header errors is counted on a per-interface basis.

Protocol Monitoring for the ATM Adaptation Layer

This section discusses protocol monitoring for the Common Parts of AAL3/4 and AAL5.

The AAL Type 3/4 supports the transport of connection-oriented and connectionless packet service. AAL3/4 processing is performed wherever the AAL3/4 is terminated.

Protocol monitoring for AAL Type 3/4 is based on maintaining counts of errors in received Protocol Data Units (PDUs). The methods employed for storing, thresholding, and reporting AAL errors are the same as those employed for the ATM Layer. The occurrence of any one of a particular group of errors or abnormalities at a sublayer is recorded in a single, thresholded counter. Because multiple error types are captured in a common performance counter, this algorithm is referred to as the sum-of-errors algorithm, and any such counter is known as a sum-of-errors counter. Below is a description of the sum-of-errors algorithm [1], [2].

The purpose of the sum-of-errors algorithm is to detect non-bursty errors (moderate error rates) over an aggregation period. There is one sum-of-errors algorithm per connection (VPC or VCC) terminating AAL Type 3/4 per sublayer (SAR or CS). Whenever an error is detected, the current counter is incremented. If the counter's value exceeds a predetermined threshold value, a Threshold Crossing Alert (TCA) message is generated and sent to the appropriate management system. If further errors are detected, the counter continues incrementing even after the Threshold Crossing Alert message is generated. If the counter reaches its maximum value, it does not "roll" but remains at that value for the duration of the aggregation period. A query of this counter may aid in determining the severity of the trouble. Only one TCA message per sum-of-errors algorithm is generated during an aggregation period. After the aggregation period expires, the queue is advanced and the current counter is reset.

SAR Layer performance monitoring is performed by collecting and thresholding counts at each point where incoming SAR-PDUs are processed. Two error detection mechanisms may be employed for each connection termination where incoming SAR-PDUs are processed. One detects invalid fields, and the other detects incorrect fields. An invalid field's value falls outside of the range permitted by the protocol. For example, if a SAR-PDU User Information Length field is not equal to 44 for a SAR-PDU having a SAR type of Beginning of Message (BOM) or Continuation of Message (COM), then it is an invalid field, because only a length of 44 is permitted for BOMs and COMs [1], [2].

An incorrect field's value falls within the range permitted by the protocol, but indicates the occurrence of a transmission or procedural error. For instance, a SAR-PDU CRC field that does not match the locally calculated CRC value is an incorrect field.

The principal difference between the two error types is that invalid fields indicate improper or incorrect implementations of the protocol, while incorrect field values indicate that a procedural or transmission error has occurred.

CS Layer Performance Monitoring

CS Layer performance monitoring is accomplished by collecting and thresholding counts at each point where incoming CS-PDUs are processed. Outgoing CS-PDUs are not monitored.

As with the protocol monitoring for the SAR Layer, errors are divided into invalid fields and incorrect fields.

Protocol Monitoring for AAL Type 5 (Common Part)

AAL Type 5 supports the transport of variable length frames up to 65,535 octets long, with error detection extending over the entire frame. The frame is padded to align the resulting protocol data unit to fill an integral number of ATM cells.

Protocol monitoring for the AAL5 Common Part is accomplished by monitoring the following error conditions at the receiving point:

- Invalid format of Control field.

- Length violations.

- Oversized Service Data Units (SDUs) received.

- Cyclic Redundancy Checking (CRC) violations.

8.2.5 Managing Multiple ATM Switches

From a user's point of view, performance is measured end to end. This implies that a critical issue in this context is to aggregate performance measurements across multiple switches. The Network Element Management Layer capability first introduced in Chapter 7 supports these network requirements, as follows:

- Accumulation of performance monitoring and traffic management data. This Network Element Management Layer capability supports the collection and storage of ATM switch performance monitoring and traffic measurement information that goes beyond what each individual ATM switch does. Some CNMAs or NMS functions may require data accumulated over a time horizon of hours or days; an individual ATM switch may store only 15 minutes worth of performance information. This capability may also have to format the data in some specific manner dictated by the OSs or agents (e.g., CNM agent).

- Analysis of performance management information and reporting of findings. This Network Element Management Layer capability supports the analysis of the set of accumulated performance management information, and the reporting of the results to the appropriate entities.

- Correlation of alerts and alarms and reporting of findings. This Network Element Management Layer capability supports the correlation of threshold crossing events with failure notification. Although individual ATM switches undertake some localized correlation and filtering of alerts and alarms, a global-level correlation is still needed to support end-to-end performance goals.

- Update/Query of switch performance management information and control information. This Network Element Management Layer capability supports the ability to retrieve (historical) performance monitoring information stored in the ATM switches in a distributed fashion. This function also supports updating the criteria, schedule, and thresholds in a global manner, for the collection of performance information.

8.2.6 Customer Network Management

Table 8.4 provides a summary of the CNM features discussed in the previous chapter, along with some potential future capabilities. Performance management aspects are indicated.

	PM
Receive event notifications (over SNMP)	X
Retrieve ATM UNI and CRS configuration information (over SNMP)	
Retrieve ATM UNI performance information (over SNMP)	X
Retrieve connection (PVC) configuration information (over SNMP)	
Retrieve general CRS CNM information (over SNMP)	X
Receive event notifications (over B-LMI)	X
Retrieve ATM UNI configuration information (over B-LMI)	
Retrieve ATM UNI performance information (over B-LMI)	X
Initiate tests (future)	X
Modify general CRS CNM information (over SNMPv2) (future)	X
Modify UNI and CRS configuration information (over future SNMPv2)	
Reconfigure PVCs (over SNMPv2) (future)	
Request event notifications (over SNMPv2) (future)	X
Retrieve usage information (over SNMPv2) (future)	
Support trouble report administration (over SNMPv2) (future)	

Table 8.4   CNM Functions, performance management

References

[1] D. Minoli, M. Vitella, *Cell Relay Service and ATM in Corporate Environments*, (McGraw-Hill, 1994).

[2] Bellcore Technical Advisory TA-NWT-001248, *Generic Requirements for Operations of Broadband Switching Systems*, October, 1993.

[3] Bellcore Technical Advisory TA-NWT-001112, *Broadband ISDN User to Network and Network Node Interface Physical Layer Generic Criteria*, August 1992.

[4] ITU-T Recommendation T.356. Geneva, CH.

chapter 9

Managing ATM Networks: Accounting and Security Management

Accounting and security are both fundamental requirements of network management. Without a capacity to bill for service, carriers are not motivated to install ATM. Chargeback procedures or "departmentalized" bills may also be crucial for corporate networks. Managers will demand a way to account for who is using ATM services and for what purpose. This is especially true if a company's traffic moves over the same small set of UNIs.

Issues include:

- *The many departments that may make up an enterprise.*

- *Different categories of traffic, such as voice, data, and video.*

Without adequate security procedures, few customers would want to use an ATM-based service.

As in Chapter 6, the techniques discussed in this chapter apply to public ATM switches as well as to customer-owned switches. Also, these techniques support CNM for hybrid or all-public corporate ATM networks. Key capabilities are discussed in this chapter.

9.1 Accounting Management

To recapitulate points outlined in Chapter 4, functions supported by accounting management include:

- Create, activate, deactivate, and delete a data collection process for service-specific charging.
- Create, change, obtain information on, and delete a tariff.
- Enable accounting limits to be set, and tariff schedules to be associated with resource usage.
- Enable costs from the use of multiple switches to be combined.
- Inform users of resources used and the associated costs incurred.

While the method of measurement is standardized to some extent (i.e., there are national de facto standards), as discussed below, the tariffs to generate bills are clearly dictated by business needs.

9.1.1 Public ATM Switches

Accounting management capabilities provide network operators with information that can be used to bill customers for their use of network resources and services. This usage information (variously called *Automatic Message Accounting* (AMA) or *accounting management data*) is also valuable for other applications. Since there are no standards for ATM accounting management per se, it is expected that these functions will be performed on a network-specific (perhaps national-specific) basis. Some of the key functions to be supported are:

- AMA data collection.

- Call assembly.

- Assurance of AMA record accuracy.

- Support of AMA recording format "standards" (Table 9.1).

SMDS
    TR-TSV-000775 (June 1991)
    TR-TSV-001060 (March 1993)

Frame relay (PVC)
    TR-TSV-001369 (May 1993)
    TR-TSV-001370 (May 1993)

Cell relay (PVC)
    TA-TSV-001408 (August 1993)
    TA-TSV-001409 (November 1993)
    TA-NWT-001501 (December 1993)

Other documents
    TR-TSY-000385 (Revision 1, February 1990)
    TR-NWT-000508 (Section 8.1 — A module of LSSGR, FR-NWT-000064, Issue 3, June 1992)
    TR-TSV-000775 (June 1991)
    TA-NWT-001343 (Issue 2, August 1993)
    TA-NWT-001110 (Issue 2, August 1993)

Note: These Technical Advisories and Technical Requirements are published by Bellcore, Livingston, NJ.

Table 9.1 Published requirements for accounting management of public ATM switches

These accounting needs include end-customer billing, CNM functions, and possibly network planning. Since the ATM switch may be deployed as a platform supporting multiple services, existing service-specific measurements must also be supported, particularly in public networks. Table 9.1 depicts the billing requirements for public ATM switches.

The view at press time (at least for PVC CRS) was to collect for billing purposes Total Cells, High Priority Cells, OAM Cells, and High Priority OAM Cells, at the egress interface of a network (i.e., at a UNI or B-ICI). There are similarities between traffic load measurements, NDC[1] (Network Data Collection) information, and usage information for AMA purposes. However, there are some differences on how the measurements are taken; hence, all the various counts must be collected. For a more complete discussion of this issue, and of NDC in particular, the reader is referred to [1].

9.1.2 Managing Multiple ATM Switches

An important issue in this context is to aggregate usage measurements across multiple switches. The Network Element Management Layer capability first introduced in Chapter 6 supports the collection of usage measurement data for use by billing applications residing at central location in the network. (In a public network, this is the Revenue Accounting Office, RAO.)

---

[1] Public ATM-network NDC measurements are collected over a time horizon to detect violations of service subscription parameters by ATM users, and to detect long-term trends in traffic patterns and loads. NDC assists the manager to plan network capacity (e.g., to establish load balancing) and to optimize network administration (e.g., to detect routing or resource allocation inefficiencies). NDC also supports CNM functions. NDC measurements are characterized by factors such as data collection requirements, types of data collected, collection methods (e.g., scheduled measurements or special-studies measurements), and reporting methods to the management system. The most important scheduled measurements for a public ATM switch are as follows:

- Traffic load measurements (e.g., cell counts) entering and leaving an ATM switch interface and VPLs/VCLs.
- UPC/NPC inconsistency measurements per VPL/VCL (i.e., measure of cells discarded due to UPC/NPC violations).
- Traffic load and congestion measurements, for the switch as a whole, or for any congestionable switch module (e.g., a switch stage). Traffic loads refer to counts of cells that are processed by a module of the ATM switch. Congestion measurements are counts of cells discarded by the ATM switch because of buffer overflows or switch-initiated drops to alleviate congestion (but excluding cells dropped because of UPC/NPC disagreements).

A supportive function is the formatting and transmission of the usage measurements. Prior to transmitting the billing information, it may have preformatted in a standardized way. (If the ATM switch already follows the appropriate billing data "standards" of Table 9.1, then this step will not be needed.)

9.1.3 Customer Network Management

Table 9.2 provides a summary of the CNM features discussed in the previous chapter, along with some potential future capabilities. Accounting management aspects are indicated.

Function	Accounting management
Receive event notifications (over SNMP)	
Retrieve ATM UNI and CRS configuration information (over SNMP)	
Retrieve ATM UNI performance information (over SNMP)	
Retrieve connection (PVC) configuration information (over SNMP)	
Retrieve general CRS CNM information (over SNMP)	X
Receive event notifications (over B-LMI)	
Retrieve ATM UNI configuration information (over B-LMI)	
Retrieve ATM UNI performance information (over B-LMI)	
Initiate tests (future)	
Modify general CRS CNM information (over SNMPv2) (future)	X
Modify UNI and CRS configuration information (over SNMPv2) (future)	
Reconfigure PVCs (over SNMPv2) (future)	
Request event notifications (over SNMPv2) (future)	
Retrieve usage information (over SNMPv2) (future)	X
Support trouble report administration (over SNMPv2) (future)	

Table 9.2   CNM functions, accounting management

9.2 Security Management

9.2.1 General Capabilities

Security mechanisms must enable carriers to offer a CNM service that guarantees the privacy of the corporation's information, and the integrity of the public network and the information provided to the corporation.

These aspects of security are of interest in a network management context:

- Authentication.
- Data and system integrity.
- Identification.
- Resource access control.
- System access control.
- System audit logs.

For a general discussion of network security, including threats and defense mechanisms, the reader may wish to refer to [2].

Security management deals with methods for protecting the network from unwanted or unauthorized intrusion [7.12, 7.13, and 7.14]. Clearly, only persons authorized by an organization should be allowed access to CNM information pertaining to that organization (and none other). This issue is even more important in the case of public CNM service. Mechanisms are required in CNM (and also in NMSs) to provide authentication and access control, including different levels of permission for network managers retrieving/modifying the CRS CNM information. The same holds for accessing network management information on a customer-owned ATM switch which is part of a private ATM network, or for accessing the "raw" management information on a public-service switch. For a general discussion of network security, including threats and defense mechanisms, refer to [2].

Initially, securing a network was mainly a matter of restricting physical access to network facilities and devices. However, as network elements have become more "intelligent," the network now resembles a large distributed computing system. Thus, each element must not only be physically secured against security threats, but logically secured as well. The major known security threats include:

- An entity gaining greater privileges by masquerading as another entity.
- Disclosure of data without authorization.

- Alteration of data.
- Access of system resources by unauthorized users.
- Degradation of a system's performance, or incapacitation of the system.

Security features fall into the following categories:

- Identification of users (e.g., use of a user-ID).
- Authentication of users (e.g., smart card verification).
- Session control (e.g., session establishment procedures).
- Resource access control (e.g., restriction of user's access of certain data).
- Data and system integrity (e.g., consistency of intelligent network node data).
- Security logging (e.g., ability to establish an audit trail).
- Security administration (e.g., overriding vendor defaults)

The first security step an intelligent network node needs to take is to identify a user as being valid or not. The user's ID must be stored in the intelligent network node for the user to gain access to the node.

After identifying the user, the authentication process is performed. This consists of verifying user attributes, such as the private identifier (e.g., password) and calling address (for remote dial access), to verify that a user is, in fact, who he or she claims to be. Mechanisms can include dial-back mechanisms and *smart card* verification.

Session control features, such as session timeouts and limiting the number of password attempts, can be implemented. Once he or she passes these tests, the user is granted access to the intelligent network node. An intelligent network node has the capability to store these security attributes and update them in response to messages from a management system.

Once a user is deemed to be valid, resource access control functionality is employed to make sure that he or she is authorized to perform the functions he or she requests. Resource access control is based on the user identity, and when applicable, on the calling address of the user. Users and calling addresses can be assigned privilege codes that restrict access to some functions and data.

To access a subset of the database (e.g., an object class in a CMIS implementation), the user's authorization level must meet or exceed the access restrictions on those data.

Data and system integrity checking provides for a level of automated security monitoring, e.g., through the detection of network management data corrupted due to viruses.

Security logs provide the ability to examine an audit trail when a security problem is suspected. Security administration deals with functions such as:

- Providing a mechanism for a security administrator to display all currently active users and review the actions of selected users.

- Providing a mechanism for the security administrator to authorize or revoke users, reset user passwords, disable user IDs, and review a user's access privileges.

9.2.2 *Managing Multiple ATM Switches*

When managing multiple ATM switches, security issues become even more critical. The distributed nature of the switch complex makes it more susceptible to security concerns. The security issues are as follows:

- *Authentication*   This Network Element Management Layer capability supports the ability to identify users attempting to access it to gain control to one or more switches for management purposes.

- *Access control*   This Network Element Management Layer capability supports system access control, which restricts system access for modifying any and all switch information, across one or more switches; resource access control, which restricts access to various resources (modules, servers, databases, etc.) associated with a switch or switches; and privilege enforcement, restricting individual users to specific functionality.

- *Audit trail management*   This capability supports auditing functions across one or more switches for a posterior investigation of security infractions or events.

- *Journaling*   This Network Element Management Layer capability supports the ability to journal and report a security infraction, a security mechanism misoperation, or an attempt at a security violation. Notification is triggered by events such as but not limited to integrity violation, indicating that a potential corruption may have occurred, such as modification, insertion, or deletion of management information on one or more switches; physical violation, indicating that a physical resource has been attached and breached; security service or mechanism violation, indicating that a security infringement has been detected by a security service or mechanism; and a temporal-domain violation, indicating that an event has occurred beyond the allowed time period.

- *System integrity monitoring* This Network Element Management Layer capability supports integrity monitoring at the hardware and software levels across one or more switches.

- *Recovery* This function supports recovery following an intrusion. Such recovery entails, among other functions, the ability to access and restore backup files.

9.2.3 Customer Network Management

Table 9.3 provides a summary of the CNM features discussed in the previous chapter, along with some potential future capabilities. All of the features in this table involve security aspects.

Receive event notifications (over SNMP)

Retrieve ATM UNI and CRS configuration information (over SNMP)

Retrieve ATM UNI performance information (over SNMP)

Retrieve connection (PVC) configuration information (over SNMP)

Retrieve general CRS CNM information (over SNMP)

Receive event notifications (over B-LMI)

Retrieve ATM UNI configuration information (over B-LMI)

Retrieve ATM UNI performance information (over B-LMI)

Initiate tests (future)

Modify general CRS CNM information (over SNMPv2) (future)

Modify UNI and CRS configuration information (over SNMPv2) (future)

Reconfigure PVCs (over SNMPv2) (future)

Request event notifications (over SNMPv2) (future)

Retrieve usage information (over SNMPv2) (future)

Support trouble report administration (over SNMPv2) (future)

Note: All CNM functions need to be secure. The use of SNMPv1 does not provide the full level of desired security. SNMPv2 extends such functionality.

Table 9.3   CNM functions, security management

References

[1] D. Minoli, M. Vitella, *Cell Relay Service and ATM in Corporate Environments* (McGraw-Hill, New York, NY) 1994.

[2] Bellcore Technical Advisory TA-NWT-001248, *Generic Requirements for Operations of Broadband Switching Systems*, October, 1993.

[3] RFC 1157, *Simple Network Management Protocol*, SRI International, May 1990.

[4] Bellcore Technical Advisory TA-NWT-001112, *Broadband ISDN User-to-Network and Network Node Interface Physical Layer Generic Criteria*, August 1992.

[5] ITU-T Recommendation I.356. Geneva, CH.

[6] D. Minoli, *Evolving Security Management Standards*, Datapro Report NM20-500-101, June 1989.

[7] D. Minoli, Building the New OSI Security Architecture, *Network Computing*, June 1992, page 136.

[8] D. Minoli, What are the Standards for Interoperable LAN Security, *Network Computing*, June 1992, page 148.

[9] D. Minoli, *Telecommunications Technology Handbook*, 2nd Edition (Artech House, 1997).

chapter 10

Telecommunications Management Network

*T*he Telecommunications Management Network (TMN) is the internal data communications network within a public ATM network that supports all management functions discussed earlier, including public switch management, management of a group of public ATM switches, and CNM.

The TMN supports a variety of applications which cover the operations, administration, maintenance, and provisioning, of a telecommunications network. From a general perspective, the TMN supports all carrier services in addition to ATM and fastpacket services.

The TMN is typically within the realm of the public network, but the corporate ATM planner should be cognizant of the internals that support the ATM service, both from the view of the carrier's ability to deliver the stated QoS, as well as from the view of making CNM data available to the user. A very large user (say a Fortune 50 company) may also have a private TMN, if its private ATM network is large enough. This chapter describes the TMN and its capabilities.

10.1 Introduction

Operations Systems (OSs) embedded in the network undertake many functions in support of network elements such as switches, ATM switches, transmission systems, etc., as well as several other functions that are not directly related to network elements. Such functions include engineering of circuits, work force management, planning for network capacity expansion, preparing bills for customers, and so on.

The TMN consists of the OSs, the portions of the network elements that interface with such systems, the optional mediation devices that are needed to facilitate interactions among the OSs and network elements, interfaces to external entities, and the data communications network that interconnects all those elements. Readers not interested in the perspectives listed above may choose to skip this chapter on first reading.

The discussion that follows is based on ITU-T Recommendation M.30, *Principles For A Telecommunications Management Network.* Figure 10.1 depicts the TMN in the context of ATM.

10.2 TMN Architecture

TMN provides the means to transport and to process management information pertaining to the public (ATM) network. The TMN is connected to net-

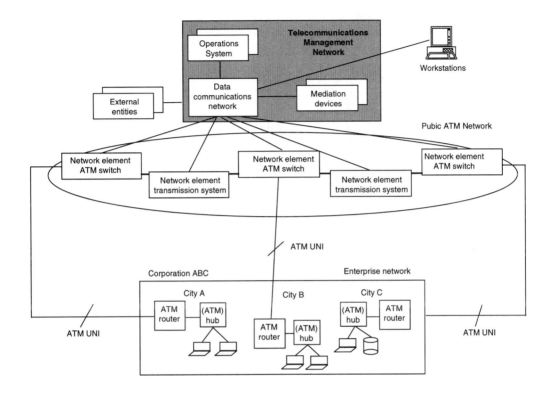

Figure 10.1   Simplified view of the TMN

work element functions (NEFs) and workstation functions (WSFs). Logically, a TMN consists of three functional groups that enable it to perform its application functions (Figure 10.2):

- *Operations system function (OSF)*   This function block processes information related to telecommunication management to support or control the realization of various management functions. The physical architecture of an OS must provide the alternatives of either centralizing or distributing the general functions, which include support application programs, database functions, user terminal support, analysis program, data formatting, and reporting. The OS functional architecture may be realized on various numbers of OSs, depending on the network's size.

- *Mediation function (MF)*   This function block acts on information passing between NEFs and OSFs to achieve effective and efficient communication; this includes communication control (e.g., polling) and concentration pro-

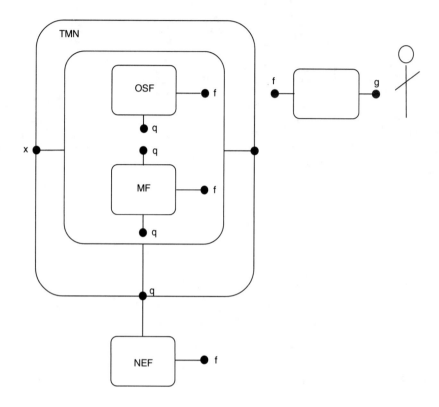

Figure 10.2   Functional view of TMN

tocol conversion (conversion between various communications protocols at lower and upper layers, formatting, etc.), and storage (including backup).

- *Data communications function (DCF)*   This function block provides the means to transport information related to telecommunication management between function blocks. Physically, DCFs are implemented in data communications networks (DCNs, the functional equivalent of wide area networks) and local communication networks (LCNs, the functional equivalent of local area networks).

Reference points define conceptual points of information exchange between function blocks, as seen in Figure 10.2. (A reference point becomes an interface when the connected function blocks are embodied in distinct pieces of equipment.) Table 10.1 describes the reference points.

Reference Point	Description
q	Connects (directly or through the DCF) the function blocks NEF to MF, MF to MF, MF to OSF
q1	Connects (directly or through the DCF) the function blocks NEF to MF
q2	Connects (directly or through the DCF) the function blocks MF to MF
q3	Connects (directly or through the DCF) the function blocks MF to OSF
f	Connects function blocks OSF, MF, NEF, DCF to the WSF
g	Interfaces the user to the WSF
x	Connects a TMN to other TMNs

Table 10.1 TMN reference points

These reference points and the subtending physical interfaces can be used to define a variety of realizations of the TMN. The interested reader should refer directly to ITU-T M.30.

In this model, operations functions are partitioned across multiple layers, including the Element Layer, Element Management Layer, Network Management Layer, and higher layers (e.g., Service Management Layer); see Figure 10.3.

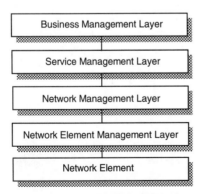

Figure 10.3 TMN layers

The philosophy of a multilayer model of operations is that each layer views the network at a different level of abstraction, and thus can manage it accordingly. The Element Layer's view of the network is the most detailed of all the layers: it has visibility of the vendor-specific intricacies of the various elements in the network. The Element Management Layer contains functions that may be used to manage resources individually and in aggregation as a subnetwork. The Network Management Layer deals with an aggregated view of network resources as presented by the Element Management Layer; it is responsible for providing management functions that require coordination across multiple subnetworks. The Service Management Layer maintains a view of the services being provided and supported by the network. The Business Management Layer provides the functions necessary to operating a network as a going business concern, e.g., billing and collection functions. Figure 10.4 depicts an example of a TMN configuration (from ITU-T M.30.)

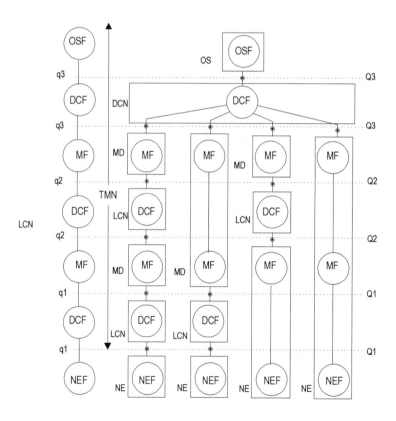

Figure 10.4   Examples of TMN configurations

10.3 Specific Functions Associated with a TMN

The functions associated with a TMN can be divided into two sets:

- TMN general functions provided by the function blocks defined above.
- TMN application functions such as:

  1. Transport, which provides for the movement of information among TMN elements.
  2. Storage, which provides for holding information over controlled amounts of time.
  3. Security, which provides access for reading or changing information.
  4. Retrieval, which provides access to information.
  5. Processing, which provides for analysis and information manipulation.
  6. User terminal support, which provides for input/output of information.

Within the TMN, the OSI management categories have been expanded in the following manner.

10.3.1 Performance Management

As discussed in Chapter 5 from a general perspective, performance management provides functions to evaluate and report upon the behavior of telecom equipment and the effectiveness of the network element. Its role is to gather statistical data for the purpose of monitoring and correcting the behavior and effectiveness of the network, network element, or equipment, and to aid in planning and analyzing. The following functionalities have been defined in Recommendation M.20 for the TMN:

- *Performance monitoring functions*   Performance monitoring entails the continuous collection of information concerning the NE/switch. While acute fault conditions will be detected by alarm surveillance methods, very low rate or intermittent error conditions in multiple equipment units may interact, resulting in poor service quality. Performance monitoring is designed to measure the overall quality on the monitoring parameters to detect such deterioration. It may also be designed to detect characteristic patterns before quality has dropped below an acceptable level. See Table 10.2.

- *Traffic management and network management functions*   A TMN collects traffic data from NEs (e.g., switches and transmission equipment), and sends

Function	Description
Request PM data	The TMN requests the NE (e.g., ATM switch) to send current PM data.
PM data report	The NE (e.g., ATM switch) sends performance data to the TMN. It may be generated routinely by the NE (e.g., ATM switch), sent upon demand by the TMN, or by exception when a parameter threshold has been exceeded.
Schedule PM data report	The TMN directs the NE (e.g., ATM switch) to establish a schedule for the reporting of PM data.
Request PM data report schedule	The TMN directs the NE (e.g., ATM switch) to send the current PM data reporting schedule. The NE (e.g., ATM switch) responds with the schedule.
Start/stop PM data	The TMN directs the NE (e.g., ATM switch) to start or stop the collection of PM data.
Initialize PM data	The TMN directs the NE (e.g., ATM switch) to reset storage registers for PM data.
Set PM attributes	The TMN directs the NE (e.g., ATM switch) to assign designated values to PM attributes.
Request PM attributes	The TMN requests the NE (e.g., ATM switch) to send current PM attributes.
PM attributes report	The NE (e.g., ATM switch) sends the currently assigned PM attributes to the TMN.
Requests protocol conversion data	The TMN requests the NE (e.g., ATM switch) to transmit the data concerning the protocol conversion performance, such as the types and their number of protocol conversions.
Protocol conversion data report	The NE (e.g., ATM switch) sends data concerning protocol conversion performance.

Table 10.2   TMN-Supported performance monitoring (PM) functions

commands to NEs to reconfigure the telecommunication network or modify its operation to adjust to extraordinary traffic. A TMN may request traffic reports to be sent from NEs, or such a report may be sent upon threshold triggering, periodically, or on demand. At any time, the TMN may modify the current set of thresholds or periods in the network. Reports from the NE may consist of raw data which are processed in a TMN, or the NE may be capable of carrying out analysis of the data before the report is sent. See Table 10.3.

- *Generic quality of service observation functions* A TMN collects generic QoS[1] information from NEs, and supports activities aimed at improving the generic QoS. The TMN may request generic QoS data reports to be sent from the NE, or such a report may be sent automatically on a scheduled or threshold basis. At any time, the TMN may modify the current or thresholds. Reports from the NE on generic QoS data may consist of raw information which is processed in a TMN, or the NE may be capable of carrying out analysis of the information before the report is sent.

Generic QoS includes monitoring and recording parameters relating to:

1. Connection establishment (e.g., call setup delays, successful and failed call requests).
2. Connection retention.
3. Connection quality.
4. Billing integrity.
5. Keeping and examining logs of system state histories.
6. Cooperation with fault (or maintenance) management to establish possible failure of a resource, and with configuration management to change routing and load control parameters/limits for links, trunks, etc.
7. Initiation of test calls to monitor general QoS parameters.
   See Table 10.4.

10.3.2 Fault or Maintenance Management

As discussed in Chapter 4 from a general perspective, fault or maintenance management is a set of functions which enables the detection, isolation, and correction of abnormal operation of the telecommunications network and its environment. The following functionalities have been defined in Recommendation M.20 for the TMN:

- *Alarm surveillance functions* A TMN provides the capability to monitor NE failures in real time or near-real time. When a failure occurs, an indication is

---

[1] In this treatment *generic QoS* refers to any service objective and metric of a public network. The term *QoS* used by itself refers specifically to ATM-specific QoS measures.

Function	Description
Set traffic data attributes	The TMN directs the NE (e.g., ATM switch) to set parameters to select traffic data.
Requests traffic data attributes	The TMN requests the NE (e.g., ATM switch) to report the current traffic data attributes.
Request traffic data	The TMN requests the NE (e.g., ATM switch) to transmit traffic data to the TMN.
Traffic data report	The NE (e.g., ATM switch) sends specified traffic data to the TMN.
Requests clock report	The TMN requests the NE (e.g., ATM switch) to transmit its current clock time to the TMN.
Clock sync report	The NE (e.g., ATM switch) sends the current clock time.
Set error analysis	The TMN directs the NE (e.g., ATM switch) to assign designated values to error analyses parameters. These are used by the NE (e.g., ATM switch) to recognize that a given unit is faulty based on the direction of errors and intermittent troubles.
Requests analysis data	The TMN requests the NE (e.g., ATM switch) to report the current error analysis parameters or resulting data.
Error analysis report	The NE (e.g., ATM switch) sends error analysis data to the TMN.
Set NM data attributes	The TMN directs the NE (e.g., ATM switch) to set parameters to generate required NM measurement data.
Request NM data	The TMN requests the NE (e.g., ATM switch) to report the current NM data attributes.
Request NM data	The TMN requests the NE (e.g., ATM switch) to send NM data to the TMN. This includes periodic measurement data and status-alerting discrete information.
NM data report attributes	The NE (e.g., ATM switch) sends required NM data to the TMN.
Sent NM control	The TMN directs the NE (e.g., ATM switch) to perform specified real-time NM controls.
Control report	The NE (e.g., ATM switch) sends NM control status information to its TMN.
Set NM thresholds	The TMN directs the NE (e.g., ATM switch) to set or change the congestion thresholds used by the NE (e.g., ATM switch) to perform automatic NM control.
Request NM threshold	The TMN requests the NE (e.g., ATM switch) to send the current congestion thresholds to the TMN.
NM threshold report	The NE (e.g., ATM switch) sends current congestion thresholds to the TMN.

Table 10.3   Traffic management and network management

Function	Description
Schedule QoS data report	The TMN directs the NE (e.g., ATM switch) to establish a schedule for the report of QoS data.
Request QoS data	The TMN directs the NE (e.g., ATM switch) to send the current QoS data reporting schedule.
QoS report report schedule	The NE (e.g., ATM switch) reports the value of an observed QoS parameter to the TMN. It may be sent on demand by the TMN or on a schedule basis.
Set QoS threshold	The TMN directs the NE (e.g., ATM switch) to set or change the QoS parameter threshold.
Request QoS threshold	The TMN directs the NE (e.g., ATM switch) to send the current QoS threshold.
Exceptional QoS report	The NE (e.g., ATM switch) reports the value of an observed parameter to the TMN when a parameter threshold has been exceeded.
Initialize QoS data	The TMN directs the NE (e.g., ATM switch) to reset storage registers for QoS data.
Start/stop QoS data	The TMN directs the NE (e.g., ATM switch) to start or stop the collection of QoS data.
Schedule QoS test calls	The TMN directs the NE (e.g., ATM switch) to establish a schedule for the execution of QoS test calls.
Request QoS test call schedule	The TMN directs the NE (e.g., ATM switch) to set the current QoS test call schedule.
QoS test call report	The NE (e.g., ATM switch) reports the result of QoS test calls to the TMN. It may be sent on demand by the TMN or on a schedule basis.
Set QoS test call attributes	The TMN directs the NE (e.g., ATM switch) to set or change the attributes of QoS test calls.
Start/stop QoS test calls	The TMN directs the NE (e.g., ATM switch) to start or stop sending test calls.
Initialize QoS test calls	The TMN directs the NE (e.g., ATM switch) to reset the storage registers for test calls.
Request QoS test call attributes	The TMN directs the NE (e.g., ATM switch) to send the current QoS test call attributes.
Schedule semiautomatic observations	The TMN directs the NE (e.g., ATM switch) to establish a schedule for the execution of semiautomatic observations.

Table 10.4   General QoS observations

Function	Description
Request semiautomatic observation schedule	The TMN directs the NE (e.g., ATM switch) to send the current semiautomatic observation schedule.
Automatic observation report	The NE (e.g., ATM switch) reports the result of automatic observations to the TMN. It may be sent on demand by the TMN or on schedule basis.
Set semiautomatic observation attributes	The TMN directs the NE (e.g., ATM switch) to set or change the attributes. The TMN directs the NE (e.g., ATM switch) to set or change the attributes of semiautomatic observations.
Start/stop semi-observation attribute	The TMN directs the NE (e.g., ATM switch) to start or stop the semiautomatic observations.
Initialize automatic observations	The TMN directs the NE (e.g., ATM switch) to reset the storage registers for automatic observations.
Request semiautomatic observations	The TMN directs the NE (e.g., ATM switch) to send the current semiautomatic observation attributes.

Table 10.4 *Continued*

made available by the NE. Based on this indication, the TMN determines the nature and severity of the fault. For example, it may determine the effect of the fault on the services supported by the failed/impaired equipment. This can be accomplished in two ways: a database within a TMN may serve to interpret the alarm indications from the NE; or if the NE has sufficient intelligence, it may transmit self-explanatory messages to a TMN. The first method requires little of the NE beyond a basic self-monitoring capability. The second method requires additionally that both the NE and a TMN support some type of message syntax that allows adequate description of fault conditions. See Table 10.5.

- *Fault localization functions* Where the initial failure information is insufficient for fault localization, it has to be augmented with information obtained by additional failure localization routines. The routines can employ internal or external test systems, and can be controlled by a TMN. See Table 10.6.

- *Testing functions* Testing can be carried out as follows: The TMN directs a given NE to carry out analysis of circuit or equipment characteristics. Processing is executed entirely within, the NE, and the results are automatically reported to the TMN, either immediately or on a delayed basis. The analysis may also be carried out within the TMN. In this case, the TMN merely requests that the NE provide access to the circuit or equipment of interest, and other messages are exchanged with the NE.

Function	Description
Request alarm information	The TMN request the NE (e.g., ATM switch) to send current alarm information.
Alarm information report	The NE (e.g., ATM switch) notifies the TMN of alarm information. It may be sent automatically on occurrence, or on demand by the TMN.
Schedule alarm report	The TMN directs the NE (e.g., ATM switch) to establish a schedule for the reporting of alarms.
Request alarm report schedule	The TMN directs the NE (e.g., ATM switch) to send the current schedule for alarm reporting. The NE (e.g., ATM switch) responds with the schedule.
Condition alarm	The TMN directs the NE (e.g., ATM switch) to assign alarm attributes, modes and thresholds.
Request condition	The TMN requests the NE (e.g., ATM switch) to report the current assignment of alarm attributes, modes and thresholds; the NE (e.g., ATM switch) responds with the assignments.
Route alarm	The TMN directs the NE (e.g., ATM switch) to send alarms to designed locations.
Request alarm route	The TMN requests the NE (e.g., ATM switch) to send the current assignment of alarm routes for a specified set of alarms; the NE (e.g., ATM switch) responds with the routers.
Allow/inhibit alarms	The TMN directs the NE (e.g., ATM switch) to allow/inhibit either local/visual alarms or remote alarms.
Alarm cut-off	The TMN directs the NE (e.g., ATM switch) to reset designated audible alarms.

Table 10.5   Alarm surveillance

Function	Description
Request diagnostic data	The TMN requests the NE (e.g., ATM switch) to send the results of a diagnostic sequence.
Stop diagnostic in progress	The TMN directs the NE (e.g., ATM switch) to stop a particular diagnostic procedure in progress.
Diagnostic report	The NE (e.g., ATM switch) reports the results of a diagnostic sequence to The TMN. It may be used in conjunction with the request and stop functions and has applications where it may be necessary or desirable to repeat diagnostic test for a period of time to catch a failure.
Schedule diagnostic	The TMN directs the NE (e.g., ATM switch) to establish a routine schedule for the initiation of a diagnostic.
Request diagnostic schedule	The TMN requests the NE (e.g., ATM switch) to report the current schedule of diagnostics.
Diagnostic schedule report	The NE (e.g., ATM switch) sends the current schedule of diagnostics
Request exercise report	The TMN requests the NE (e.g., ATM switch) to send the results of a particular exercise.
Exercise report	The NE (e.g., ATM switch) sends the results of an exercise to the TMN.
Stop exercise	The TMN directs the NE (e.g., ATM switch) to stop a particular exercise in progress.
Schedule exercise	The TMN directs the NE (e.g., ATM switch) to establish a routine for the initiation of an exercise.
Request exercise report schedule	The TMN directs the NE (e.g., ATM switch) to send the current schedule of an exercise. The NE (e.g., ATM switch) responds with the schedule.
Operate/release loopback	The TMN directs the NE (e.g., ATM switch) to establish or release a specific loopback. It may be activated either remotely by the TMN or locally by craft action.
Test internal access path	The TMN directs the NE (e.g., ATM switch) to connect a termination on the NE (e.g., ATM switch) to another termination by a specified path within the NE (e.g., ATM switch), then test the path.

Table 10.6   Fault localization

Function	Description
Hold network path	The TMN directs the NE (e.g., ATM switch) to hold a particular network path.
Start/stop program traps	The TMN directs the NE (e.g., ATM switch) to start or stop a specific program trap.
Program trap report	The NE (e.g., ATM switch) automatically reports the occurrence of a program trap to the TMN.
Start/stop program trace	The TMN directs the NE (e.g., ATM switch) to start or stop a specific trace.
Program trace report	The NE (e.g., ATM switch) automatically reports the results of a trace to the TMN.
Start/stop audit	The TMN directs the NE (e.g., ATM switch) to start or stop an audit.
Audit report	The NE (e.g., ATM switch) automatically reports the results of an audit to the TMN.
Schedule audit	The TMN directs the NE (e.g., ATM switch) to establish a specific schedule for a given audit.
Request audit schedule	The TMN requests the NE (e.g., ATM switch) to send the current audit schedule. The NE (e.g., ATM switch) responds with the test schedule.
Start/stop loop insulation test	The TMN directs the NE (e.g., ATM switch) to start or stop a loop insulation test.
Schedule loop insulation test	The TMN directs the NE (e.g., ATM switch) to schedule a loop insulation test.
Request loop insulation test schedule	The TMN requests the NE (e.g., ATM switch) to send current loop insulation test schedule. The NE (e.g., ATM switch) responds with the schedule.

Table 10.6 *Continued*

10.3.3 Configuration Management

Configuration management provides functions to control, identify, collect data from, and provide data to NEs. In the TMN context this includes:

- *Provisioning functions* Provisioning consists of procedures which are necessary to bring equipment into service, not including the installation of user equipment. Once a unit is ready for service, the supporting programs are initialized over the TMN. The state of the unit, e.g., in-service or stand-by, may also be controlled by provisioning functions, as are selected parameters. For some NEs, these functions are used initially and rarely again; for other NEs, such as ATM switches and cross-connect systems, one requires frequent use of these functions as circuits are brought on line and dropped. See Table 10.7. In addition, there are administrative and data management functions associated with provisioning.

Function	Description
Request configuration	The TMN requests that the NE (e.g., ATM switch) report the current configuration of each entity.
Configuration report	For each entity, the NE (e.g., ATM switch) reports status, capacity of the entity, optional parameters, type of entity (in sufficient detail for TMN identification), and the version and revision of the version.
Grow	The TMN notifies the NE (e.g., ATM switch) of the presence of a newly installed entity.
Prune	The TMN notifies the NE (e.g., ATM switch) of the disconnection of an entity.
Restore	The TMN notifies the NE (e.g., ATM switch) to begin monitoring the newly installed entity.
Assign	The TMN notifies the NE (e.g., ATM switch) that a previously unequipped entity is now equipped.
Delete	The TMN notifies the NE (e.g., ATM switch) that a previously equipped entity is no longer equipped.
Set service state	The TMN directs the NE (e.g., ATM switch) to place the specified entity in one of the following states: in service (available for use), out of service (unavailable for use), standby (not faulty but not performing normal function), or reserved.
Request assignments	The TMN requests that NE (e.g., ATM switch) reports the identity of each assigned entity. The request may be for a specified entity or for all equipped entities.

Table 10.7   Provisioning: NE configuration

Function	Description
Assignment	The NE (e.g., ATM switch) reports the identity of each assigned channel for each equipped entity or for a specified entity.
Set parameters	The TMN directs the NE (e.g., ATM switch) to set parameters associated with a specified entity.
Set service threshold	The TMN directs the NE (e.g., ATM switch) to set performance thresholds for the specified channel.
Add/drop	The TMN directs the NE (e.g., ATM switch) to insert or remove a channel from the complement of through-channels.
Cross-connect	The TMN directs the NE (e.g., ATM switch) to interconnect two specified channels operating at the same rate.
Disconnect	The TMN directs the NE (e.g., ATM switch) to remove the interconnection between two specified channels.
Start transmission test	The TMN directs the NE (e.g., ATM switch) to begin a transmission test on a given circuit.
Balance	The TMN directs the NE (e.g., ATM switch) to perform a balance test/adjustment.
Start transponder test	The TMN directs the NE (e.g., ATM switch) to look for a transponder signal on the given circuit.
Set report periods	The TMN directs the NE (e.g., ATM switch) to set or change report periods.
Request report periods	The TMN requests the NE (e.g., ATM switch) to send the current periods to the TMN.

Table 10.7 *Continued*

- *Status and control functions*   The TMN provides the capability to monitor and control aspects of The NE "on demand." Examples include checking or changing the service of an NE or one of its subparts, and initiating diagnostics tests within the NE. Normally, a status check is provided in conjunction with each control function to verify that the resulting action has taken place. The TMN will enable the exclusion of faulty equipment from operation, and it may rearrange equipment or reroute traffic. See Table 10.8.

Function	Description
Request status	The TMN requests the NE (e.g., ATM switch) to send current status information.
Status report	The NE (e.g., ATM switch) reports the value of a monitored parameter to the TMN. It may be sent on demand by the TMN or on a schedule basis.
Schedule status report	The TMN directs the NE (e.g., ATM switch) to establish a schedule for the reporting of status information.
Request status report schedule	The TMN directs the NE (e.g., ATM switch) to send the current schedule of status reporting. The NE (e.g., ATM switch) responds with the schedule.
Allow/inhibit automatic restoration	The TMN directs the NE (e.g., ATM switch) to allow or inhibit automatic restoration in an M+N or duplex system.
Operator/release	The TMN directs the NE (e.g., ATM switch) to switch a specified line or equipment to the redundant unit, or release it from the redundant unit. For an M+N system, service is placed on the redundant unit and taken off the working unit. For a duplex system, the main unit becomes standby and the unit becomes the main unit.

Table 10.8   Status and control

- *Installation functions*   The TMN can support the installation of equipment which makes up the telecommunication network. Some NEs call for the initial exchange of data between themselves and the TMN; other NEs/services require the installation of programs into NEs from database systems within the TMN.

10.3.4 Accounting and Security Management

The TMN also supports accounting and security management functions. In particular, an OS within the TMN can collect data from NEs which is used to determine charges to customers' accounts. Security management functions are shown in Table 10.9.

Function	Description
Change channel class	The TMN directs the NE to change the security user data class of an operations channel.
Change terminal class	The TMN directs the NE to change the security class of the NE terminal.
Dial capability	The TMN directs the NE to initiate a secure dial-out/dial-back capability to the TMN.
Log off	The TMN directs the NE to terminate communication on a channel.
Change	The TMN directs the NE to change the log-in code assigned to the NE.
Change dial number	The TMN directs the NE to change the auto-dial-back number that the NE uses to call back the calling party upon receipt of a dial-out call.

Table 10.9   Security management functions

10.4 Conclusion

Carriers have been putting TMNs in place to support all the network management features needed to run a telecommunications network, including the ATM portion of that network. Users benefit from the TMN through improved service (up-time, fast restoration, quick provisioning, service QoS, etc.). Additionally, the TMN is used to support ATM CNM functions. Even if the corporate users were to obtain only dedicated lines from a carrier (e.g., DS3/T3 and SONET) and purchase their own ATM switches, the TMN still supports functions aimed at maintaining the integrity of the underlying transport component of the organization's network. The reader should refer to [1] for an up-to-date assessment of this field.

References

[1] Special issue, Making TMN a Reality, *IEEE Communications Magazine,* September 1996, pages 55-90.

Part IV

Planning of ATM Networks

chapter 11

Emerging Computing and Communications Environments

*P*atterns of demand for networking have been changing more rapidly than the underlying hardware and software. These changes have been driven by the following trends:

- The increasing need for split-second decisions in many fields.

- The evolution of LANs from low-utilization localized networks to high-utilization intranets.

- The changes in corporate structures and management philosophy that raise rates of communication outside the immediate workgroup.

- The continuing improvements in microprocessor performance and memory/disk capacity on the desktop.

- The emergence of switches or routers as collapsed backbones that supplant high-capacity campus backbones.

- The growing adoption of client-server strategies that lead toward the global virtual corporation.

- The introduction of clustering and other cooperative computing strategies.

- The launching of new projects aimed at reducing management overhead.

- The introduction of visualization-based applications like multimedia, teleconferencing, and telecommuting/virtual offices that require relatively high bandwidths.

11.1 Introduction

ATM technology is maturing toward true ubiquity by the final years of this century. This chapter addresses the demands and capabilities that will determine the direction of network management environments as this transition to new technologies takes place. These environments will in turn define the demand for ATM to new technologies.

What are the major trends in corporate networks? What developments are driving and shaping market trends? Where will those trends lead during the next few years? What will networks look like ten years from now?

In networking as in related fields of high technology, long-range forecasting is a doubtful exercise. Intelligent planning based upon a systematic examination of present tendencies and their implications for the future are, nevertheless, especially crucial in networking. The selection, establishment, and management of corporate information systems have usually been defined first in terms of computing equipment. Networking has received secondary attention in some companies.

Early LANs started with a few PCs or workstations wired together, with no policies governing planning, management, and operations. The technologies were fragmented, and the horizons were local. Even after networking became more diverse, as LANs were joined using backbones, planning was usually ad hoc. This could be tolerated because studies showed consistently that about 80% of total traffic was transmitted within the LAN. As it became evident that a wider reach was necessary, attention focused on specific solutions, and on equipment that permitted LANs of different kinds to exchange traffic with one another. Comprehensive networking planning was the exception. When it took place, planning for the future focused primarily on bandwidth, and gave little attention to formal policies and network-management issues.

The obsolescence of these day-by-day, year-by-year strategies is now increasingly evident. In many corporate settings, these ill-defined strategies have resulted in a degree of chaos, in networks that rarely work well up to specifications, and too often, not up to the users' expectations. The advent of ATM makes it even more urgent to adopt more systematic and farsighted strategies of network management.

What major changes are propelling this evolving market?

11.2 Present Market Drivers

Networks move from the background to the foreground of corporate consciousness when it becomes apparent that the right kind of network strategy can provide a significant competitive edge. This awareness has begun in a few sectors where competition is especially intense. Success can be determined by delivering data a few minutes or even a few seconds before the same information reaches competitors. This is especially true in the financial services sector, where billions of dollars' worth of foreign exchange transactions and other trading is carried out on a global scale, continuing at a 7-day-a-week, 24-hour-a-day pace. Adequate bandwidth, is of course, an essential precondition for communications-enabled competitive advantage, but is not sufficient by itself. Delays due to contention, congestion, and slow interconnections between networks can also dull one's competitive edge.

Trading support systems now go far beyond providing real time updates of market changes. These applications are especially complicated, now that declining revenue from sales commissions have increased the motivation for financial houses to trade on their own accounts. The trader may require instant access to a multiplicity of applications, including credit management, risk potential, and risk management. These applications can be used to guide the trader's decisions and reduce the chance that a move could cripple a trading category within the institution—or destroy the entire corporation overnight. Similar challenges exist in other industries.

11.2.1 LAN Intranet

The strictly local LAN was a simple, relatively tidy community. It was used within a self-contained workgroup. Network software like NFS (Network File System) and Novell's Netware was used to take care of backup requirements and storage housekeeping. Client workstations were mostly left to themselves. This model has been supplanted by the LAN intranet, which may link dozens, even hundreds of LANs. These LANs can be local, within a building, or can be remotely located in other cities, states, and countries. Many changes in business organization and management practices have altered traffic patterns. More people find it necessary to exchange information with others within the corporation but outside the immediate business unit served by a LAN.

In the past, communication among business units was primarily the function of middle managers. Corporations are now pruning or eliminating their middle management, to be replaced by a much larger, far reaching, and diverse volume of communication over the LAN intranet by more junior staff. As a result, at an increasing number of corporations, the traditional traffic flow paradigm of 80% internal, 20% external is being radically altered, and in some cases, even reversed.

Computational power and disk space are shooting up at every point on the network, from the desktop to compute and storage servers. Only a few years ago, the typical desktop system was a 386-level PC or a relatively low-powered workstation like the early Sun SparcStations. Servers were somewhat more powerful versions of the same technology. The typical volume, speed, and file-lengths of data sent over the network were proportionately modest. Now, desktops are equipped with machines that are four to ten or more times as powerful, with comparably large memories and storage resources, capable of dumping large quantities of data onto the network at high speeds. The full-bore output of a single mid or upper level workstation with an advanced microprocessor can choke traditional LANs like Ethernet.

Microprocessors now available—from the IBM/ Motorola/ Apple PowerPC to the Pentium Pro, the Sun UltraSPARC, and the MIPS R10000—will increase capabilities of today's most advanced microprocessors by two or more times. In both the commercial and scientific markets, servers are increasingly multiprocessor systems having tens of gigabytes of storage. In these changed circumstances, a LAN serving a thousand people—all trying to download software from the same server—becomes a significant bottleneck.

On a larger scale, the traditional model presumed that LANs, perhaps a hundred or more, were linked to larger capacity backbones, or indeed to a pyramid of backbones having a high-capacity communication channel at the apex. The conceptual model was a pattern similar to the circulation system in the body. Now, however, managers are adopting the collapsed backbone alternative on an increasingly wide scale. This means that a switch, or in some cases a router, takes over the functions of the backbone. In a router, the bus becomes the backbone. In switches, which provide a much faster solution, the switch fabric becomes the backbone.

Differences arise because a switch operates at level 2 in the OSI seven-layer stack, where it is not concerned with networking protocols and routing. A router functions at level 3, where it must adapt to these considerations. The rapidly growing popularity of graphical user interfaces (GUIs) like X-Windows, increases demands on network capacity due to their bandwidth-hungry visual philosophy and high interaction rates. This is especially true when operators attempt to cut desktop investments by providing individual users with relatively inexpensive X-Terminals of limited intelligence and storage capacity. Any heavy lifting must be done at the server end, adding to the requirements for bandwidth and quick, assured, response.

11.2.2 Intranet Services

As demand for services and connectivity has grown, bandwidths have increased, and technology has advanced to the point where, corporate networks have become more sophisticated than the public Internet. They continue to grow and improve, while the outlook of their public counterpart remains dimmed by untested assumptions about mass demand. Indeed, a number of corporations prefer to ignore the public Internet, even though their staff may use it frequently for e-mail, access to public reference sources, and other purposes. This does not mean, however, that corporate managers are indifferent to the potentials of networking tools developed for the public Internet. For example, some corporate users have utilized the World Wide Web (WWW) application to distribute technical reports, including color diagrams and sometimes video, to hundreds of employees simultaneously. Detailed product information, maintenance manuals, troubleshooting protocols, and other internal communications can be made available to employees, trainees, customers, and potential buyers on Web servers.

This decreases the cost of assigning qualified engineers to answer 1-800 numbers, e.g., for help desks; accelerates the dissemination of new information; and could reduce sharply the delay, bulk, and inevitable disorder of printed materials.

WWW technology can be used, for example, to inform busy financial traders about new financial products and tax developments that can affect profitability and legal liability. Investment advisors and mutual fund managers are becoming involved more deeply in enticing unpredictable financial markets in developing countries suchas Poland and Hungary. WWW technology can make analysts, researchers, and managers more fully aware of the political and economic contexts in these countries—and can do so with fresh news in an easily understood, concise package. Visual interfaces like the WWW also make it easier for those running networks—whether or not they may be highly qualified network managers—to follow visual representations of traffic trends and incipient problems.

Image compression algorithms like JPEG (Joint Photographic Expert Group) make it possible to show pictures (with high resolution if need be) and video (using for example Motion JPEG) to display with high precision the details of a product, part, or process. Bitonal office documents can be compressed to 0.05 MB per page (at 200 dots per inch); color office documents (e.g., pictures) produce 0.2 MB per page. High-quality graphics produce files in the range 1.2–20 MB per scan [1]. Motion JPEG produces quality video at 2 Mbps. MPEG-1 (Motion Pictures Export Group) produces VCR-quality video at 1.5 Mbps, while MPEG-2 produces "network-quality" video at 6 Mbps. HDTV produces a stream of 21.5 Mbps [2].

Applications of this kind may not be critical to immediate business requirements, but they can affect overall efficiency. Their appetite for bandwidth is nevertheless acute.

11.2.3   The Global Corporation

Client-server has been both a slogan and a strategy of information management reengineering in recent years. The concept continues to be the subject of discussion and redefinition, but it also continues to become a widely used reality. Proponents and critics agree on one point: a corporation that has wholeheartedly embraced client-server computing simultaneously commits itself to total dependence on network capacity and efficiency. Client-server is not just a matter of plugging in new computers. It requires sweeping changes in the network, and its management.

Demands on networks will grow further as product development, manufacturing, and marketing are pursued in the wider context of department- or division-based groups. In addition to involving larger numbers of participants, departmental groups are also likely to have a wider geographical scope, to other sites in the headquarter's city or over much longer distances. Client-server strategies are expanding toward a corporate-wide or even global basis. This trend is accelerating, as more and more parts of corporations develop interest in a wider variety of information from more sources.

The realization of global collaboration on the basis of a 24-hour day and 7-day week is close at hand. There is also the emergence of the *virtual corporation*, where employees are geographically dispersed, connected only (or mostly) through communication links. Such connectivity is not the exclusive realm of ATM, however. Fundamentally, what would make virtual corporations a reality is the availability of ubiquitous, inexpensive, and convenient communication bandwidth. To the extent that ATM supports these three requirements, it can serve this useful purpose; otherwise, other technologies may present themselves as possible solutions. A true virtual corporation would add flexibility and adaptability to continuous global collaboration.

Historically, restructuring a major corporation has been a protracted, distracting, painful operation that often has an uncertain outcome and may require a long post-operative recovery. Restructuring networks has been one of the ancillary issues as management structures are changed and workgroups are rearranged, merged, sundered, and eliminated. It has been necessary to rebuild or reconfigure networks to conform to a new table of organization. This has involved a tedious and costly effort to rewire, relocate switches from one place to another, reinstall the equipment, and get everything working once again.

The virtual connection capability of ATM makes it possible to restructure a corporation's network whenever the need arises. Hypothetically, design/production divisions could be restructured periodically, or continuously, during the successive stages of the product cycle. Sales forces could be restructured—every few months, if need be—to respond to changes in the market and mobilize for new competitive threats. But the virtual corporation will not work unless it adjusts to, and persuades, its human participants. Even the most technology-oriented people are concerned above all with other people, who are far more important to their welfare and sanity than networks or other inanimate parts of their environment. They will need to adjust to a new community in which shared objectives (even if temporary) become as important a definer of personal roles and value as physical propinquity.

New generations of managers must grasp the implications of this information revolution, which in this context could have consequences as profound as the industrial revolution.

Thus, the transition to the virtual corporation will not be short, is not likely to be easy, and may remain incomplete for a number of years. This transition will require sweeping changes in the philosophy and operations of network management that reflect and support changes in corporate management styles. Interoperability with wireless networks will lead to additional requirements for managers of next-generation broadband communications.

11.2.4 Cooperative Strategies

The assumptions of client-server strategies may become irrelevant as corporations adopt cooperative strategies in which there are no clients and no servers. Because of the growing capabilities of individual units on the desktop, every system could become both client and server.

Added desktop power pleases individual users, who view the machines at their fingertips as personal property that must be protected and should, whenever possible, be expanded. It distresses system managers, who note that desktop resources are typically utilized for only 1500 to 2500 hours each year, only about 20% of the total annual availability of 8760 hours. Low-return investment on the desktop may be accompanied by increased investment in overworked servers, so a manager's information services budget is assaulted from two directions.

For example, backroom operations on Wall Street have, for a number of years, put this idle nighttime capacity to use. Workstations are linked together to crank out the reports and other documents required by SEC regulations. This work has typically been done in a batch mode: machines that have finished a task are assigned another job from a queue. The queuing software and network capacity required for this application are relatively simple. The cooperative computing paradigm (also called clustering)—in which the idle desktop systems are connected to work together as a parallel computer—raises the ante substantially. The software is much more complicated than queuing or load-distribution systems (one widely used solution is called *PVM*, for *parallel virtual machine*), and generates considerable overhead on the network.

Clustering is nevertheless attractive. Linking together a farm of servers operating in a cooperative state allows for parallel computing. For example, a financial company needing a great deal of compute power to scrutinize packages of mortgages would find clustering an attractive alternative to the purchase of an expensive high-performance computer. But there are disadvantages. Because of the latency inherent in clustering, it has been successful primarily with applications that require relatively limited data exchange among computational units. Clustering also encounters social problems, especially ownership attitudes about desktop systems. In some organizations, notably universities and similar settings, there is a strong tradition of departmental and professorial autonomy, and many people work on irregular schedules. In these cases, negotiating the terms for access to unused desktop capacity is an issue. This is less frequently an issue in businesses with more vertical hierarchies and fixed hours; although staff in the R&D operations of those same businesses may behave more like university researchers.

Reduction in latency is being sought along two paths: higher capacity networks connecting the workstations/nodes and less burdensome intercommunications protocols, supplanting the use of the high-overhead TCP/IP for clustering software like PVM. As the price of ATM adapters for workstations descends through the $1 thousand level, ATM is becoming the preferred method to enhance bandwidth and offering service guarantees. A network that is operated part time in a fully parallel mode can, however, be a significant challenge for network managers.

Some managers with very large storage system requirements, as well as other mounting demands, have turned to high-performance systems from Convex or lower end Cray Research machines. Both vendors sell value-added file server or network manager packages. This is, however, an expensive solution.

Meanwhile, the tasks placed upon networks have grown in complexity and in demands for capacity. When networking was a novelty, users were delighted with services that could be defined as virtual device support: printers, file servers, backup facilities, and modems that could be located at considerable distances from the individual desktop could be made to appear as if they were right at hand. Communications such as ordinary e-mail and occasional file transfers within and beyond the workgroup were relatively simple in form, and placed modest requirements on bandwidth. Network products from vendors like Novell and Apple and basic file-management systems such as NFS or Andrew met these needs.

Information sharing applications, exemplified in software products like Lotus Notes, are rapidly supplementing and in some cases supplanting ordinary e-mail. This trend could be described as the growth of wholesale rather than retail access to information. To turn this metaphor inside out, consider a large chain of retail stores. In the e-mail model, managers at headquarters would send messages to individual store managers, alerting them to trends, criticizing shortfalls, exhorting them to do better, and so on. Broader information would be conveyed through mailed or faxed summaries, or left until the quarterly regional sales meetings. This information-flow pattern may be carried out over electronic networks, but it is not significantly different from the flow of management information originally carried verbally, by telephone, or on paper.

In the information-sharing model, the key information available to central management is also delivered simultaneously to store managers and other key staff. Local and regional trends in demand for categories of stock or individual items are highlighted. Local managers can in turn share sales results and trends with their nearby colleagues as well as central management.

It now appears that the World Wide Web, which offers the added flexibility of hypertext as a tool for exploring connections and relevance, is beginning to gain ground at the expense of software like Lotus Notes, but it is difficult to be definitive about the future. In any event, these new modes of communication add greatly to the demand for bandwidth and network efficiency.

11.2.5 Network Management: An Indispensable Burden

Network management, quality control procedures, and security measures, are opportunities that can grow into dilemmas. Improved management can increase efficiency, reduce costs, and simplify operations, but it also places burdens on the network. Every byte devoted to diagnosis or management is a byte that does not transmit business information. It is not easy to strike the correct balance, and the ideal solution will vary from one network to another. Probes, protocol analyzers, and other diagnostic tools can provide the manager with valuable information about management on the lower levels of the OSI seven-layer stack. They can also outline traffic patterns and improve understanding of the applications in use by indicating what is happening on the higher (applications) level.

Nevertheless, if the manager unleashes too many probes through the network, these add to the pressure on bandwidth and switching capacity. Experience and common sense can reduce this burden. In addition, researchers are exploring network protocols that reduce overhead while providing improved feedback. The Bianchini network protocol for example, is geared at synchronizing information around the network and drawing on available resources without excessive overhead. This is especially relevant to information-sharing and message-replication applications. Development of the Bianchini concept remains in early stages, but it is typical of solutions that are being sought for the management/burden paradox.

11.3 Emerging Applications

The revolutionary transition from data+voice to data+voice+image+video imposes unprecedented demands upon networks, complicating network management as well as requiring significant increases in bandwidth.

For corporate users, teleconferencing, real time collaboration, and telecommuting (the virtual office) will offer opportunities for raising productivity that would be costly if ignored. They also raise substantial problems for network planners and managers.

11.3.1 Visualization and Multimedia

Computer people and Wall Street market analysts who constantly seek formulas to justify buy and sell recommendations speak reverently of *killer apps*. They mean applications so appropriate, so timely, meeting a widespread need so well, that they power the acceptance of a whole new class of technology. The usual historical citation is the spreadsheet applications for early PCs.

There is not yet an evident killer app for next-generation networking, but one far reaching trend could have similar importance. This is the trend toward *universal visualization*. This has a double effect upon the demand for network capacity, and hence upon the role of ATM. People respond more enthusiastically to communications media that use pictures as well as words. Human beings are, after all, vision-oriented creatures optimized for the high-bandwidth input that images make possible. If a medium includes pictures, people use it more, increasing the amount of traffic over a network. At the same time, images increase the bandwidth needed to communicate. If pictures are to seem realistic—and, especially, if the pictures are expected to imitate natural motion—the demand for network bandwidth grows further. Today's rapidly maturing techniques for image compression reduce this demand for bandwidth, but it remains high nevertheless.

Visualization technology was born in the scientific/technical market, where visualization was the only comprehensible way to depict simulations of phenomena like the El Nino effect on global weather and the airflow around the engine nacelle of a jet aircraft. Over the past ten years, the explosion in computational power and increasingly sophisticated software have sharpened these visual tools. Reliance on visualization has spread within the corporate world, shaping workstyles, cost/effectiveness, and time to market in design and manufacturing, as well as R&D. As implied from the JPEG/MPEG discussion above, the guaranteed delivery of 6 Mbps to each desktop is more than adequate to support network-quality real-time video. Naturally, there has to be an assessment of the required throughput to download stored files to (other) applications running on the desktop.[1] For example, a 6-Mbps dedicated link would support a throughput of 0.8 MBps, which is a fairly significant amount of data.

Increasingly, real time video is joining simulation as a tool for information exchange and cooperative work on a work group, departmental, or broader scope. Eventually, Virtual Reality applications may also become widespread.

---

[1] It may well be the case that the server is the bottleneck rather that the communication link, particularly in a local environment.

11.3.2 From Teleconferencing to Dynamic Collaboration

In its most basic form, real time video means teleconferencing, an idea that has been the subject of occasional episodes of enthusiasm since the invention of the TV camera more than 50 years ago. Its advantages were obvious. Widely separated decision makers, technicians, or other staff could meet together on short notice on a quasi face-to-face basis without requiring the time and expense of travel.

Until very recently, the drawbacks were many: cumbersome, usually unreliable technology that delivered low-quality images at very high cost. Benefiting as in other fields from the steep escalation of computer power, these disadvantages have been reduced or eliminated. The current bottom level price for a simple package, adequate for a conference of reasonably acceptable visual quality among a few participants, is now $5–$10 thousand and dropping. More sophisticated systems suitable for larger conferences are now priced in the low tens of thousand of dollars. Objections, however, have persisted. Skeptics point out that any committee is inefficient. A committee whose communication is squeezed through TV cameras of moderately low resolution and echo-prone speakerphones is doubly or triply unsatisfactory.

The maturation of low-cost multimedia systems banishes most of these objections. In addition to talking heads and blackboards, up-to-date teleconferences can display in real time images of design concepts or product components, simulations in progress, and videos, real or simulated, of the part in action.

Such sessions tend to be informal and highly interactive, as one engineer or work-group and then another explores in a try-it-and-see; if-not-try-again fashion how their work fits together. This change in style, and the probability that all participants are on about the same level within the organization, tend to contradict the formal implications of the term *conference*.

Applications like this are especially well-suited to ATM because of its capacity to establish virtual circuits and so create virtual work groups whose members may rarely (or never) meet face to face. Engineers and marketers in a product-specific task force that consult several times each day as they work cooperatively to iron out all the last-minute problems in bringing their new product to market may be best suited by a permanent connection. In earlier stages of development, when consultation may be less frequent and involve a wider, changing roster of participants, ad hoc virtual connections can meet their needs flexibly. Consultative episodes of this kind are in effect an example of virtual connectivity, whose duration may range from ephemeral to quasi permanent.

11.3.3 Telecommuting and Virtual Offices

Telecommuting is another application whose advantages have long been recognized. It can reduce investment in office space. If adopted on a wide scale, it could have a significant impact on road congestion and smog creation. It may offer an option to retain staff members with key skills whose family responsibilities preclude a full day of work at the office. Each additional new mode of communication—the fax, e-mail, videoconferencing—has been hailed as the key to telecommuting. All have contributed, but they do little to reduce telecommuting's most fundamental problem: isolation from the constant, informal, highly personalized communication within workgroups.

In any business organization, the most important single kind of knowledge is knowledge about the organization itself. This is typically acquired in nonofficial, face-to-face corridor talk about personalities, new decisions rumored or anticipated, and all the other daily topics of office life. This constant flow of information helps each individual to maintain confidence as a fully functioning member of the group and assess prospects for advancement (and, in the era of downsizing, continued employment). The spontaneous interactivity as well as the low cost, versatility and multimedia reinforcement of today's technologies for informal consultation (the virtual office) could take another long step toward reducing the sense of isolation from the workgroup that has hindered adoption of telecommuting.

11.4 Service Model for Networks

To further explain the advantages of new technologies like ATM, we have developed a three layer model that includes a Physical Access Layer, a Logical Access, and a Service Layer. The middle Logical, or Virtual, Layer reflects the unique features of the ATM architecture, and is at the heart of this model. The features and functions of each layer of this model are explained in detail below. Planning and management of this model as it relates to ATM are described in Chapters 14–15.

Each of these model layers exists independently of its adjacent layers. The actual design and management details of each are completely transparent to the other layers. They are similar to the OSI Reference Model Layers, and can coexist with those seven layers; nevertheless the differences are significant. These layers respond to the more concrete perspectives of users, planners, and managers—a practical view of network computing as it is shaped by business requirements, as well as operational issues. The OSI reference model is an abstraction which was driven by technical communication requirements and protocols.

11.4.1   Physical Access Layer

The Physical Access Layer is the foundation of the network. It provides the management of information flow from one node to another node. A multitude of media, typically optimized to the scope of the network (e.g., WAN, metropolitan area, campus, building, floor, desktop) are supported transparently. This layer includes physical signaling, traffic shaping, congestion control, and the policing of management policies.

11.4.2   Virtual Layer

The Virtual Layer acts as a flexible, adaptive intermediary between the Physical and Service layers. Its versatility is made possible by ATM's capability to create virtual networks. The Virtual Layer supports a *view* of the network, as required by the Service Layer. A transformation function occurs at layer adjacency points (i.e., a specific application may think the network topology is a star; however, the physical network is actually a mesh).

This layer manages virtual network mappings and logical groupings of end devices without a physical-to-logical correlation. Application service level requirements are mapped into class of service and priority levels supported by the Physical Access Layer. The Virtual Layer sets the network policies that are implemented by the Physical Access Layer.

11.4.3   Service Layer

The Service Layer provides network application functions and supports the business-specific applications. The latter include naming services, security, APIs, object management, and middleware components.

References

[1] D. Minoli, *Imaging in Corporate Environments, Technology and Communication* (McGraw-Hill, 1994).

[2] D. Minoli, *Video Dialtone Technology, Approaches, and Services: Digital Video over ADSL, HFC, FTTC, and ATM* (McGraw-Hill, 1995).

[3] O. Eldib, D. Minoli, *Telecommuting* (Artech House, Norwood, 1995).

chapter 12

Corporate Network Management Goals

What should be the goals of the next generation of corporate networks? Corporate planners and network managers are concerned with costs and efficiency. Those in this group who have been skirmishing along the frontiers of advanced networking are aware of other requirements that will enable corporations to obtain better service and more value from the bandwidth they are buying.

The potential of ATM technology, considered in the context of networking experiences, suggests additional needs and potentials—immediate and over a longer term. These different sorts of goals are summarized in the Ten Requirements, which can be divided into three headings:

- *Fundamental requirements*

    1. Availability; 2. Reliability and serviceability; 3. Seamlessness; 4. Performance; and 5. Responsiveness

- *Cost Considerations*

    6. Lower system costs; and 7. Reduced operational costs

- *Management issues*

    8. Feedback and diagnostics; 9. Integrated proactive modeling; and 10. Flexibility

12.1 Introduction

Technologists generally prefer to talk about the technological wonder of their products—the hardware and software that does remarkable things. Even more than other chapters in this book, this one chapter focuses upon the human element of networking: the people who use them, run them, pay for them, and take responsibility for them during crises as well as on happier occasions. Like other lists of desiderata, the Ten Requirements differ in priority and achievability.

Requirements must also be considered on a time scale: some are of crucial importance, demanded from the outset, while others may not be accomplished for some time to come. Nevertheless, none of these requirements can be ignored in current or long-range plans. Networking strategies that fall short in too many of these criteria cannot be expected to endure.

The five fundamental requirements are crucial to everyone involved in networks, including the mailroom clerk ordering additional envelopes, traders making profits out of slight differences in global prices, and the executive trying to decide whether it makes sense to authorize that additional few million dollars requested by his network specialists.

It is useful to remember, however, what ATM really is. ATM is nothing more than a Data Link Layer protocol, (much) like HDLC, SDLC, LAP-D, etc. It specifies how a block of data coming down the protocol stack is partitioned into small frames, and which header needs to be added. Recently an individual told one of the authors that he could not wait for ATM to be deployed in a certain company because his spouse is a network manager at this company and she comes home grouchy and with a headache every night, because of today's technology. The author could not but think how naive this person's thinking is, and how he will be utterly disappointed to find out that ATM will not cure headaches for many years to come, but actually cause them! This author, however, could not bring himself to alert the individual to be prepared to come home and find headaches for another eight years.

By *ATM* some mean the entire technology that goes with this new kind of communication, not just the protocol. ATM is nothing more than 1970s technology (network infrastructure and customer premises equipment) of statistical multiplexing in which all the vendors have agreed how to support such multiplexing. The industry has agreed to use small frames and a certain header format. For statistical multiplexing to be worth anything, it must support statistical gain and bandwidth overbooking. ATM aims at doing that, and this is why complex traffic management methods have to be incorporated in the network, and usually not in the user's, equipment.

In deploying a new network infrastructure, it would be desirable if it also supported video and voice; hence ATM must also support a constant bit rate of 1.5 Mbps (or 6 Mbps, or 21.5 Mbps). To deploy a technology that obsoleted overnight all of the embedded equipment would be castastophic[1]. Hence, ATM must support legacy systems such as Ethernets, Token Ring, private lines, and Frame Relay.

In the end, ATM is nothing more than another transmission technology. ATM does not create or provide any bandwidth: it is only a (Layer 2) administrator of the bandwidth already made available by fiber media. It does not provide any more bandwidth-on-demand that the underlying access transmission link, trunk-side transmission links, or ATM backplane already can provide. It does not scale up for free: a user who has purchased (for example) 25-Mbps NICs cannot scale up (nor get bandwidth-on-demand) to 51 Mbps, 155 Mbps, or 622 Mbps, without replacing the cards in the PC, hub, router, or switch,

---

[1] Studies indicate that the embedded base of computing equipment in corporations equates to about 5–8% of their annual revenue. A $5-trillion economy would (approximately) have about $250 billion of computing/communication equipment on the books.

unless he or she has already purchased a very expensive all-speeds card and the connecting PC-to-hub wire can support the higher speeds. (Both of these assumptions are unlikely to hold before the year 2003: at press time OC-3 cards purchased by one of the authors for 2-Gbps workgroup switches cost $17,000.)

Virtual LANs are not really virtual: they are real LANs, with real hardware, real cards, and real wires; they only give the appearance to the user (not even the administrator) of providing location-independent connectivity.

12.2 Availability

Definitions of acceptable availability differ, from one extreme—network-caused downtime must be zero, or very close to it—to the other—occasional failures can be tolerated, at a frequency of once a day, once a week, once every month, and so on. Satisfactory availability is the foundation of a network's acceptability.

Many will complain if downtime exceeds whatever limits are perceived as acceptable. At a minimum, users expect that any new technology will equal the availability rate of existing equipment. In reality, users will be strongly inclined to expect that any new technology will also deliver better availability. Steady improvements in technology make it possible, in principle, to satisfy these expectations. Nevertheless, especially in the earlier stages of a transition to a new higher performance system, managers must be prepared to endure the consequences of an unexpected reduction in performance.

12.3 Reliability/Serviceability

These two interdependent desiderata are, in turn, the principal immediate determinants of availability.

Networking, like computation, is able to take advantage of a broad trend: improvements in system design and microprocessor technology have led to mean times between failure that were only hypothetical a few years ago. Serviceability is much better, and less costly, because improved modularization makes it possible to replace defective components through simple, quick pop-out pop-in procedures, often without interrupting work. Diagnostic systems that can be monitored from a central service center make it possible to sustain historical or improved levels of reliability without the expense of onsite maintenance specialists.

For networks, however, these gains in hardware reliability are not sufficient in themselves. Networks are much more complex than computational systems, and they sprawl all over the place. Incompatibilities between different networking technologies that may cause few problems under ordinary loads can become significant if demand peaks suddenly to unanticipated levels. These crises are especially serious because peaks in demand almost invariably arrive when the need for a reliable network is most acute. True reliability requires that software and management procedures approach the basic downtime-avoidance capabilities of hardware. Improvements in this respect can only go so far if the complete network system is made up of components from different manufacturers operating under different standards.

12.4 Seamlessness

Consistent high reliability is much easier to achieve if the entire network is composed of hardware and protocols that conform to a single standard from one desktop, through the series of intervening networks, to another user. This ideal, the seamless network transparent to the user, has been the El Dorado of networking ever since large networks were first assembled two decades ago.

On some levels, seamlessness is already a fact. When everything is working right, ordinary e-mail goes to its destination with a high rate of reliability and at an adequate speed. This is accomplished despite the tangle of networking standards, proprietary equipment, and varying bandwidths of the networks that must be traversed en route. The qualification *when everything is working right* is, however, not a formality. Congestion and backup at bottlenecks are more likely to cause trouble than outright equipment failure. For example, recent sharp increases in subscribers to some popular on-line services have led to rush-hour delays as facilities are inadequate to cope with the traffic.

On the one hand, the capacity and growing universality of optical fiber, combined with a parallel growth in digitalization, provide foundations for seamlessness that are far superior to the narrow wire pipes and analog environment that have prevailed for so many years. Contemporary demands for higher bandwidth, multimedia, higher reliability, and improved security nevertheless make it more difficult to deliver seamlessness across of the whole range of network services and the existing multiplicity of LANs, MANs, and WANs.

ATM is beginning to make it possible to move toward seamlessness. By the end of this century, ATM and related technologies will offer the prospect of a single set of standards across all parts of the network. Maintenance, servicing, reliability, and cost should become less dependent upon the quirks of individual vendors. Seamlessness in fundamentals does not, however, imply total uniformity. Applications are bound to increase in diversity as well as in their demands upon networks. Consequently, seamlessness may be feasible up through the middle layers of the networking stack but is less likely at the higher layers. Even with that reservation, however, operations and management procedures must be improved greatly in order to approach seamlessness with any technology, including ATM.

This is an acceptable tradeoff. Seamlessness for network means providing a consistent view of the network for all applications. However, each application may require a distinct view of the network. This can be accomplished with ATM by leveraging its ability to provide virtual networks.

12.5 *Performance*

When corporate customers consider a new network technology, their initial expectations are likely to be concentrated upon improved performance, expressed initially in bandwidth. After all, if it isn't faster, why bother? As has been noted earlier in this book, improvements in bandwidth capability are among the most important distinguishing features of ATM. Today, however, demands for improved performance are qualitative as well as quantitative. As outlined in Chapter 11, corporate users are increasingly adopting visualization-based applications that require transmission of images, sound, and moving pictures as readily as voice and data.

Performance, like reliability, is not an absolute measure. It is affected by a wide range of influences that extend far beyond the rated capabilities of a network architecture or its underlying circuitry. Measuring performance in terms of equipment capabilities, which in principle should be the easiest dimension, is in fact very difficult. The ostensible throughput capacity of a switch, for example, may be reflected ambiguously in its actual ability to move traffic that is structured by a specific protocol.

Bandwidth alone is not really a very illuminating measure. In principle, a four-lane highway would have twice the bandwidth of a two-lane highway. Its actual carrying capacity for large trucks would, however, be constrained if its route included too many steep inclines. Its efficiency for all vehicles could be degraded if too many high-capacity on-ramps delivered so much traffic that the added bandwidth became saturated while no one got anywhere.

It is difficult to develop *metrics* (criteria of relative performance, usually expressed numerically) for networks. In computing, benchmarks can measure throughput or the time required to complete a particular real-life or artificial task. Networks are too protean. Does one measure productivity in terms of time or cost per standard page or per minute? The ultimate test of performance is on the mouse level, in the subjective judgments of individual users. Toleration of workable but mediocre performance may mean an easier day for network managers, but it is not always the best measure of acceptable efficiency. Performance that seems delightfully revolutionary to users in companies, industries, or countries accustomed to slow, primitive networks may seem inadequate to other users with wider exposure and more sophisticated expectations.

Improved capabilities for network monitoring can improve gauges of performance, but monitoring strategies require extensive improvement before they can perform acceptable evaluations. If performance is measured in terms of quality of service—video, voice, data, and special requirements—does each receive reliably the levels of service they require?

Benchmarking can also imply a detached comparison of one corporation's network performance, measured in terms of a few objective and relevant criteria with the performance of another corporate network with a similar workload. This may be difficult because many corporations consider this to be a matter of proprietary information. Consultants, system integrators, and market analysts may, however, be able to carry out illuminating assessments of this kind.

12.6 Responsiveness

Technologists are understandably inclined to think first in terms of their technology and then, as a secondary consideration, user-utility and user-friendliness.

It is clear that the most significant metric by which network operations are judged is the mean time to stabilize. Networks are complex tools having many interworking parts. Many of these parts depend on each other, or affect other parts of the network. If one of these parts fails, the network could experience a temporary glitch, or a more significant outage.

The traditional metrics used to judge an operations team are the time to respond and the time to repair. Since networks are very complex, the time to repair may not be indicative of the time to stabilize the network and restore the fully operational environment. The challenge in network planning and management is to recognize this difference and to focus on reducing the time to stabilize, not just the time to repair.

12.7 System Costs

All of the Ten Requirements affect costs in some fashion, but two variables can raise or lower costs most directly. These are:

- Lower system costs or capital costs—buying hardware components, software systems, installing circuits, and making sure it all works.

- Operating costs are less evident but may be more expensive. Expenditures can be shaved by reducing the costs of equipment moves and network changes, and simplifying corporate data centers, which too often are cluttered with gear and wires that have accumulated over the years. Training and hiring services from outsiders (outsourcing) may also reduce costs.

The most evident network cost is for the hardware that is purchased and carted in through the door. These costs are being reduced steadily by the same trends that bring about improved price/performance for computers. Prices keep going down for adapter/connector cards and other commodity items, especially on the lower levels of the seven layer stack. Lower sticker prices do not, however, always imply improved usability.

The latest connector cards have considerable built-in intelligence, but only an expert can understand how this intelligence is applied. The better components, having a full suite of diagnostic indicators and other refinements, remain expensive.

If an entire network is being built from scratch, or if an existing network is being reequipped on a large scale, the expenses have only begun when the machinery has been uncrated. New or replacement cabling is not a trivial cost. Vendors may charge extra for systems integration services to bring everything on line.

Extensive and costly training for users and support/management staff may be necessary before the new hardware (and associated software, if a change is made) can be put to effective use. Adjustments may be needed in essential applications, which may lead to additional requirements for training.

Experienced managers foresee these requirements, and make sure that they are provided for as the budget is drawn up. All too often, however, early planning may concentrate so intently on the dazzling price-performance and versatility of the new technology that these additional costs are taken for granted or minimized.

ATM brings the promise of more commodity components, some of which are inherently scalable. With ATM the technology remains the same regardless of bandwidth considerations; however, as discussed earlier, new hardware may well be required to support scalability. Legacy technologies such as Ethernet and Token Ring required substantial upgrades and costs each time major additions to the network were required.

12.8 Operating Costs

Current operating costs for networks are high. One estimate places expenditures at $1100 per year for each PC on a network. Thus, over the service life of a PC, operating costs will exceed the cost of the PC itself. Today's networks, which typically evolved from ad hoc growth, are labor intensive. This labor is moreover expensive because specialists are needed to repair or maintain each different type of equipment. The most important dimensions of operating costs may not be apparent to bookkeepers.

12.8.1 Time to Market

Time to market delays can mean the difference between a successful leading-edge product and a mediocre me-too offering. Time to market is an obvious consideration in manufacturing, where development cycles in most industries are shrinking swiftly. Delays can be even more damaging in service industries. A new model car will be on the market for several years. A PC with some new feature may be able to command a price premium for six months. A new way to package or present investment products may enjoy an even briefer exclusivity. High-bandwidth connections joining distant design and engineering centers are playing increasingly important roles in reducing development cycles in manufacturing. Innovative products in service industries can be even more dependent upon network resources.

Network-dependent procedural advantages may persist a bit longer but are still short lived. Examples include better ways to track inventories, reducing both overstocking and inability to meet local demand, and matching price changes—for example, in mark-downs on seasonal merchandise—to alterations in demand.

If full weight is given to these less obvious cost factors, new technologies like ATM, which permit rapid adaption and reconfiguration, can become a preferred choice even though immediate acquisition costs may be higher than those for conventional solutions.

12.8.2 Opportunity Loss

Opportunity loss can also be caused by routine activities like moves and changes. Workers do not stay in one place, and network access must follow them. Moves and changes are a major cost factor. One large financial institution that maintains close controls over networking costs estimates that changes total 1.5 per person per year.

Ordinary plug-out plug-in changes may not be possible. The user may be moving to a corridor or floor that is not served by the network that must be accessed. Moves are typically made during off-hours or on weekends—itself a costly practice due to overtime. This may cause acceptable disruption if a change is limited to client machines that are in use only during regular business hours. In many corporate settings, however, key servers have no off hours but are accessed, often on a global basis, at all times. Managers are faced with a choice between a shutdown, which may be expensive in lost business opportunities, and equally expensive temporary database transfers and rerouting to a substitute machine.

These difficulties can be reduced in present-day networks by using switched methodologies, but problems remain. With ATM, virtual moves and changes can occur with minimal effect on the network. Changes can theoretically occur at any time with the mean time to stabilize measured in minutes, not hours.

12.8.3 Simplifying the Data Center

Most large corporate information services operations have a central facility devoted to network operations, shared infrastructure, and shared servers. The data center has evolved from a classical glass house intended initially to pamper and oversee mainframe computers. These new breed data centers focus specifically on the corporation's networks. They typically provide a secure environment with conditioned power and proper environmental controls for the housed equipment. They also provide the termination point for cable plants running throughout the building.

In too many cases, however, servers, routers and other equipment simply have accreted in the data center—each addition made with the best of intentions—as LANs grew in number and overall capacity increased. This jumble may be complicated by a wiring nightmare if, as is often the case, switching or routing of a large number of LANs is carried out in the data center. Many data centers have run out of space. Corporate planners are faced with a painful choice: a disruptive rebuild-in-place in the midst of operations or an expensive move to a new center constructed from the floor up.

In the data center, as in the moves and changes problem, ATM's virtual connections, enabling flexible and changeable virtual workgroups, are an encouraging pathway toward reduction of cost and clutter.

12.8.4 Expenses

Expenses for people, usually considered a cost factor in networking, can be a canny investment that reduces costs substantially.

Most corporate networks are overseen and maintained by a specialist staff that was acquired ad hoc over the years, just like the networks themselves. Once the staff was on hand, it was necessary to keep them busy. As long as they are watching flashing lights on the networks display, they appear to be usefully employed. Current and forthcoming technologies like ATM could cast doubt on this assumption. Following possible problems in the lower levels of the network stack will become less pressing, while the upper layers—and the effect of applications on network performance—become more crucial.

It may be advisable to outsource (bring in contractors) to look after remaining lower level issues, while experienced staff members who really know the inner reaches of the corporate network are redeployed to focus upon higher level requirements. Assistance acquired through outsourcing was once considered in about the same class as temporary help brought in for a few days to fold, stuff, and mail the marketing packets for a new product. This concept is shifting toward a partnership model. Outsourced staff are viewed as doing important tasks efficiently, at long-term costs that are lower than regular employees.

One of the tasks of experienced staff members might be to improve in-house training for users or junior support persons. Careful analysis of help-desk queries and network problems may indicate recurring difficulties that arise because users have not been taught to do it better. One goal, of course, would be to reduce time-wasting repetitive queries to the help desk. More important, targeted training could reduce the time loss for users while they struggle in frustration before calling the help desk.

Simple and inexpensive updates of operational guides, procedural prompt cards, and minirefresher courses pay off in better network efficiency without siphoning too much profitable time away from users condemned to sit through long, windy lectures.

Analysis of frequent fluffs and real requirements could be utilized to train new hires more effectively without wasting time—and save money in the long run.

The final three of the Ten Requirements are primarily of interest to managers seeking to obtain the best performance from their networks—into the future as well as in the present:

- Improved feedback and diagnosis to acquire better information about what is going on in the network. Issues include accountability in terms of service levels, better accounting for chargeback as well as other purposes, and improved event correlation, which would enable managers to connect anomalies, defects, and faults accurately with the causes of these troubles.

- Interactive proactive modeling, which makes it possible to make better sense out of this information.

- Flexibility in meeting the service requirements of different types of users, which refers back to the needs of users as well as network overseers.

12.9 Improved Feedback and Diagnosis

12.9.1 Chargebacks

Chargebacks and other procedures that allocate network costs to divisions and profit centers according to usage or other criteria are a fundamental dimension of network accounting. (For a detailed discussion of accounting issues, see Chapters 6 and 9.)

This information gratifies accountants in the finance department, who need to allocate network costs among branches and support functions. Network managers must look beyond this essentially mechanical function. They need a broader definition of feedback, diagnosis, and accountability. The means toward this end could be comprehensive monitoring of the network. Options can be considered, and the manager can evaluate the consequences of alternative courses of action. It is not a simple balance to strike. Monitoring raises overhead and, if carried too far, may impact upon capacity to carry the data that is the network's real job.

Accounting procedures have in most cases been the tools used to acquire feedback from networks. These are not necessarily the best way to accomplish this—or even adequate. Managers and finance departments insist that vendors provide accounting capabilities, however, and some vendors have responded with useful packages. Unfortunately, many network managers do not know how to use these facilities effectively for purposes that go beyond chargebacks.

12.9.2 Event Correlation

Event correlation is an important issue in network diagnosis. In networkese, *event* is a term, referring to an anomaly, defect, fault, or downright breakdown that affects service at some level—from a possible degradation of efficiency to a total disruption. Traditionally, network management and data centers are concerned with detecting such problems, determining their cause, and maintaining service by rerouting or other means. Unfortunately, it is often very difficult to locate the real cause. The correlation between a service-threatening event and its apparent cause—a LAN switch that happened to lose a few ports at the same time, for example—may be misleading. This is another example of the limitations of a management philosophy focused upon the health of the network's physical levels.

With five or six major applications in use, each impacting upon the network in a different way, port outages on a LAN may be insignificant and irrelevant. All these applications, reaching flashpoint levels at the same time, may be the real cause of congestion, cell/packet loss, or other difficulty.

Event also has a broader meaning: any change in normal network behavior that may take place without any apparent service degradation or disruption. Events of this kind may be very revealing about the network's overall efficiency and changes in patterns of usage.

Improved feedback and diagnosis, as touched upon in the preceding section, should provide the means that enable managers to track, understand, and correct these unusual occurrences.

For example, a manager may note with satisfaction that an Ethernet LAN has been operating at 60% efficiency—very close to the practical maximum. One day, however, utilization drops to 10%—hardly a catastrophe, but an acceptable level of performance that is very common on Ethernet LANs.

Nevertheless, a substantial change has taken place. It may have been brought about by a new application, termination of a high-priority, work-around-the-clock project, or a local invasion of a mutated flu virus. Whether the change marks a new trend in demand or an unidentified hardware problem, it may deserve attention from network managers.

Tools now available are not adequate for the task of consistent, accurate diagnosis of subtle problems like this. Network managers are like detectives forced to identify a suspect when only the shadow can be seen. In networking, the shadow is the information provided indistinctly by accounting tools intended to deliver numbers for chargeback purposes.

12.10 Integrated Proactive Modeling

Modeling is one way to make use of feedback and, in the short run, to compensate for inadequate feedback. Modeling is also necessary because networks are too expensive and too necessary to be used as proving grounds. In a network, changes can have widespread and often unforeseen consequences. A passive model, like an old-fashioned depiction of a new car in a full-sized clay mock-up, is insufficient. Managers are interested above all in the effects of adjustments in the hardware infrastructure of the network, in applications and other software, and in management procedures. Whenever possible, changes should be modeled, and their consequences evaluated, before they are put into practice.

Modeling must thus be proactive. For example, it could be obvious that a new application would change traffic flow, but to what degree? In what portions of the network? This can be done through mock-ups in the laboratory and in simulations that reflect the unique characteristics of the actual network rather than some ideal that exists only in diagram form.

12.11 Flexibility

Flexibility is sought by network managers but is also important to users, making it doubly important for managers.

Managers can, of course, assume that they know the needs of various parts of their user constituency. It is easy to classify them by function, assess their requirements for different classes of service—voice, data, images, etc.—and factor these presumed requirements into network planning and administration.

Such assumptions can, however, obscure crucial distinctions. A user's requirements for service levels may be shaped according to the application in use, and many users may juggle five or six applications at once.

It may be assumed that a unit devoted to long-term research may be able to tolerate a level of service that includes substantial delays. Yet it may turn out that this unit also does occasional high-priority jobs that require both maximum speed and top quality in delivery. On those occasions, the researchers can in principle call up the network managers and tell them: "give this one your express treatment." In practice, this is unlikely and inefficient: networks and overnight delivery services are different species. In a perfect world, it would be possible to provide users with a catalog of service levels. Users could pick the class of service that suited each specific requirement. Care must be taken, however, to avoid priority QoS creep, which means that almost everyone attaches a high priority QoS to almost every transmission, just to keep even with everyone else.

The equivalents of network administrators in foreign ministries and other government departments issue frequent but usually empty threats intended to prevent embassy staffs from applying a *SECRET* (in principle, second only to *TOP SECRET*) classification on nearly any cable of any importance. They then send it at the next-to-highest priority (the highest being reserved for acts of war and similar grave events.) The most common counterattack is self-defeating: inventing higher than top secret classifications and hierarchies of exceptional priorities. An ordinary unclassified cable about some unfortunate citizen whose passport was stolen may be overwhelmed.

In the more rational world of corporate network administration, QoS creep can be controlled by giving chargeback reductions for lower priority transmissions. Post offices around the world stumbled upon this subtlety long ago, when they discovered that they could charge extra for air mail. They also provided an incentive for letter writers to use special lightweight airmail formats that (with some difficulty) could be folded into a poor imitation of an envelope. Networks should be able to adjust more readily than post offices.

The ideal is described by networkers as flexible provisioning, which includes providing, in an adaptable and easily adjusted way, everything from ports on a concentrator or LAN through network services to applications. ATM adapts to flexible network management more readily than a typical mixture of current network architectures. Whatever the technology, however a corporate network that assures genuine flexibility is well on the way toward meeting users' hopes and requirements.

chapter 13

Managing the Deployment of ATM

Corporate strategists eager to attain a competitive advantage by adopting a new network technology, whether it be ATM or something else, could do more harm than good if new equipment is installed too quickly on too large a scale. Network specialists tend to focus upon technical aspects, considering issues progressively from the lower to the upper levels of the protocol stack. They then presume that everything important has been taken into account. Network upgrade activity should be accompanied or preceded by close consideration of broader corporate management issues. Initial deployment is a crucial stage—in many respects the most important stage. The start must be planned and executed systematically, with close attention to the people involved as well as hardware and software.

Issues that should be considered with special care include:

- *Well-conceived, simple, well-executed pilots.*

- *A lab testing environment dedicated to ATM oriented products, services and applications.*

- *An effort to focus upon people that support an ATM pilot and will be important for further deployment, emphasizing education, and partnerships.*

- *Emphasis on industry standards, and a lean protocol policy on the Logical Control Layer.*

- *Orderly priority-setting, and awareness of interdependencies on the Applications Layer.*

- *Realism, which includes recognition that things will break, and readiness to decide that the human and institutional infrastructure is not yet ready to adopt ATM.*

13.1 Pilots: Start Small, Start Simple

This is hardly a new concept, but it is overlooked too often in networking deployment. The first stage should be a pilot, kept as simple as possible, rather than moving immediately to wider adoption—even partial deployment on a test basis. This is sound practice with any new technology. It is doubly true for ATM, which differs in many important ways from earlier technologies.

In particular, the most distinctive characteristic of ATM could be described as *soft functionality*. This term is used to underscore ATM's virtues that go beyond bandwidth: congestion management (needed to support statistical multiplexing and traffic overbooking[1]), a better class of service management (providing a service better than on today's LANs, to support video and multimedia [1]), and so on. These virtues may be overlooked in a test deployment in some selected offices, where higher bandwidth and just getting it all to work may be the only agenda. If ATM's soft features are leveraged adequately, networked managers will be able to design around problems that may arise. The network will scale better and more economically. If these aspects are ignored, network planners may simply increase the bandwidth—at considerable cost. The results may still be mediocre network services, and much money could be wasted.

A well-conceived pilot that limits and controls variables makes it easier to evaluate all aspects of ATM in terms of the user corporation's distinctive corporate goals, organizational structure and applications requirements. Pilots should be realistic and disciplined: Equipment should be limited to a single vendor. As time goes on and ATM standards become more elaborate, interoperability among equipment from different vendors is being improved, but problems may still remain. If equipment from multiple vendors is used in a pilot, it is difficult to tell whether the pilot network is ill-conceived or badly operated—or if the problem is inherent in the heterogeneous hardware.

The number of protocols should be limited. TCP/IP is an easy, reliable way to start out. The number of applications should also be limited to one or two per application class. Examples of application classes would be message-based applications, transaction-based, general file and print server-oriented, database replication and clustering, or cooperative applications. Selecting one or two applications which fall into these classes (or others which are user-defined) will give a good representation of how the network will behave.

Try the simplest things only. For example, the manager can start by replacing an FDDI-based campus backbone with an ATM campus backbone. This is accomplished by replacing the FDDI trunk cards in the backbone routers with ATM-based trunk cards. The manager can replace multiple DS3 private lines in a WAN with a carrier-provided ATM service.

The manager should not attempt to bring in equipment which does not yet conform to a standard. (For example, at writing time standard-conformant LANE equipment was not yet widely available.) Pertaining to this last example, why would the manager want to be the debugging shop for the vendor? What resources does the manager have that can be invested this way? What does a post-doctoral experiment prove, anyway? The manager should bring in only

---

[1] Traffic overbooking is important because this way, the still-scarce network bandwidth can be allocated more efficiently to a population of users — in principle, this implies lower transmission costs to the population of users.

equipment that has gone through several cycles of maturation: unless the manager wishes to do publishable research, he or she should stick with technology that has been tested for a couple of years. This includes: cell relay equipment for data WANs (e.g., switches and routers); and cell relay campus backbone equipment for data (e.g., switches and routers). Examples of the other type of equipment included are: P-NNI systems (trying to make switches from two vendors interwork), LANE, VLANs, voice-over-ATM, and multimedia. These are all possible in the laboratory, but are far from being production-mode technologies. The issue about ATM to the desktop is an issue of cost rather than technology: the technology is fairly simple in that it basically involves implementing the ATM UNI interface on the end system and hub board.

Complex traffic flows should be avoided if possible. Eventually the manager can graduate to more complex applications of the technology. For example, in the near future, the corporate manager looking for production-grade mission-critical technology can begin to investigate LAN Emulation and existing traffic flows to simulate the traffic behavior when ATM is introduced as a legacy-support technology, or as a method of delivering personal LAN connections among two sets of users, one set having moved up to native ATM right of way and the other set still on legacy LANs. This will simulate production traffic, and help managers to begin to understand the requirements and possibilities of congestion control.

Virtual LANs based on LANE should be introduced with caution—two or three at most to start. Specifically, the manager should inquire to what extent these VLANs conform to standards or whether they are vendor-proprietary. Remember that even if a vendor implemented 50%, 80%, or 95% of a standard, there likely still will be lack of compatibility between systems, and interworking will not be possible. Hence, the operative question is not if the vendor has implemented some ATM/LANE features in its newly introduced equipment, but whether they are *fully* conformant with the standard. VLANs can intrude upon one another or take parallel paths. If the pilot is overly ambitious, it may be difficult to discern what is going on.

Throughout the pilot, managers should ask themselves repeatedly: Is this configuration realistic? Are we discovering, step by step, how a full-fledged ATM network would actually operate? Are the objectives practical?

This discussion is nothing more than common sense, but it may nevertheless be overlooked in the fascination with new technology—and awareness of the eagerness of top management to get moving with this new killer technology.

The value of an ATM pilot can be negated by improper planning. In particular, the planner needs to consider the following:

- The purpose of the pilot must be well-defined and socialized to all participants.

- The goals and expected results of the pilot be also be predefined. This will be matched against the real results.

- The interaction of the operating systems and device drivers should be observed and tuned where appropriate. ATM traffic profiles may be unlike the existing networks, and will cause problems if drivers are not written specifically for ATM. This is particularly true for native ATM servers.

- If possible, trunk links (i.e., between switches) and links to servers should be monitored. These are the most likely links to experience congestion.

- If using LAN Emulation devices, monitor the legacy input traffic flows versus the legacy output flows. This will give a relative assessment of the impact of LAN Emulation.

- Traditional performance testing will be inappropriate, especially if comparing ATM against legacy networks. Quantum leaps of performance will not happen if applications and drivers were originally written for existing networks. To achieve optimal performance with ATM, the drivers and applications should be written to take advantage of advanced features of ATM.

13.2 People and Technology: The ATM Lab

A pilot should be supported by an ATM lab that focuses primarily upon end users, their practical requirements, the applications they actually use, and training. Education should be ongoing as network managers, selected users, and then the larger user community become familiar with ATM and with its implementation in the corporation's distinctive setting. Investments in people are likely to have more satisfactory, long-lasting benefits than over-investment in technology.

The ATM Forum is a possible source of education. Corporate memberships are relatively inexpensive and need not place a burden on the time of network managers. The ATM Forum has an Ambassadors program that is available to members for ATM education on various levels. Experts from vendors and other sources are available to address specific issues on the scene and hold seminars. Printed guides and reference materials are also available.

The Enterprise Networking Roundtable (ENR), the user category of membership in the ATM Forum, is also a source of information. Involvement in the ENR allows users access to the ATM Forum and its resources without the substantial commitment of the principal members category. The work performed by the ENR is focused on the real-world deployment issues facing ATM network managers. These include technical issues and business issues, such as business justification, ATM outsourcing, and development of RFIs.

ATM remains at a stage in which vendors of hardware and software are still in a process of learning and exploration. They welcome partnerships with users that help them to assess user needs while the participants in the partnership jointly seek solutions. In particular, everyone involved with ATM needs to gain experience in scaling ATM upward to larger, more complex networks. It is also important to make sure that vendors of routers and switches, for example, are talking to one another. If services from full-scale system integration to specific tasks are outsourced, this relationship should also be a partnership in which the education function is as central as simply getting the work done.

Outsiders, however knowledgeable and well-intentioned, tend to focus upon the supply side of networking—the hardware, software and procedures that enable a network to operate well. To understand the demand side, a corporate staff must look inside the corporation—its immediate and longer term objectives, organizational structure, level of sophistication about networking, and history of network implementation. Network planning and network management must work closely together—in effect, educate one another—as they explore the demand side of working with ATM. This is yet another instance of a common-sense step that is neglected too frequently.

An even more basic requirement is also often overlooked—the need to remain aware of developments within the corporation and outside it. The danger point is reached when a network has begun to operate smoothly, when outright outages have become very rare and complaints are few. In network management, even more than in most other jobs, it is easy to become routinized. This is a dangerous condition, because requirements within the corporation are certain to be changing, very likely at speeds and in directions that are not easy to discern. Technology will be changing with equal speed and unpredictability.

This tendency toward routinization highlights the importance of partnerships and sources like The ATM Forum that can be constant sources of stimulus as well as knowledge. Comparisons with competitors and occasional assessments by objective outside consultants can help maintain a high state of awareness, in effect, another form of partnership.

13.3 Transitioning the Physical Layer

The virtues of simplicity also apply to the specifications and operation of the network itself, on the Physical, Logical, and Applications layers. Specifics include:

- On the Physical Access Layer, modularity and a tiered topology.

- On the Virtual Layer, stress on industry standards and reduction in protocol divergence.

- On the Service Layer, establish policies and understand application interdependencies, keeping close track of traffic flows and setting priorities.

Plans for deployment of new technology must start with a careful assessment of existing networks. This holds true for any change in technology, including alternatives to ATM that also offer relatively high bandwidth.

At most corporations, networking started small and then sprawled. Diversity reached down to the physical substructure: twisted-pair lines of various levels, Ethernet, and other coaxial circuits, FDDI and other solutions based on optical fiber, and so on.

The immediate future includes choices like various physical foundations for ordinary ISDN, fast Ethernet, Frame Relay, and others, in addition to ATM. Farther into the future, ATM operating over fiber has the potential to replace all of these current technologies. No other single technology that now receives wide support has a similar potential for universality. In the real world, this potential will become reality slowly, due to the costs of replacing existing physical resources and the time required before ATM will become a fully elaborated, fully integrated, mature networking technology.

Especially in the pilot and deployment stages, attention should be concentrated upon the elimination of complexity, and the avoidance of adding new complexity that does not serve a well-defined and necessary purpose. The first rule of thumb is to keep away from proprietary solutions. If they are in use, seek to prevent their proliferation. The second is to standardize wherever possible. Category 5 twisted-pair is remarkably versatile for bandwidths up to 155 Mbps, which may be quite sufficient for the final stages to the desktop. FDDI makes use of fiber optic capabilities, offers relatively high bandwidth, and has good prospects for medium term usefulness. Both physical foundations are able to span a wide range of switching and routing technologies.

If physical diversity is a fact of corporate life, networks for basic corporate units—workgroups—should be standardized on a local basis as far as possible. This makes it easier to practice modularity: portions of the corporate network can be treated as replacable, self-contained units. This can simplify the overall structure, reducing the requirement for devices that provide interoperability. Routers and bridges cost money. They inevitably reduce overall network throughput and can be important causes of bottlenecks and congestion.

Modularity can in turn provide a foundation for a multitiered topology that provides a flexible model for both heterogeneous and relatively homogenous network environments. A tiered hierarchy is most practical. This strategy differs from the common assumption that a single backbone serves an entire campus, building, division, or other large unit. A model based on physically independent tiers will offer flexibility and performance in the short term. Long term goals of technology upgrades become easier since the solution is modular.

The tiered approach also eliminates the dependence on a given technology. Technologies can be replaced when appropriate without adversely affecting the operation of the network. An example of the tiered approach is given in Figure 13.1, where each tier is connected to its parent via a bridge or router.

The tiers go from the work group, to the backbone, to the building, and then optionally to a campus network. Note that all tiers are independent from each other, and that a tier technology can be swapped out and replaced with a different technology. Later in this chapter, we will discuss how to leverage this design to deploy ATM with minimal risks.

Many corporate network infrastructures already possess most or all of the physical prerequisites for implementing a multitier modular environment of this kind. Much can be accomplished by moving, redirecting, or acquiring servers and fitting them into this model. Existing wiring within the building or campus may be largely sufficient, requiring few expensive changes.

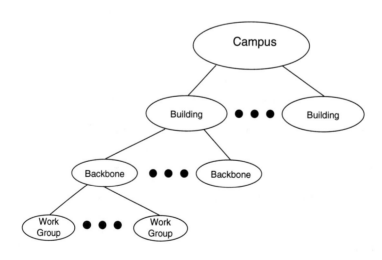

Figure 13.1   Tiered network design

CHAPTER 13: MANAGING THE DEPLOYMENT OF ATM

13.4 Physical Topology for ATM

As with the physical transition strategy discussed in the previous section, the model for the full ATM network consists of three tiers within a site.

On the first tier are the workgroup LANs. These LANs support user workstations and shared workgroup print devices. This tier is the easiest to manage and troubleshoot. If a company performs many physical changes to the workgroup, it may lead to cable sprawl. The workgroup tier is connected to a backbone tier through the use of some network device. This network device could be a bridge, router, or switch. In Figure 13.2 is labeled *FS* (for *floor switch*).

The point of adjacency between the first tier and the second tier is where the translation will occur between legacy networks and ATM. For example, a user may be connected through a personal Ethernet connection. In this case, the user has a 10-Mbps link to the network, without the inherent Ethernet contention problem. The device where the user connects could be an Ethernet switch, a LAN Emulation device, or some other type of edge device. The output into the backbone is ATM.

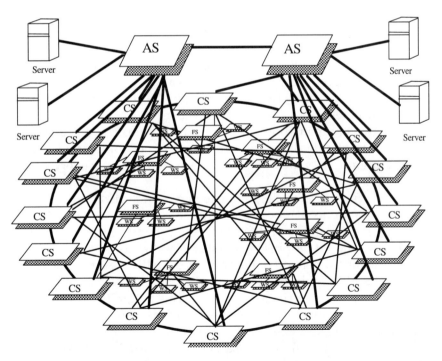

Figure 13.2   Three-tiered physical structure

The second tier is the backbone tier, labeled *CS* (for *convergence switch*) in the figure. This tier supports the convergence of traffic from the workgroup tier. It manages the traffic between first tier devices and shared services on the third tier. The best practice is to allow only infrastructure devices to be located on this tier. In a pure ATM environment, this would include only switches. In a mixed network, this would include bridges, routers, ATM and non-ATM switches.

The third tier is the apex tier (*AS*, for *apex switch*), which is where all shared services would be placed. These would include database and e-mail servers, gateways, WAN access devices, connection to the Internet, etc. Only traffic destined for these shared services would flow onto this tier.

Notice that at each successive tier, the links are thicker in Figure 13.2. This represents the increased bandwidth required for heavier traffic flows. This assumes that the traffic volumes are heaviest to the shared services, then to interworkgroups, and last to intraworkgroup.

Tier 2 devices are partially meshed to each other to minimize the latency for workgroup traffic, as well as to implement additional redundancy for sustained operation in multiple failure scenarios.

13.5 *The Logical Control Level*

The same basic principles of simplification and modularization apply to the logical control level. Simplifying the Logical Control Layer will improve the chances of a successful ATM deployment in the short term, since ATM is significantly different from a logical perspective.

Layer two encapsulation is an important issue. There is a movement toward industry standards, as many providers of network hardware offer a variety of solutions. They are not likely, however, to support every variety of encapsulation.

A trend is nevertheless beginning toward standardization on the RFC/1483 specifications for SNAP encapsulation.

Protocols also tend to proliferate excessively, and corporations are seeking to curb this trend. At the present, the sturdy and well-proved IP—with or without the accompaniment of TCP—appears to be the most satisfactory solution. Alternatives like Appletalk, Novell's IPX, and DECNet seem likely to be relegated to niche or proprietary solutions. This is significant for ATM deployment because it is difficult to implement ATM in conjunction with, for example, Appletalk or DECNet.

Protocols which will not be explicitly supported by ATM standards will need to be bridged. As shown in Chapter 1, bridging will be implemented using LAN Emulation. LAN Emulation is an effective solution, but it imposes a nontrivial performance penalty. Routers may not provide a solution as elegant and cost-effective as a seamless ATM environment, but they will not be abandoned in the near term. Scaling networks throughout the corporate environment will need to rely upon routers to make connections through a heterogeneous network structure.

Thus it is important to move toward uniformity and standardization in routers and in routing schemes. Proprietary solutions should be avoided or minimized. The Routing Information Protocol (RIP) was an early attempt toward standardization. Some implementations of RIP—Novell's, for example—have less potential than others.

Open Shortest Path First (OSPF) and Intermediate System to Intermediate System (IS-IS) are two additional standards that are becoming more important in the ATM environment for IP. Novell's Link State Protocol (NLSP) is Novell's version of IS-IS. It will eventually become the major routing protocol for all Novell environments.

Orderliness and self-restraint in terms of protocols and other variables on the logical control level can benefit any network, whatever the technology. These principles become even more important when managers must adjust to the new potentials made possible by ATM.

13.6 The Service Layer

Application behavior policies make it possible to avoid or minimize applications that place exceptional burdens on the network. Policies should be considered as early as possible, whatever the current networking technologies. During the ATM pilot, policies should be reviewed in the light of experience gained from the pilot and from the ATM lab.

For example, some database applications utilize virtual disks that reside on the client while the application is in use. This information must be downloaded to the client whenever the user opens that application, creating a substantial, sudden lump of data flowing over the network. Appropriate policies can require or encourage applications that use network resources more efficiently, for example, using SQL-type transactions with a database server.

This leads to another important partnership—with programmers who develop custom applications for the corporation. Developers are always in a rush, trying to complete tasks by specified deadlines. Developers also tend to write in the highest possible class of service priorities.

Object-oriented techniques can be used to set up classes of service priorities within objects. Each defined object could have as its attributes QoS promontories which would map to the ATM QoS model. Such a policy can be defined as a general business requirement rather than a restriction enforced specifically for developers.

These considerations may not seem important when the local level usage consists mostly of ordinary IP transmission over 10-Mbps Ethernet. For many applications, this is adequate; however, simple extension of even this basic configuration across a metropolitan area, a region, or the nation has heretofore been limited by the unavailability of sufficient WAN bandwidth. As discussed elsewhere in this book, requirements are growing in two directions: higher bandwidth all around (because of new applications), and international reach. Policies of this kind can, however, prepare the organization for a future in which each business application will broaden its scope, possibly including support of users worldwide. Bandwidth and other network resources become more severely strained. Capacity-based bottlenecks may become a serious issue.

Interdependencies must be examined closely. Different categories of interdependence may be involved: among applications, among traffic flows, and within a corporation's organizational structure. For network planners and managers, these interdependencies must receive appropriate consideration.

Other key issues include the determination of QoS and the establishment of priorities for different applications and types of traffic. A way to map these application requirements and priorities has to be defined. At the service level, ATM supports ABR, VBR, CBR, and UBR (for Cell Relay service), and a variety of other fastpacket (e.g., Frame Relay and SMDS) and legacy services (e.g., LAN bridging, FDDI bridging, and LANE). The assignment of priorities in ATM is more difficult. As discussed in Chapter 1, ATM does not explicitly support a differentiation of priority, only Class of Service (for cell relay service); furthermore, for other services, e.g., LAN bridging, there is no concept of priority intrinsic in the legacy stream approaching the switch. Switches from different vendors implement QoS classes in different ways; cell treatment within a switch is strictly a vendor-specific function.

A debate now underway pits those who believe that the application developers should have control against those who believe that policies should be enforced outside the application. Both sides have legitimate arguments, and some hybrid will probably emerge. For some time to come, an application-centric view of the communication service is probably more realistic than to expect the ATM network to develop enough intelligence to adjudicate QoS based on inferred user needs. (Recall that ATM controls only the Data Link Layer; from a user's point of view, QoS must be secured at the Application Layer, the Presentation Layer, the Session Layer, the Transport Layer, and the Network Layer. All of this is outside ATM, and so cannot be controlled by an ATM network.)

The application camp maintains that there is sometimes a need to negotiate service levels involving tradeoffs between costs and performance levels. It is also argued that the application should determine where and when tradeoffs take place and how they happen. This is fine, but again, an ATM network supports services related only to the Data Link Layer, whose job is to relay data over a single hop in an effective and (somewhat) reliable manner. The tradeoffs that the user application has access to relate, in an ATM network, to the service features at the Data Link Layer, as exemplified (at least in SVC service) by things such as bearer capability (e.g., forward bandwidth, backward bandwidth, forward QoS class, and backward QoS class). A small set of other parameters can also be negotiated, but this is done end-to-end, end system-to-end system, outside of ATM (at least when there is no service interworking). These parameters include AAL type and subparameters, subaddresses, and broadband HLI/ LLI. A thorough discussion of these topics may be found in [3].

In the other camp, it is asserted that if applications determine service levels, then it is not possible to enforce corporate policies. For example, batch-oriented file transfers could be given a higher QoS class than mission-critical information transfers. If the switch has limited capacity, this could become a problem. Users with private ATM networks need to undertake the required complex capacity and performance planning (accounting and performance management) to deal with this. Users relying on public ATM carriers simply need to hold the carriers to the service contracts that they have promised.

Long-term business requirements and current needs should be fundamental considerations as an advanced network is planned and deployed. Otherwise the network may remain an undifferentiated service.

13.7 ATM WAN Deployment

WAN implementations have dominated in early deployments of ATM. These cases have focused primarily upon gaining higher bandwidth. For WANs, as on the LAN level, the broader capabilities of ATM should be given careful attention.

13.7.1 WAN Service Offerings

Deployment of ATM in the WAN depends upon the service offerings of the carrier. A corporation considering such an implementation should request an overview of the service offered by the carrier. In this, the carrier should specify what is offered in services based on ATM as well as proprietary, value-added offerings.

It should be noted that many carriers offer not only native ATM UNI services, but also native-speed LAN interconnection, native-speed FDDI interconnection, network or service interworking for frame relay, and circuit-emulation services, all over an ATM-based platform. For the purpose of this book, these are all considered to be ATM-based services.

Services arising from ATM architecture could include:

- Support for a variety of fastpacket services.

- Support for permanent virtual circuits.

- Support for point-to-multipoint connections.

- Support for ABR, CBR, VBR, and UBR.

- QoS guarantees.

- LAN emulation.

  Value-added offerings might include:

- Managed services.

- Custom reports.

- Professional services

13.7.2 Managed Services

Many services offered by carriers are now PVC-based because user equipment typically is not ready to support SVC; carriers will be adding SVC services in the 1996–98 timeframe.

The carrier should specify the context of its QoS offerings. For example, as the discussion relates to SVC service: Is QoS specified at call setup time? As a call is initiated do the switches evaluate the call service contract in the context of the carrier's entire network? This would mean that all customers using the carrier's network would be competing against one another. The carrier must undertake appropriate capacity planning to meet the QoS and the service contracts, just as they do for other services, e.g., voice, frame relay, etc. Carriers are planning to do just that. However, users should not expect carriers to undertake a polemic with the user, to discuss the minutia of how ATM is supported and what equipment will be used, no more than users expect carriers to discuss how they plan for digital cross-connect technology (and the vendor/equipment they use), for SONET technology (and the vendor/equipment they use), for end-office voice switching technology (and the vendor/equipment they use), or for interoffice voice trunking technology (and the vendor/equipment they use), to list just a few.

Some offer another alternative: the QoS context is limited to other SVCs set up by the customer. This would mean that the customer's SVCs would compete only against other internal company traffic, not with external traffic on the carrier. If this is the case, how does the carrier maintain this context? This can be done in two ways—SVCs encapsulation and circuit trunking. In SVC encapsulation, each SVC for a particular customer is encapsulated in an existing PVC or SVC established between two sites of the same costumer. The call setup would then be processed only at switches in the local environment at the two end sites. The carrier would thus not be involved in the setup of individual calls.

In any event, when the customer subscribes to an ATM carrier service, he or she can safely assume that all of the necessary capacity planning, QoS support, and related activities will be attended to by the carrier. Naturally, the customer should check (as appropriate, and using appropriate tools) that they are getting the service for which they have contracted.

13.7.3 Contingency Strategy

A question that may arise, but that is no different from other carrier services, is, "What is the carrier's service continuity strategy?" An adequate service continuity strategy must address partial as well as full contingency scenarios. Attention is usually given to a disabling disaster, but partial losses of service should be taken into full consideration. Here the end user may refer to other contingencies plans that have been put in place by the organization for the failure of carriers' digital cross-connect technology (for example, in support of private line services), for SONET technology (for example, in support of private line services), for frame relay technology, for end-office voice switching technology, or for interoffice voice trunking technology, and apply the same principles to ATM technology.

13.7.4 Professional Services

The end user may want to find out which categories of professional services are available, if any. What skill sets and levels of experience are included in the professional services offered by the carrier? Skills that may be offered include (but do not expect them to be free): physical and logical network design, tuning of routing metrics, developing routing policies, developing policies for edge devices, and ATM network planning skills.

13.7.5 VLAN Offerings

Virtual local area networks are another critical issue. Carriers have not been offering LANE or VLANs, but could well do so in the future. However some carriers, e.g., Teleport Communications Group (TCG), have been offering native speed LAN/FDDI interconnection over ATM.

Questions that could be asked in reference to LANE or VLANs (discussed in more details in the next chapter) include:

- Does the carrier offer support for virtual networks?

- How does the carrier handle virtual networks?

- How does the carrier treat broadcasting and multicasting?

- Does the carrier support a broadcasting/multicasting server? If so, does it provide redundancy for protection against disruption by outages? How does the carrier handle propagation delays? (One solution is to support regional broadcast servers that execute the distribution of broadcasts to local devices.)

- If the carrier does not use broadcast/multicast servers, then does it support fully meshed point to multipoint connections? If so, how scalable are the multipoint connections in terms of number of devices?

Does the carrier offer virtual networking only for data services? The concept of a virtual network can be extended to include voice and video. Video/voice conferencing can be handled using the concept of a virtual network.

13.7.6 Edge Device Support

Various technologies and products can act as the edge or boundary between the carrier's network and a customer's local network. Examples of interfaces supported at edge devices include Frame Relay, Ethernet, FDDI, Token-Ring, DS1 and DS3, as well as ISDN and voice-related technologies.

The customer should ask: "What type of services does the carrier support at the customer's point of access?"

Remember: carriers offer UNI services not NNI-based services. "Does the carrier's switch interwork with an users' ATM (campus) switch?" can be an ill-posed question: the carrier switch interworks as long as the user's switch supports a standardized UNI (e.g., ATM Forum's UNI 3.1 or 4.0). Carriers do not currently offer a NNI-based service; hence the fact that the user's P-NNI (which is very useful to the user in interconnecting his or her campus switches) does not (necessarily) interwork with the carrier's P-NNI (if it even exists), is not relevant to the discussion about public carrier ATM services. A user with two separate campuses (each of which may have several ATM switches interconnected over P-NNIs), will have to achieve an interconnected network utilizing the carrier's UNI service. They can "tunnel" through the carrier's network.

An analogy might help to clarify this issue. An organization may have two remote PBXs. It could not interconnect these two PBXs by asking the carrier to provide access to the end-office switch on the network side (i.e., on the CCSS7 side) of the switch. Such multi-campus PBX interconnection is achieved in two ways: by connecting each PBX to the line side of the respective end offices, and then dialing directly the remote location PBX via the public switched network; or by providing tie lines between the two PBXs. In no case is a PBX ever connected on the network side (call it NNI even here) of the central office switch.

13.7.7 Billing Considerations

A question worth investigating is, "What types of billing would be offered?" The principal alternatives are:

- Fixed-rate billing (more appropriate to a MAN or campus environment).

- Usage-based billing.

- Billing based on structured usage. In the billing context this includes the resource needed by different QoS required by open connections; it includes SCR, PCR, and BT considerations.

- Real time contracts. The routing of a call would take into account the overall cost. During the call setup process, a specific service-level contract would be drawn up. If a customer has links with multiple carriers, each carrier would respond—with a quote on costs—to a request for a call setup. The customer could then negotiate cost structure dynamically. This billing model is not expected to be available soon.

Fixed-rate billing has been prevalent. This approach is reasonable for PVC service; SVC service will likely be billed based on usage.

13.7.8 Testing Facilities

Other questions worth investigating are, "Does the carrier maintain a testing environment? What does it include?" Major issues are:

- Does the testing environment include the capability for integration, certification, and simulation of what-if scenarios?

- What types of equipment are supported?

- Are their facilities capable of simulating the customer's production network?

- Are they able to simulate distance for propagation delay and switch/router latencies?

- Can the carrier's test facilities generate simulated traffic whose shape is similar to the customer's production network?

- Can test facilities generate a realistic call setup/call termination load on the customer's network?

A carrier testing facility may also make it possible for customers to bring ATM-enabled applications into the lab for certification/simulation testing. This would include:

- Certification that the application is stable in an ATM environment.

- Simulating the impact of the application on a simulated production environment.

13.7.9 Training

The importance of training has been emphasized throughout this book. Carriers—especially those with extensive, varied experience in ATM planning, deployment, and operation—may be an efficient and cost/effective source of training. However, do not necessarily expect the training to be free. Important issues are:

- Does the carrier offer training?

- What types of training are offered?

- Does this include managerial as well as technical training, focusing on techniques that lead to applications suited to ATM?

- Do offers stress proactive rather than purely reactive operation, advanced troubleshooting techniques, and planning issues?

13.7.10 Network Management: the NOC

Network management strategies and the carrier's Network Operation Center (NOC) are critical issues in the relationship between a customer and a carrier.

Network management for ATM can and should be set up in partitions. There are a variety of technical options. The details are, however, much less important than the quality of support. At a minimum, management partitions should divide customer from carrier. A number of partitions may be appropriate within each environment. A regional strategy should be in place within the carrier that makes it possible to oversee regional management from a local perspective.

The carrier's NOC is the single most important aspect of the carrier's network support services. During crises, customers turn to the NOC. The NOC must have complete knowledge of the network on the logical level, as well as on the physical level. Close coordination between the NOC and the carrier testing environment is essential. This assures that knowledge, experience, nuances, and peculiarities learned during testing are shared fully with the NOC staff.

Users may feel compelled to ask questions such as these, but it is unlikely that carriers will provide specific answers (any more than these questions are currently being asked or answered about digital cross-connect systems, SONET systems, end-office voice switches, etc.):

- What is the change control process? Is there a regular maintenance window that could cause an outage or decrease the level of service? Are there standard test plans for changes?

- What is the version control process? What testing is done prior to upgrades? Are new features implemented on a purely technical basis, or are priorities and objectives discussed in advance with the carrier's clients?

- What are the overall management policies and procedures? How are these implemented in the NOC?

13.8 Transition Issues

How does ATM apply to the various subtopologies that make up a complete network? This crucial issue must be understood by the prospective user. In the sections that follow, these subtopologies are classified on the basis of the lines of demarcation that separate them.

13.8.1 ATM on the Desktop

Extensive adoption of ATM will come last on the desktop. ATM will, however, meet a need of niche users whose applications require multimedia or other requirements generating high traffic volumes. In many cases, such users will turn to a hybrid solution: ATM for special-purpose applications and legacy LANs for connection with backbones. (Production-ready products that support convergence between ATM and non-ATM hosts are not expected before 1997.)

In the near term, for most applications and users on the desktop, ATM will not provide an economical or practical solution. Most workstations and work group servers cannot utilize fully the bandwidth made possible by ATM. Consequently, a desktop upgrade to ATM will not only be costly; it will also provide much more bandwidth than is likely to be needed in 1996 or 1997.

The industry is working on low-speed ATM access to support Category 3 UTP. Two proposals have been advanced: one, promoted by IBM and standardized by The ATM Forum, calls for a speed of 25 Mbps. The other, promoted by AT&T and also standardized by The ATM Forum, operates at 51.84 Mbps. Equipment supporting 25Mbps is now widely available.

Most corporate networks currently rely on a suite of protocols. These protocols include TCP/IP, Novell IPX, Apple Talk, NetBios, and SNA. So far, ATM vendors of products for the desktop support only one protocol—TCP/IP. Desktop products that support the full range of protocols now in use were not expanded to be production-ready until early 1996.

The operational subtleties of ATM remain unclear. To date, ATM has not been used widely in production environments on the scale of most corporate networks. On the simplest level, this is yet another example of problems encountering those in the forefront of adopting any new technology.

13.8.2 ATM on the Backbone

Backbones within buildings are good candidates for ATM. This depends, however, on the ability of ATM vendors to deliver production-ready products capable of high-speed, low-latency protocol conversion from legacy to ATM, including LAN bridging or emulation. LAN Emulation means that an ATM switch supports traffic in several circumstances:

- From legacy LAN-based hosts to ATM-based hosts.

- Traffic through an ATM network to legacy LAN-based hosts.

Management and support of ATM on the backbone encounter the same problems that influence adoption of ATM on the desktop. Corporate users do not typically outsource the management of backbones. Thus, talent must be developed in-house or hired from the outside. Due to the unfamiliarity of ATM technology, finding experienced outside talent may be difficult. However, routers (e.g., Cisco has 80% of the router market) now have ATM plug-ins that make use of an ATM backbone transparent to the user.

13.8.3 ATM in the MAN

MAN's of building-to-building or campus scope are good candidates for ATM, but they also encounter the problem of supporting legacy networks. If MAN ATM environments are to be managed with in-house talent, the problems would be the same as those expected for backbone implementations.

Corporate customers are, however, more likely to turn to outsourcing (e.g., carriers) to meet staffing needs for MANs. Carriers such as Teleport Communications Group and a number of RBOCs provide metropolitan-level ATM. Outsourcing contractors would also encounter difficulties finding qualified staff, but their business depends on developing personnel pools to meet challenges like this.

13.8.4 ATM in the WAN

So far, the marketplace for ATM products able to support the global WANs typical of large corporate networks is small and underdeveloped. Outstanding problems include support for intercarrier traffic flows, and the convergence of ATM and non-ATM networks. Several causes contributed to these circumstances, including multivendor product interoperability, network management, security, and billing methodology. ATM-based WANs represent movement in the correct direction, but it is too early to tell when it would be feasible for corporate networks to adopt that course on a large scale. One-to-one replacement of leased lines with ATM PVCs and LAN Emulation could provide a reasonable user migration strategy (e.g., a migration from frame relay to a higher speed WAN). As intersite flows become more dynamic and ATM moves to the desktop, SVCs may eventually be used to communicate from workstation to workstation across the WAN.

13.9 Consider Every Possibility

Planning and preparations for deployment of ATM technology and the evaluation of findings which have emerged from the pilot project should be based on a no-outcome-ruled-out philosophy.

Every once in a while, something will break, and a pilot or early partial deployment will fail. This does not mean that ATM was a bad idea; it simply proves once again that all networks, especially new networks, are vulnerable.

This prospect can in fact be made a valuable feature of the piloting process. A forensic team may be designated to examine systematically each outage and its implications—rather than just patching it up and going on. And of course, the results of a pilot may show that ATM is not yet the appropriate solution for the requirements of a particular corporation.

Even then, the effort need not be wasted. Experience gained during the pilot stage can guide the decision to adopt ATM and provide a head start toward eventual deployment. Sooner or later, for most corporate networks, the maturation of ATM technology, the inevitable rise of corporate demands upon the network capabilities, and the need to obtain the best results at the least cost will dictate that ATM be reconsidered.

References

[1] D. Minoli, B. Keinath, *Distributed Multimedia Through Broadband Communication Services* (Artech House, 1994).

[2] D. Minoli, M. Vitella, *Cell Relay Service and ATM for Corporate Environments* (McGraw-Hill, 1994).

[3] D. Minoli, G. Dobrowski, *Principles of Signaling For Cell Relay and Frame Relay* (Artech House, 1995).

chapter 14

Managing the Deployment of Virtual LANs

An ordinary physical network is composed of a number of users connected to the same wiring, usually within a defined, more or less limited geographical or organizational area. It is relatively stable; changes take place infrequently. In the past, the technology of wiring hubs greatly simplified LAN planners' and managers' jobs by providing a structured cable plant. Most work currently done on LANs involves the cable plant. Because of structured cabling, most of this work is confined to the centralized wiring closets. Still, in most LAN segment work, physical changes to the floor wiring closets and possibly even data center hubs are necessary. These procedures are tedious, time- and labor- intensive, and expensive. They are also prone to errors as volume increases.

Virtual LANs (VLANs) make it possible to change this, after an initial wiring of the premises and the deployment of VLAN switches. The Virtual LAN concept offers solutions to many of these issues. Virtual LANs can be implemented using switching technology for legacy networks such as Token Ring and Ethernet. VLANs have, however, been overlaid on these technologies, not architected into them. This limits the scalability of deploying VLANs on legacy networks. ATM technology (LANE in particular) can be used to support VLANs.

14.1 Benefits and Drawbacks

VLANs have been defined in different ways, usually for different purposes. A Virtual LAN can best be defined as any collection of network devices that have been grouped together by a well-defined policy. This policy is typically defined by a network planning organization and enforced by a network support organization.

VLANs help to optimize bandwidth and enable creative network design. They also lead to challenges for management. VLAN technology gives users the flexibility to reconfigure their networks dynamically according to changing needs. This strategy enables users to establish logical workgroups regardless of their physical connections and locations.

This technology provides significantly greater freedom for Adds/Moves/ Changes than legacy LAN technology. Legacy LAN technology required changes in at least one hub and sometimes at several hubs. Frequently, new physical cabling was also needed. For each change, the host devices would sometimes also require new Network Layer addresses.

One of the major drawbacks of VLANs to date has been the fact that they are strictly vendor-proprietary, forcing the user organization to buy enterprise-wide technology from a single vendor. ATM-related technology, and LANE in particular, provides the possibility of developing standards-based solutions. However, it should be noted that LANE was principally developed to support non-ATM-to-ATM interworking at the LAN level, not strictly for VLAN purposes. Hence, many of the required higher level functions to support Adds/Moves/Changes in a user-friendly, controllable, and secure manner remain to be developed. Characteristics of VLANs include:

- VLANs are reconfigured through software. This enables end devices to retain Network Layer addressing.

- VLANs connectivity exists independently of the end devices' physical connections.

- VLANs restrict broadcast traffic to the end devices supported on each virtual domain. This has a positive effect on bandwidth as well as security. Broadcast traffic is confined to each logical subnetwork.

- VLANs allow planning and management to provide more flexible network services. File servers and print servers can be located anywhere without limiting accessibility by users, even if physical changes have been made.

- Users and servers can be defined as parts of more than one VLAN. This enables users and servers to collaborate more easily on cross-organizational projects. Setting up, breaking down, managing, and troubleshooting are nevertheless significant issues in VLAN management. Some of these issues are:
  - How do you plan and maintain Virtual LANs?
  - How scalable are VLANs?
  - How secure are VLANs?
  - How does one model the traffic flows for in a VLAN environment?
  - How does the virtual plane map onto the physical plane?
  - What procedures should be followed when failures occur?
  - How are VLANs monitored? Does one use a dedicated protocol analyzer per port, or does one use RMON?

14.2 Planning the Virtual Environment

The concepts in this chapter will be described at a high level, and will be used to illustrate the various key areas of concern when deploying Virtual LANs.

Sets and set theory make it possible to identify potential points of congestion. They help in describing the routing relationship between Virtual LANs and in the mapping of the virtual plane to the physical plane.

It is mandatory that all sets be ordinary finite sets; that is, all sets may have sets as members, but no set may be a member of itself.

A few key definitions are needed before discussing the actual policies:

- At the atomic level, a member of a set is defined as a port on an ATM-enabled network infrastructure device. This includes ATM switches, router servers, and emulation devices (such as LAN Emulation).

- All members will belong to one or more Virtual LANs. No restrictions are placed on them with respect to logical addressing—with the exception that each port on any device providing a Network Layer routing function must be on a separate Virtual LAN.

- A set is a collection of member elements. These member elements may be individual members (as defined above), or can be a set themselves. A simple set contains nothing but individual atomic members. A compound set has one or more sets as members.

- Every Virtual LAN is a set. Using these definitions as the baseline for the network, the following statements may be derived:
  - For each port on a network device that is a member of more than one Virtual LAN, a point of intersection exists between two or more sets.
  - These points of intersection between sets can be active (i.e., propagating routing updates), or passive (i.e., not propagating routing updates).
  - Routing policies are defined at each active point of intersection.

14.2.1 Establishing Policies

As previously discussed, VLANs are groupings of devices according to a predefined policy. Defining this policy is fairly straightforward; examples can be found in current networks, including grouping users on a common Ethernet segment to share a common server and placing users on the same Token Ring for SNA access to a mainframe.

Policies may be technical in nature or may be related to a business function. In an ATM network, deploying multiple policies will be a common practice. Workstations and servers will frequently be members of multiple VLANs. Once policies have been established, a standard mechanism needs to be implemented regarding the enforcement of policies. Some examples of how to define members of specific VLANs follow:

- *By physical address*   Use the IEEE 802 MAC layer address or use the ATM address. Problems include: difficult maintenance; users do not normally know the specified address; and the network becomes flatter, leading to potential scalability problems. Benefits include: absolute addressing; no duplication; this approach is not protocol specific; and switches are simpler.

- *Segregating VLANs by protocol*   For example, all Novell IPX users reside on one VLAN, IP users on another, and Appletalk users on another. Problems include: scalability; addressing limitations (especially with IP); propagation of broadcasts could bring the network down; and lack of security. This approach is, however, easy to manage.

- *By Layer 3 address*   Using a specific network protocol such as IP, IPX or Appletalk. Problems include: this method is protocol-specific; switches need to be more intelligent; and Network Layer addressing schemes currently in use may become obsolete. Benefits include: more flexibility; this method is similar to the routed environment currently in wide use; and logical management is similar to logical management in today's networks.

- *Application-specific*   Each application has its own VLAN configuration. A business application would define the topology of its own view of the network. The VLAN is set up according to the policies and requirements of the application. Problems include: management is complex; this method requires more proactive planning (which should, however, be done anyway); and may require sophisticated modeling tools. Benefits include: flexibility; the network will be dynamically tuned to fit the needs of each application; security, QoS, and prioritization mechanisms all fall under the domain of the application (which is where they should be).

- *By user*   VLANs are segregated according to the specific user ID as the user signs on. For example, a user sits down at a workstation anywhere within the corporate network (even spanning geographic boundaries). The user proceeds to login to the network (using Kerberos, DCE, or another single login method), and is then assigned to a predefined VLAN for the duration of the session. Problems include: users may require applications that are not appropriate for this VLAN; this may lead to the proliferation of cross VLAN traffic (which is what we were trying to avoid in the first place). Benefits include: easy deployment of a single login; and users are able to suspend their sessions and resume from anywhere on the network (including a remote location).

- *By user and application*   This is by far the best method. A user will sit down at a workstation and login to the network as in the previous method. The user will be joined to his or her associated Login VLAN. As users executes different applications, they will join the appropriate VLAN for each individual application. A user could thus belong to multiple VLANs simultaneously. Problems include: scalability limitations for workstations, and possibly for the network. Benefits include: reduced and predictable traffic flows for VLANs.

14.2.2 Logical Topology

What is the best way to monitor Virtual LANs to detect exceptional traffic concentrations and anticipate possible problems? A choice is necessary because there is no efficient way to monitor all traffic. If that were attempted, managers would be swamped with data, and the cost in additional network overhead would be too high.

The best solution: focus on intersections. For example, two applications having the same priority contend for passage into a trunk line. One solution would be to overengineer the network, providing enough capacity to take care of extreme cases. This method, however, is unnecessarily and unacceptably costly.

Set theory provides a solution. Policies should be defined for the intersection points between sets. Policies can also govern access in terms of protocols—IP is more suitable than IPX for this approach.

This is not a new concept. Terrestrial traffic engineers discovered long ago that monitoring and controlling traffic at crossroads is cheaper and more efficient that doing so during the straight-running stretches between one crossroad and the next. Defining policy makes it possible to extend this analogy, determining who gets green, who gets red, and the length of each phase in the cycle. These policies are set in terms of QoS and congestion control. Thus traffic can be shaped to fit a predictable model.

Above all, the monitoring process and the policy stipulations should be kept as simple as possible. These principles, combined with concentration on intersections, make monitoring easier and reduce costs.

14.2.3 Physical-to-Logical Mapping

Mapping must be considered in various planes: physical and virtual, backbones, floor and apex, with policies governing traffic flows on each plane.

In addition, mapping VLANs from the physical to logical levels is determined by choices among the alternative policies summarized earlier. Mapping becomes more difficult if it is done by application or by user. A user may move in and out of the VLAN to move from application to application.

The mapping process is easiest if done in terms of physical addresses or Layer 3 addresses. It becomes more difficult for more complex policies. This leads to a conflict, however, because the more sophisticated policies—like definition by both user and application—have the greatest overall advantages. Difficulties of this kind may be reduced by the use of a well-known configuration server. This server can provide the ATM device with all the necessary information to carry out the mapping of setups.

Complications grow when users roam widely among VLANs. This makes it even more difficult to define the issues in static terms. Solutions to these conundrums are being considered by The ATM Forum. A satisfactory definition may not be reached before the next two years or so.

14.3 Managing Virtual LAN Sprawl

14.3.1 The Challenge

One of the key problems that network planners will face when deploying Virtual LANs will be how to manage the resultant logical sprawl. Logical sprawl is a result from the everyday changes which take place on a network. In existing networks these changes can translate into logical sprawl, however, they most likely translate into physical sprawl.

Let's take a step back and look at the standard business-as-usual in the current network environments. In today's network environment, most network planners and managers face constant changes in their networks. Much of these changes are related to real estate activity and organizational adjustments.

The result of these changes has been physical sprawl. Many companies have floors in building which have the presence of two or more distinct LANs. Thus complicating the physical topology of a network.

For example, suppose a user is on the 12th floor, connected to LAN12. Now if the user moves to the 11th floor, the planners may be faced with a decision whether to add the presence of LAN12 to the floor, or add the user to an existing LAN on the 11th floor and bridge/route them to their logical workgroups. This creates traffic flow changes, physical cable plant changes, etc.

In the ATM environment, the cable plant problems associated with the user workstation can diminish greatly. This does not imply that all problems are solved. Some of the issues will be discussed in the next several sections.

14.3.2 Traffic Flow Chaos

The physical cable plant is just part of the sprawl problem. Maintaining consistent traffic flows is certainly a major priority of most corporate network planners. Many corporations have chosen to deal with the physical sprawl, rather than tackle the logical sprawl created by inefficient traffic flows. There are good reasons for this.

The industry found in the 1980s that bridged networks do not scale well. Traffic can be blocked by broadcast storms—too much data addressed to too many recipients simultaneously. The result is that many devices on the bridged network may receive inappropriate packets, which can lead to system resource problems on those devices. In addition, point-to-point traffic between two devices will also be received by all devices on that physical LAN.

In an ATM Virtual LAN, broadcasts and multicasts will only be sent to the devices configured to be on that Virtual LAN. This is done by a point-to-multipoint connection (see Chapter 3). Traffic between two devices is done using a point-to-point virtual circuit. Thus, point-to-point traffic will only be received by the destination device, and not any other devices.

This effectively removes the end station congestion problems experienced by the legacy shared media technologies such as Ethernet and Token-Ring. The end station problem may be solved, however there is still potential for problems in an ATM based Virtual LAN.

VLANs can be afflicted by similar problems. VLANs have intersection points and problems of on-ramp access to trunk circuits. This may seem manageable on the logical level, but on the physical level it may mean a number of data-filled VLANs competing for the same bandwidth.

This may not be too important in static situations, in which a different physical path can be designated for each VLAN. It can become serious indeed when VLANs are reconfigured frequently—perhaps very rapidly. One consequence could be serious complications due to broadcast storms. Changes also impact upon call setups.

Fixed VLANs using assigned physical paths make it possible to avoid these difficulties, but how are moves and changes to be accommodated? If these are carried out physically, that means costs of $1200 or so for each change, versus perhaps $40 or $50 dollars for virtual changes.

Additional bandwidth is, of course, one way to avoid or mitigate such problems. If management is alert and monitoring is effective, such difficulties can be identified before they become too serious. Bandwidth is an increasingly cheap resource, but it is not cost-free. If problems are anticipated successfully, bandwidth can be added productively, rather than as a hasty (and, probably, more expensive) fix after the fact.

One additional problem which network planners need to consider is the difference in the fill rate versus drain rate of the traffic flowing through each switch. By *fill rate* we mean the rate at which traffic enters the switch, and *drain rate* refers to the rate at which traffic leaves the switch. In a perfect world, the aggregate fill rate of all input ports will equal the aggregate drain rate of all the output ports.

Of course networks are not perfect, but let's examine what both the perfect world would look like and what issues come up in the real world. Consider a 4-port switch. Assume that every port supports an OC-3 interface for connecting to another device.

An example of a perfect situation would be if the input of point 1 is only destined for the output of port 2, the input of port 2 is only destined for the output of port 1, the input of port 3 is only destined for the output of port 4, and the input of port 4 is only destined for the output of port 3. With all ports divided into input/output pairs, traffic engineering becomes very easy.

An example of the worst case situation would be if the input of ports 1, 2, and 3 were destined for the output on port 4. The potential fill rate destined for port 4 greatly exceeds the real drain rate on port 4. One way of solving this would be to increase the port speed on port 4 to OC-12. If this is done, then the potential fill rate destined for port 4 is less than the real drain rate. This situation presents a problem in the reverse direction. The potential fill rate on port 4 is OC-12, yet at any given time, a large amount of information may be destined for port 1, which has a drain rate of OC-3, significantly less than the fill rate.

In reality an ATM network should fall somewhere in between these two cases. These cases show that traffic flows are still very important considerations in an ATM network. In particular the physical connections between switches (or trunk links) are potentially the main congestion points in your network, so sizing and monitoring of these links is critical to a successful ATM network.

14.3.3 Broadcasting and Multicasting

Since VLANs emulate the existing shared LAN concept, a facility for broadcast and multicast communication is necessary. Broadcasting is heavily used in corporate networks for both administrative tasks and application functions.

For example, the IP protocol uses an ARP (Address Resolution Protocol) request to resolve an IP address to a Layer-2 MAC address. Novell's IPX protocol uses a get nearest server request for the client workstation to identify either its home server, or a path to get to its home server.

Some corporate applications use broadcasting as a method to share information among many systems. In the financial industry, market rate information is typically received from a WAN connection and redistributed to many systems using broadcasting. There are many additional examples, however they are beyond the scope of this book. It is important to note that the ability to broadcast information is both necessary and very useful.

Broadcasting on a shared media, connectionless technology like Ethernet and Token-Ring is easily facilitated. ATM is usually deployed as a point-to-point, connection-oriented technology. This makes it more difficult to send broadcasts.

Broadcasting in ATM can be implemented in three ways. The first is from a single point to multiple addressees. This means a separate circuit to each destination, thus creating an excessive number of circuits. Imagine that there are 50 systems on a VLAN. To implement broadcasting between these systems using this method would require fully meshed virtual circuit for all 50 systems. Each system would thus have 49 VCs, and when broadcasting, would need to send the broadcast message out 49 times, one for each VC.

The second method is to create point-to-multipoint circuits between all 50 systems. This would greatly reduce the number of VCs, to one point-to-multipoint VC for each system. Each point-to-multipoint VC would have 49 leaves on the tree. This reduces the overhead required for each system; however, it does increase the overhead for the switched infrastructure, since the switches would need to maintain 50 point-to-multipoint VCs (with 49 leaves each).

The third method is to use a root broadcast server. This is the method described in Section 3.5. This method uses a broadcast server which maintains a single point-to-multipoint VC to all the systems on the VLAN. Each system maintains a point-to-point VC to the server. When a system needs to broadcast information, the information is sent to the broadcast server on the point-to-point VC, which then sends the information out on its point-to-multipoint VC. This greatly reduces the overhead required by the end systems and the switched infrastructure.

The third method does have some issues which network planners need to address. The first issue is redundancy. Does one implement a single root, or does one implement redundant roots? Of course, this will depend on the criticality of the information being broadcast. In the case of two or more servers, there is no current standard on fail overs to a secondary server. The choices will be a transparent fail over implemented by the switches, parallel VCs to the redundant servers, or signalling software in each workstation to fail over.

Another issue is how servers will be deployed in cases where there are workstations in multiple physical sites on the same VLAN. A decision must be made on the deployment of broadcast servers in all sites on the VLANs. This may not be economically justified if sites are small and the amount of traffic is very low. On the other hand, if the sites are far apart, propagation delay may become a critical component of the overall latency, especially for broadcast information which may have time criticality associated with it.

14.3.4 Proliferation of Call Setups

Another factor in controlling the sprawl of the VLAN environment is the number of call setups which will be present in a corporate network at any given time. Along with how long each call lasts this can introduce significant overhead in the network.

Most planners are concerned with the overall latency in their network, which is very justified. Latency in ATM switches is very important, especially considering that reduced latency is a big selling point of ATM. This is not the only latency factor which needs attention. In reality, the cumulative latency of ATM switches may be significantly less than the overall signal propogation delay when communicating between continents.

The "other" latency involves the latency and overhead involved in call setups. This is obviously not a problem when using permanent virtual circuits, since they are static and do not use the setup signaling like switched virtual circuits.

Various vendor companies have performed measurements on call setups and have found that latency can be over 100 milliseconds in a lightly loaded network. As a network becomes more loaded, this latency can rise exponentially to unacceptable levels, as well as adding to the overall load on the network.

Even in a moderately loaded network, applications may time-out waiting for a call setup to complete. These applications would then begin their retry and recovery mechanism, thus adding to the problem.

And remember that call setup is not the only process which adds to the overhead. Call termination also consumes valuable network resources.

14.3.5 The Use of Routers

As discussed in the previous section, the corporate network environment can potentially become quite complex, and will definitely look and behave differently from today's environment. There is a risk that it will become overly complex and chaotic; however, remembering the expansion of corporate networks in the late 1980's, the horizon looked quite similar.

As corporate networks became more complex, network planners began to leverage bridges, routers and gateways to gain control of the situation. Policies, traffic shaping, protocol conversion, and congestion management were performed in these devices through various features offered by these products.

ATM has been architected to allow network planners to deploy similar practices to gain control over the network. There are tradeoffs associated with these practices just as there are tradeoffs today. A measurement of the cost/benefit must be assessed to evaluate the impact of these tradeoffs and their associated value to the corporate network.

In the previous section, we described the overhead associated with frequent call setups on a large ATM network. One way to prevent the proliferation of call setups to occur is to use a route server (which is similar in function to today's routers).

Route servers can be used as a convergence point for systems on one ATM domain to talk to another ATM domain. Note that the work domain is used loosely as a collection of ATM systems which have interdependencies. An example would be systems which have TCP/IP running and are in the same subnet.

Figure 14.1 illustrates how a route server can help in reducing network overhead. WSn is workstation 1, 2, 3, or 4. RSn refers to route server 1 or 2. The solid lines indicate physical links between a native ATM device and an ATM switch. The dashed lines indicate a virtual circuit between two native ATM end points.

In this example, the route server would maintain virtual circuits to all systems on the ATM domain it manages, as well as other route servers in the network. This is indicated by the dashed lines between WS1 and RS1, WS2 and RS1, WS3 and RS2, and WS4 and RS2.

All interdomain traffic flows will flow from the workstation to its associated route server. the route server will pass it to the appropriate partner route

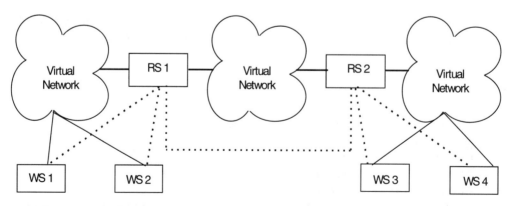

Figure 14.1   Routed VLAN example

server, which will pass the information to the destination workstation. This approach will solve the problem of virtual circuit proliferation by narrowing the scope of a VC to an intradomain role. For any amount of inter-domain information flows, a workstation will only require a single VC, to its local route server.

There is, however a drawback to this approach. There is no guarantee that service levels will be maintained end to end. The quality of service parameters are associated with a single virtual circuit from end to end. In this case, a route server is considered to be the end system and will terminate the VC and its associated required QoS.

Figure 14.2 illustrates another example of a logical design. This time we have added an additional virtual circuit from WS2 to WS5. This is known as a *cut-through* circuit, because it "cuts-through" the route server.

Cut-through VCs enable end systems to communicate directly without the intervention of a route server. A cut-through VC preserves all service levels as specified by the originating end system. For applications which require strict QoS guarantees, cut-through may be the only option.

14.3.6 Dynamic VLANs

As discussed in the previous sections, VLANs are primarily static in nature and emulate the existing shared media infrastructure most corporations have deployed. This will not always be the case in the future.

In the future, ATM VLANs will be setup dynamically as the need arises. In the future, the VLAN model will be used for applications such as

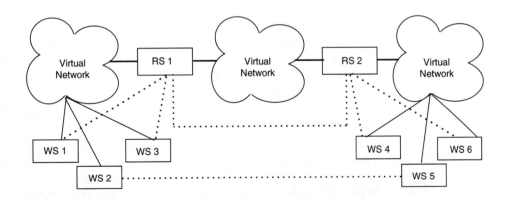

Figure 14.2   Routed and cut-through VLAN example

videoconferencing, dynamic broadcast applications (such as broadcast television), voice conferencing and electronic whiteboard applications.

This situation, which the authors have termed *dynamic VLANs* will be a big challenge for network planners to manage. The nature of these dynamic VLANs could be that they require fixed, dedicated bandwidth (such as videoconferencing), or they can be highly bursty and chaotic (such as the electronic whiteboard application).

Tools are not in existence today to model such network behavior. New processes or algorithms will be required to model the integration of the many diverse applications and information representations (such as video, voice, and data) which can be supported by ATM. The use of Wavelet-based algorithms may be one way to approximate traffic behavior through a switched network. There may be others.

14.3.7 Performance Issues

Latency in a LANE environment is the time it takes to send data across a switch or across a network. It is an important dimension for the measurement of ATM switches. ATM is reputedly able to mitigate the latency problem, compared to earlier switching technologies (e.g., packet switching and frame relay). Thus testing to assure that vendors' ATM switches do in fact deliver low latency under stressful conditions appears to be a mandatory starting point.

Nevertheless, the intense emphasis placed on measuring and comparing the latencies of ATM switches is misplaced, if not misguided. Most switches tested showed latencies well under 30 microseconds under normal loads. All switches had a latency below 150 microseconds when under stress. That is a minor consideration when compared with latencies that WAN or LAN managers normally worry about. At these levels, for any well-designed network spanning a continent, delays due to cumulative ATM switch latencies will be hundreds of times less than delays due to propagation delays. The latency that really matters in ATM is in the time it takes at the outset to establish a virtual channel before any user data can be transmitted.

PVCs are a network management function. The set-up of SVCs using ATM standard Q.2931 signaling is consequently the only case in which latency, in any ordinary sense of the word, comes into play. Several recent tests by Digital Equipment have studied various software implementations of the ATM standard Q.2931 signaling packages running on fast RISC processors. For a simple, single switch, ATM network elapsed times from 40 milliseconds to over 100 milliseconds per SVC set-up have been measured on an otherwise unloaded CPU. Since the CPU will usually be busy, the throughput of a single processor in this ideal case is likely to be no more than 20 to 30 call setups per second.

Naturally this is related to the processor power and mode of setup (serial versus parallel). Carrier switches are expected to handle significantly more setups per second than workgroup switches.

Large, more complex ATM nets will display longer latencies. These are due to route processing (which could add about 20 more milliseconds) plus about 30 milliseconds for signaling to each switch for each additional ATM switch in the route.

On a large private network supported by a single call/route processor on a "slow" workgroup switch, throughputs could easily decrease to less than 10 call setups per second, with latencies under light loads of several hundred milliseconds per call setup. Naturally, if a call processor in the workgroup switch becomes loaded with a sudden burst of setup requests, SVC setup latency can rise rapidly without limit, affecting all users in the network.

14.4 Dynamic Virtual LANs

The present mode of operation for VLANs, where network managers set them up and then eventually take them down, will not always be the prevailing mode. In the future, ATM VLANs will be set up dynamically. Static VLANs would be used primarily for specialized purposes such as conferencing that may include visual peripherals—video, whiteboard, etc.

The issues include:

- How is the VLAN set up? Who is responsible for doing so?

- Does everyone have a point-to-multipoint virtual circuit, or is one broadcast server sufficient?

14.5 Virtual LANs and Multicasting

The most common conception of a network assumes point-to-point communication, including applications from e-mail to large-scale data transfer. Especially in corporate environments, however, many crucial applications involve multicasting: transmission on a point-to-multipoint basis. That is, multiple users are sent the same message simultaneously. Point-to-point messages to individual addressees can also be transmitted over Virtual LANs that are assembled primarily for multicasting.

Multicasting is selective. This distinguished it from broadcasting (like conventional TV or radio) in which a signal is made available to anyone equipped to receive it. Pay-per-view TV is an example of multicasting. Multicasting can be accomplished over Virtual LANs that establish a subset of addressees who can make productive use of specific messages or classes of messages. For example, efficient multicasting is essential for a global financial-services corporation or a large manufacturing company with numerous plants, warehouses, and dealers. It can increase the productivity of a retail chain.

It is, of course, possible—and much simpler—to send the same information to all points. This may be an adequate solution in small organizations, but it becomes unsuitable when only a moderate degree of internal specialization and geographical spread is reached.

The most important single factor in the dissemination of information is the attention and comprehension of the recipient. This is the *last few inches* factor, referring to the distance from eye or ear to the appropriate part of the brain. It is a constant preoccupation for specialties that range from advertising agencies to designers of data displays for the cockpits of fighter aircraft. Elimination of clutter and irrelevancies is one way to improve transmission over those few inches. In today's information-saturated world, a large part of a uniform package of information sent to all addressees would be clutter for most users. In addition, a great deal of transmission capacity would be wasted when information of interest to only a few users is sent to the entire population. Finally, especially in a large organization, even the largest conceivable package may not contain all the information required by every recipient.

The solution: highly discriminating selectivity. The definition of *useless information* varies from place to place, from one job to another, and at different times, defined by the march of events as well as the 24-hour cycle. Thus key information on leading markets like London, New York, or Tokyo—especially those open for trading during the current portion of the 24-hour cycle—would be sent to a substantial portion, perhaps a majority, of all users.

Full trading data on smaller, localized markets like Djakarta or Caracas would be transmitted to much more restricted lists of addressees. Others would receive it in summary form or not at all. Different patterns would apply for commodities and other specialized markets like, for example, the petroleum or shipping businesses. Normally, an office in Moscow would take little interest in the Mexican stock market or the value of the peso. This data may acquire immediate significance, however, if a dramatic unwinding of the Mexican economy affects investment and exchange rates around the world. The Moscow office might then complain that it was not receiving sufficient detail on Mexico.

Corporations have responded to these requirements since the days of teletype—indeed, even longer. For the most part, they have done so through labor-intensive methods that were not considered expensive at the time but would be prohibitive today. Additional costs included severe redundancy combined with inadequate information flows to many recipients, especially those in remote locations having low densities of traffic and revenue. Repeat transmissions eat up carrier and switching capacity, and cause delays, often leading to serious consequences.

14.6 VLAN Technologies

Virtual LANs based on conventional technology are an improvement over traditional LANs, but also have significant limitations. It is possible for members of one LAN to participate in other LANs as well, but this has required separate adapter cards for each additional LAN. ATM is an efficient technology for virtual LANs, because a single adapter can make connections with many other networks. In addition, helper addresses can provide for transfer from one network to another.

The efficiency of multicasting can now be enhanced by new data-delivery tools that permit all recipients to customize their own data uptake. Today's browsers and navigators, used with services like the World Wide Web, also make it easier to place the selection process with data consumers, where it is most efficient. Managers at a central or regional office may be adept at making informed guesses, but choices should be shifted as much as possible to consumers, who know exactly what they want. They are also able to restrict the flow to the volume they can find time for at that moment. Data consumers trust technology like this only if the selection/delivery process is very fast. This places additional demands upon network management, including prioritization as well as overall efficiency.

Virtual LANs involve substantial investment, and they may also be critical for a corporation's overall productivity. Flexible, well-targeted, rapid transmission through multicasting can have a direct impact on the effectiveness of data consumers who must use this data to make split-second trading decisions or restock their showrooms with timely orders in carefully calibrated quantities and specifications. Slow, sparse, or redundant information can have equally significant adverse effects. For these reasons, VLANs are not solely a technical issue. As in other spheres of ATM implementation, planning for Virtual LANs must be shaped by close consideration of the corporation's business objectives. Continuous consultation is essential among information producers, information consumers, applications developers, and network managers.

 *chapter 15*

Collateral Tools for Effective Network Management

Widespread adoption of ATM networks will require improved planning, scalable management and operations infrastructures, systematic network modeling, more sophisticated analysis of support costs, and an efficient, responsive help desk operation supported by thorough, dynamic on-line documentation.

Network plans should include close attention to the appropriate balance between reliance on in-house staff—who should concentrate on broader, longer range issues, mostly on the logical and applications levels—and outsourcing—who should concentrate on the physical level and for other routine functions.

15.1 The Planning Function

Just as in the deployment of ATM technology, management of network operations must be based firmly on an assessment of the corporate goals and business processes of the user organization. The mission definition, composition, structure, and procedures of the network planning organization should conform to corporate objectives and characteristics. Planners should set and enforce network policies.

Even in large corporations, the network planning group should be small and highly skilled. This also qualifies planners to act as troubleshooters when complex issues arise. In addition to its obvious putting-out-fires benefits, this role can also be exploited to give planners a better grasp of the network, including its shortcomings as well as its capabilities.

The management and operations infrastructure should be scalable. When compared with other network architectures, ATM is more easily scalable than other technologies, adapting to the complexity of the network—in its diversity in terms of equipment and requirements as well as in its scalability across a wide range of physical media and bandwidths. For operations staff, scalability means more than increases or decreases in the network management workforce. The skills and outlook of the staff should be able to scale upward to match the requirements and capabilities of the new technology. Scalability of this kind should be supported with training and tools.

Training should not be limited to specialized staff. Selective, sharply focused, task-oriented training for end users—available on-line or delivered in seminars and other more formal settings—can also contribute significantly to network efficiency. In addition to building awareness of new network technology, this can also inform users about the costs as well as benefits of various levels of service.

15.2 Making a Network Model

Assessments of the characteristics of the business and of the flows of information over the network should also serve as a foundation for the development of a network model. This is an indispensable aspect of network planning, because flows translate into network traffic requirements. The characteristics of new applications and their implications for network requirements should also be modeled—preferably before the new applications are deployed.

Reliability modeling requires appropriate modeling tools and algorithms that are not yet available but are now being developed. Metrics for the evaluation of reliability can be developed and applied. An initial strategy is to reduce the probabilities of failure by monitoring sensitive areas—such as selected trunk lines—chosen because of their susceptibility to exceptional stress or failure. Analysis of this kind could reveal, for example, that the most important users—those for whom even a brief interruption may cause great damage—are on the least reliable portions of the network. In these cases, the preferable solution is to change the network.

Well-designed modeling makes it possible to predict traffic flows. Planning and operations functions must work closely together to assure that traffic flows are as predictable as possible during partial outages. It should be possible to treat an outage in the same light as a planned shutdown for maintenance, rather than as an exceptional event. Traffic would be routed around the affected area, and other steps should be taken to make sure that the rest of the network still operates efficiently. Through careful planning and application of these concepts, it should be possible to develop an early warning system that detects probable causes or vulnerable areas before an actual fault or outage takes place.

None of these models will be perfect, but a less-than-perfect model is better than no model at all. Systematic modeling may not necessarily reduce staff, but it will improve service.

15.3 Support and the Help Desk

Support costs are a large—often the largest—portion of the lifetime costs of a network. The forecasted costs of support should be an important aspect of the planning process. Actual costs should be monitored and then applied to refine the original estimates. This process can be based upon a simple mathematical model. It is founded on a common-sense proposition: the simplest network, the one with the fewest variables, will be the cheapest to support.

The number of nodes should be multiplied by a set of complexity factors. These include:

- The network technology or technologies.

- Operating environment.

- The number and characteristics of protocols in use.

- The number and nature of applications, including custom applications, and the relative importance of each in the total workload.

- The number of vendors involved.

As a first approximation, it is evident that support costs can be reduced by shrinking the numbers of variations in any of these categories. The gains will, however, vary considerably from one category to another. Experience will make it possible to apply monetary figures to each category. Careful monitoring will make it possible to determine which categories contribute most significantly to higher support costs.

At least in the short run, some factors—like the complexity of technologies and number of vendors—may be beyond immediate control. Attention could focus on other categories—custom applications, for example—that might be controlled more easily. Meanwhile, cost figures should show which longer-term changes—in technology diversity or number of vendors, for example—would yield the most cost reductions. A well-designed, suitably staffed, and responsive help desk can contribute greatly toward increased efficiency and reduction in support costs, while reducing frustration and dissatisfaction among users.

The help desk should be based upon a strategy of triage. Complex cases should be passed on to level-two and level-three support. Minor problems would receive deferred attention. Attention would then be focused upon complaints, requests, and problems that can benefit, soon and substantially, from the resources of the help desk. A help desk should not be an isolated, hierarchical structure. Maintaining ties with all parts of the business will lead to an active awareness of specific organizational problems or strengths throughout the organization. This kind of familiarity should be a fundamental part of the responsibilities of the help desk staff.

Help desks should be built upon a core of full-time specialists but should be considered a flexible, scalable resource. Scalability should move down as well as up. During a major transition in technology, a change in applications, or an increase in the network's geographical reach or complexity, staff could be borrowed from other duties to help meet bursts of demand on the help desk. When routine is restored, help-desk assignments can be reduced while staff are freed to focus on longer term issues.

As in a medical practice, skill at diagnosis is at least as important as the ability to cure. Case-based reasoning should be applied to determine the complexity and severity of the problems reflected in user complaints. A flexible, easily accessed database, updated day to day, should be used to identify common symptoms and connect them with solutions that are known to be effective. One useful tool is the FAQ (Frequently Asked Question) file. The main issues are the organization and prioritization of the FAQ file. A long list of problems and responses jumbled arbitrarily together, that scrolls onward for page after page, is of little use to a confused, impatient user. The FAQ resource should be structured for emphasis on the most common problems and easy identification of other issues.

15.4 Information and Support Flows

The improvements in network capacities and capabilities that have taken place in the past 40 years or so have been stimulated, especially in the earlier stages of technological development, by the requirements of military establishments. In the United States (and, at a lower level of technology, in the Soviet Union), vast sums were spent to assure effective central control over military assets, especially nuclear weapons. This led to a highly centralized pattern of traffic flow as well as network management that might be termed the Pentagon model.

Many corporate structures have—unconsciously, for the most part—emulated the Pentagon model, which implies a highly centralized corporate structure as well as centralized network management. These models are obsolete for a corporation with widely distributed concerns, especially if it operates globally around the 24-hour cycle. In this case, management responsibility should follow the patterns of traffic. Consider an example:

For a large American financial services company, New York would be in charge while the major markets in New York and Chicago are active. Traffic would be dispatched globally, but most would go to Western hemisphere users. As the US markets close down, the usual assumptions would imply that New York would remain in control while night-shift staffs received information from all over the world and rerouted it to data consumers everywhere. This can lead to poor management and inefficient use of network capacity. As business activity shifts to Tokyo, Singapore, and other Asian markets, network responsibility should follow. Once again, demand for information will be at a peak in that region. Staff on the scene will be in a better position to make timely decisions on dataflow management and redefinition of virtual networks to adapt to the hour-to-hour pulse of the global economy.

The focus and responsibility would then shift to Europe, where the predominance of intraregional traffic would be even more marked. The hand-off of responsibility from Europe to New York would be complicated by the overlap of trading peaks in the two regions. In that event, New York might start the day as a redistributor for Frankfurt or London as well as a major originator of traffic. At some defined point, or simply in accordance with the flows of traffic, New York would take over primary responsibility as Europe winds down.

15.4.1 Decision-making at the Consumer End

This strategy reflects a simple principle: network management resources—the capability and responsibility to make immediate decisions on information flow—should be concentrated where the decisions need to be made. The validity of this principle has been increased, not decreased, as global communications facilities have grown. A strategy of this kind also has far-reaching implications for corporate structure and the process of decision-making on issues of all kinds.

Many corporations have now turned away from the Pentagon model and decentralized their operations. Regional and specialized subsidiaries may be managed on federal rather than unitary principles. The central authority concentrates on common issues like setting corporate objectives, coordinating policies, including network policies, establishing and monitoring budgets, and selecting key personnel. Day-to-day management of networks and dataflows as well as overall policy remain excessively concentrated at headquarters; the door is opened to inefficiencies.

A global, decentralized model aimed at efficient use of virtual networks and their multicasting capabilities also requires very close communication and collaboration between staff familiar with the content of traffic, and network managers more likely to concentrate on flow patterns. These considerations should be at the top of the agenda as corporations prepare for the transition from legacy networks to networks based largely or entirely on ATM.

15.5 Dynamic Documentation

The usefulness of a help desk—and indeed, the efficiency of the entire process of network planning and management—are greatly dependent upon the adequacy and accessibility of documentation. Most major users have adequate documentation of their cable plant. Comprehensive documentation of the networks' Physical Layer is much less likely to be satisfactory, especially in terms of accurate depiction of routers, router interfaces, Virtual LANs, and protocols. The logical level is at least equally important, and more likely to be ignored in documentation, or represented sketchily, with outdated information. Documentation should also view the network on the service level—naming, addressing, and message handling.

Network documentation should be three-dimensional: the conventional network, Virtual LANs, and protocols each give a different view of the complete network. Some sites are using the hypertext features of Mosaic or similar software to create a dynamic, automated multidimensional picture. The operator can isolate specific LAN segments where utilization is exceptionally high or other anomalies exist. Information available from automated documentation can be used as a development tool by application developers. It may also be used to determine network capabilities.

Applications should also be reflected in documentation. At many sites, this information is simply penciled on the margin of a chart of the physical underpinnings, kept in the head of a system operator, or ignored completely. The characteristics of applications, and changes in their use, nevertheless have far-reaching impacts on traffic flow, overall efficiency, support costs, and practical problems such as congestion. Documentation that fully depicts all these levels of the network should be available on-line. This encourages end users to contribute more actively to sound network management.

When dynamic, multilayer, automated documentation is made available, employees involved with the network in a wide range of capacities find their own uses for it. When one site made this service available on an internal Web server, it was accessed at a rate in the thousands of hits every day. If users are enabled to use data in this form to solve problems on their own, there are multiple benefits. Satisfaction over solving their own problems increases users' emotional stake in the network. When any immediate crisis is passed, users can apply their new knowledge to exploit the network's capability more efficiently on a daily basis. Finally, by reducing direct appeals to the help desks, costs of maintaining a help service can be reduced.

Even the best automated documentation should not, however, be considered a sufficient substitute for an effective help desk. As noted above, knowledge gained during service on the help desk can help to make planners and managers more effective. Furthermore, for psychological as well as practical reasons, users with problems or complaints should be able to discuss them with help-desk specialists. Procedures should assure that this can be accomplished without interminable delays or passing through a gauntlet of arbitrarily defined questions that must be answered in the correct sequence—otherwise, the inquirer might be forced to start over.

15.6 Prioritization: Levels of Service

In many current corporate networks, every user and every function is accorded equal priority, which is not a reality of business. This causes congestion and delays, which in turn lead to complaints bombarding the operations staff. At many network sites, the situation can be compared to the water supply system of a building in which the only effective differentiation is provided by the size of the pipes. In a hotel, adequate water supplies to the laundry and kitchen/ dishwashing facilities will in principle be assured by pipes that are larger than those that serve individual guest rooms. In today's networks, the parallel would be an Ethernet connection that might be replaced by an FDDI circuit for a workgroup with exceptional requirements. This provides only a crude means for matching supply and demand. In allocating network capacity, a distinction may be drawn between low end workstations and high end workstations and servers. This is, however, a rough-and-ready guide that is becoming even less useful as low-end workstations also have enough power to require a great deal of bandwidth.

This style of management also imposes no penalties on users who may be imposing unnecessary burdens on the network. For example, at one site a user was generating an exceptional amount of traffic by continuously polling other locations for trading data. Demand smoothed out when the frequency was reduced to one poll every ten seconds—which satisfied the user's requirements just as well. Allocations can also be structured so that business units making more efficient use of network resources are rewarded with rebates, bonuses, or other concrete benefits.

Services can be defined through a hierarchy of criteria that combine volume with specific or implied priority:

- A variable bit-rate service (of ATM) would be appropriate for a trading desk, a law department that is usually routine but has episodes of frantic deal-closing or litigation, or the central dispatching/control office of a large, widely dispersed manufacturer committed to just-in-time principles that must cope with frequent crises. The service would include congestion control. This could define a minimum level of throughput and an anticipated maximum, with an added factor that allows for a probability of higher burst rates. A typical minimum might be 500 kbps, with an average rate of 1 Mbps.

- Available bit-rate service (of ATM) could be provided to workgroups that operate at a less hectic, more predictable pace or for services like e-mail. The concept is similar to stand-by service at an airport, except that delivery, although not immediate, is assured within some agreed delay. Congestion control is also provided.

- Unspecified bit-rate service (of ATM) are more directly comparable to stand-by service or third-class mail. It does not include congestion control.

15.7 Outsourcing and Insourcing

Outsourcing has become a familiar practice, although awareness tends to lag behind the growing extent and changing scope of outsourcing [1]. Insourcing is a newer concept; it is a different perspective on a familiar resource, in-house network management and operations staff. The rationale is straightforward: the skills, cost/effectiveness, and overall efficiency of in-house network staff should be evaluated with the same rigor that management applies to bids for outsourcing services.

In considering both alternatives, corporations should carefully define distinctive, basic capabilities that differentiate them from competitors and support long-term growth. These core competencies should be provided by direct-hire staff. Noncore services should also be defined systematically. As an integral part of drawing up network management plans, the most cost-effective way to perform these services should be established.

In its earlier years, from the 1960s through the mid 1980s, outsourcing was a life raft sought by companies in financial or managerial difficulties. Healthy companies that wished to improve their efficiency further, began to consider outsourcing as a way to concentrate their resources in the most productive fashion. Within the past few years, outsourcing has become a routine tactic, employed by companies of all kinds.

Corporations have found that outsourcing can bring a number of benefits, many of them not obvious at first glance. One is to improve service provided by in-house staff. In an apparent paradox, contractors providing outsourced services can be easier to control than internal operations staff. Direct-hire personal may follow established (and very likely outdated) procedures without being required to meet any cost-effectiveness criteria. Explicit goals can be set for outsourcing contractors, with penalties for shortfalls. It is often difficult to apply similar discipline to in-house staff. Commitment to an outsourcing solution may also reduce squabbling and delay over spending decisions on procurement of technology.

An efficient outsourcing operation can erode "this is how we do it, always have, and always will" attitudes among direct-hire staff. Outsourcing can help to provide a bridge between current and future technology like ATM. This can be a short-term function, accelerating the transition and maintaining satisfactory service while changes are made. Outsourcing can also perform an educational function, helping to stimulate growth of in-house expertise as future technologies are assimilated.

Cost benefits of outsourcing may be substantial. One study found that savings of 20% are still possible. Fixed equipment costs can be transformed into contractual costs that are more variable and spread out over time. Many of the costs of fixed investment can be transferred to the contractor. Functions that are not specific to the corporation's core business are the most obvious candidates for outsourcing. Maintenance of the cable plant, including moves and changes, is at the top of the list. Surveillance of network operations at the physical level is another leading candidate. Traditionally, this has been the principal concern for network operations staff, partly because this was the only readily-available perspective on traffic patterns and utilization.

Especially in an ATM environment, however, in-house staff can make greater contributions to network performance by focusing upon the higher, logical levels of the network profile. Routine functions on the logical levels may also be outsourced, leaving in-house network staff free to concentrate upon planning, the effects of applications, and other broader issues. Insourcing should be investigated as a viable option.

A direct-hire network operations staff that works in accordance with the insourcing concept will offer catalogs of services to users, specifying levels of service and chargebacks. Charges should be based on the depreciation of capital investment in the network and the costs of future acquisitions, as well as staff salaries and other current costs of network planning and management. In addition, insourced staff should broaden the definition specialization. Traditionally, network staff would have technological specializations—concentrating, for example, on hubs or routers.

Staff must also specialize in terms of their customers, becoming familiar with the operations and requirements of specific business units. Network specialists could then take a better-informed part in modeling application behavior in the network laboratory or in actual service. They could then focus on the specific needs of the business unit that has become their speciality. Generic attention to widely used applications is not enough.

It should be remembered that outsourcing carries with it one additional cost. It is essential that qualified staff resources be dedicated to monitoring the performance of the outsourcing contractor. Outsourcing is far from a sure thing. In many cases, a contractor may possess adequate overall competence but lack sufficient familiarity with the requirements of the user organization's business or indeed with the entire industry in which it competes. Adequate contractor performance should not be considered a routine matter of technical compliance, left in the hands of the purchasing or legal departments. Like network management itself, supervision of outsources should be a dynamic process. Contracts should provide for rigorous periodic reviews with options for revision if the review finds unsatisfactory results.

The solution is, in principle, obvious—a suitable balance between outsourcing and insourcing. Striking that balance is, however, not necessarily easy. This should be considered an important part of the responsibilities of network planners as well as day-to-day managers.

References

[1] D. Minoli, *Analyzing Outsourcing, Reengineering Information And Communication Systems* (McGraw-Hill, 1995).

 *chapter 16*

Summary of ATM Network Management Platforms on the Market

*T*his chapter[1] provides a short review of some of the key systems now available. Although more systems are expected to evolve in the next few years, the systems listed herewith have gained some amount of market share, and will therefore continue to be of relevance.

The last few chapters focused on some predeployment considerations that should be taken into account when planning the initial deployment of an ATM network. Many of those considerations focused more on affiliated corporate management issues than on exact operational issues and performance issues. These plenary functions are mandatory, since a corporate network upgrade will cost the corporation money and resources, and because ATM will not live up to the exaggerated expectation that it is a total panacea for all application, networking, financial, and people problems that may ail a company.

However, once an ATM network is deployed, routine operational responsibilities become an imperative. As discussed in Chapters 4–10, technical management covers the areas of accounting management, security management, performance management, fault management, and configuration management. Readers interested in analytical performance modeling in ATM may wish to consult reference [1].

The systems discussed in this chapter principally support fault management; they also may support some performance management, and to a lesser extent, configuration management. Many switches come with their own NMSs which support the specific element management of the switch. These NMS typically support configuration, accounting, and performance management. Switch fault management is also supported, but end-to-end connection (that is to say, network) management, end-to-end performance, end-to-end routing, and end-to-end diagnostics may be more difficult to support with the localized NMS. There is also the issue of ATM network management integration with other corporate systems. This will be difficult to achieve in the next couple of years. The manager may be left with a system to manage the (pre-ATM) hubs, another system for the routers, another system for the carrier's service (if any such system is made available), and yet another system for the voice network. Eventually, network management systems should become more integrated.

---

[1] This chapter is based on work done by Mr. Minoli while at Bell Communications Research (Bellcore), a leading telecommunication services and consulting company, whom the author thanks.

16.1 Some Aspects of Performance Management

The preface of Reference [1] made the following points, which merit consideration:

Users have seen an accelerated introduction of new networking technologies in the past five years. Unfortunately, usable network design tools, textbooks, and techniques have not kept up with these developments, in order to assist users to discriminate between cost savings which the new services might possibly afford and over-inflated expectations. In today's austere climate, users should be punctilious in their pursuit of cost-effectivness over unnecessary or marginally needed capabilities that appear to exhibit great efficiency in no domain other than in the trade press or in multicolor sales brochures.

The 1990s is the decade of broadband services, from megabits per second (such as Switched Multimegabit Data Service) to ATM to gigabits per second (so called Gigabit Networks). Given the relatively high cost of these technologies compared to 9.6 kbps services, which have been the data communications staple for the past quarter of a century, it is critical that design methodologies be applied to demonstrate to any internal or external auditor that cost-effective use is indeed being made. Broadband affords economy of scale, particularly for large backbone applications. One T1 is cheaper than twenty-four DS0s; one T3 is cheaper than twenty-eight DS1s; one OC-3 is cheaper than three OC-1s. However, the judicial use of analytical methods to design such networks remains critical.

Of course, all techniques, models, formulas, and approaches described in this book are equally applicable to narrowband services. However, the cost implications are more critical on a broadband level.

For some aspects of modeling, the techniques listed may be valuable to corporations planning to enter the ATM arena.

16.2 Hewlett Packard—OpenView Distributed Management Platform

Hewlett Packard's (HP) OpenView Management Platform products support both SNMP and CMIP interfaces with SNMP management applications. HP is targeting small corporate networks as well as carriers. HP's Openview has the second largest installed base of network management systems. HP contributes significantly to NMS standards, and is working towards developing an Element Management Layer (EML) management system. HP OpenView's management platform provides common management services that are accessed through standard application programming interfaces (APIs). HP OpenView provides for an open, modular, and distributed solution. HP OpenView's products are then built on this base platform.

The HP OpenView Management Platform Architecture is built on the following components: a distributed management infrastructure that allows management applications and services to be located on different systems throughout the network, a graphical management user interface, management applications, management services, the communications protocols and interfaces for communicating with the real resources, event forwarding and filtering services, a management data repository with SQL access, and metadata services; and managed objects: abstract representations of the real resources.

HP OpenView is intended to support Open Software Foundation's (OSF) DME (Distributed Management Environment). The DME is a set of distributed management services, accessed through well-defined APIs, that allows users to manage their multivendor distributed environment. HP has had significant input in the development of OSF DME. HP OpenView's APIs and management services, which are based on DME-selected technologies, enable HP to offer DME-based products today. It also provides for a fast migration to full DME in the future.

HP OpenView's Management Platform products consist of the following products, all having many common components:

- *SNMP Management Platform*   An SNMP-based management platform for developing and distributing management applications for managing TCP/IP networks using SNMP.

- *SNMP Developer's Kit*   A development environment for developing network and systems management applications to manage TCP/IP devices and networks using SNMP. Provides APIs for HP OpenView Windows graphical user interface and HP's SNMP protocol stack.

- *Distributed Management Platform*   A platform for applications managing heterogeneous networks using standard management protocols and services (a superset of HP OpenView SNMP Management Platform). It has fully interoperable SNMP and CMOT (CMIP over TCP/IP) stacks, but also offers an option of OSI CMIP over a full OSI stack. With the OSI CMIP option, it conforms to both the OMNIPoint 1 specification and the US Government Network Management Profile (GNMP).

- *Distributed Management Developer's Kit*   A development environment for developing network and systems management applications for networks using multiple management protocols and/or multiple communications stacks. In addition to the components of the SNMP Developer's Kit, this includes HP's implementation of the current X/Open Management Protocol (XMP) API specification and XMP-based access to HP OpenView Event Management Services.

- *SNMP Agent* Provides capabilities to manage HP 9000 and Sun SPARCstation workstations via SNMP.

- *Network Node Manager* Provides fault, configuration, and management for multivendor networks.

16.3 AT&T/Lucent Technologies—BaseWorX

AT&T's BaseWorX object-oriented platform provides a run time and development environment for building management applications. The emphasis of this platform is to facilitate the development of a managing system rather than an agent system. The services offered by the platform are in support of the Management Application Architecture which has been evolved from the AT&T Unified Network Management Architecture (UNMA) in order to support distributed processing environments. The architecture identifies four layers: Managed Object Layer, Distributed Management Layer, Management Application Layer, and User Interface Layer and application program interfaces between the layers. The services defined by the architecture and supported by the platform include:

- Common management services (e.g., event service and application process service).

- Management distribution services (e.g., object request broker, locking, and concurrency control in accessing the objects).

- Communication services supporting both CMIP and SNMP.

- MIB services that supports persistent storage using different relational databases (referred to as internal MIB services), and those that provide the external interface using CMIP to the managed objects (referred to as External MIB services).

Tools are provided in the development environment for processing the GDMO definitions and generating the library of managed objects, for developing products using multiple national languages, and rapid generation of graphical user interfaces. Future releases are to include libraries of managed objects that are available in the standards.

The run time environment supports procedures required commonly across several object oriented applications.

The platform is to be available on different hardware: Sun SPARCStation, HP 9000/800 processor and NCR 3445/3450. Applications developed using the platform can support a variety of protocols (X.25, TCP/IP, Datakit VCS, Starlan, UNIX Sockets, and UNIX Pipes). The storage for the objects may use relational database management systems such as Sybase, INFORMIX, or Ingres.

16.4 OSF—DME

The Open Software Foundation (OSF) Distributed Management Environment (DME) product is a suite of integrated management tools for its Distributed Computing Environment (DCE). DME features APIs that developers can use to write their own object request brokers (ORBs). ORB's act as management information "traffic managers," recognizing and directing requests for management information from various protocols, including SNMP, CMIP, and RPCs (remote procedure calls).

16.5 IBM—NetView/6000

NetView/6000 is similar to Hewlett Packard's OpenView. They have similar capabilities, including the following:

- Based on HP OpenView.

- GDMO compiler for CMIP.

- Includes SNMP management applications (none for CMIP).

- Supports SNMP API for application development.

- Supports SNMP and CMIP interface protocols.

- Will merge platforms with DEC's PolyCenter.

- Will support DME.

In the 1980s corporate computing was dominated by mainframe systems and the networks they controlled. Many of the networks used IBM's System Network Architecture as their only transport protocol and SNA Management

Services as their only management protocol. NetView was IBM's SNA manager product. However, in 1990s an increasing amount of information processing is being done by networks of smaller computers using SNMP as the management protocol. To accommodate this trend IBM extended the function of their SNA managers to manage these networks. The SNA Manager was used to save SNA investment and customization.

The mechanism for this cooperative network management of SNA and TCP/IP networks is an SNA Service Point that converts protocols of one network into the other and supports communication between the SNA manager and the non-SNA devices. Its set of programs performs SNA MS functions for non-SNA devices. NetView, the IBM SNA Manager, uses IBM's AIX NetView Service Point as an SNMP gateway to communicate with non-SNA devices.

IBM introduction of AIX SystemView NetView/6000 (AIX NetView/6000) and complementary set of products aims at supporting IBM's new network and systems management strategy. The AIX NetView/6000 applications provide configuration, fault, and performance management functions. Recent releases provide an open network management platform that enables the integration of SNMP and CMIP applications. One of the supported industry-standard APIs is X/Open Management Protocols (XMP) API. (X/Open provides SNMP and CMOT.) However, while it supports SNMP and CMIP interface protocols, it initially only included SNMP management. AIX SystemView NetView/60000 runs on a RISC System/6000 POWERstation and POWERserver. It manages all IP-addressable SNMP devices.

16.6 NetLabs—DiMONS 3G

This network management platform[2] offers a development environment for implementing both manager and agent applications. The platform has features to support the development of integrated and distributed management applications. The product is designed to be independent of hardware and operating systems. The components are:

- *Kernel* Supports retrieving information using either SNMP or CMIP in addition to storing the information using an object-oriented approach.

- *Map service* Allows customization by the user to present the collected management information.

---

[2] Trademarked by NetLabs Inc.

- *NerveCenter* Used to define event correlation and obtain the current status of the events in the network.

- *Log service* Used for storing and viewing historical information.

- *Object tool box* Parsers for object definitions using either the SNMP format or GDMO (for CMIP) so that new definitions can be created, tested, and stored in the data repository and object editing and browsing capabilities.

- *A variety of Application Program Interfaces are supported* Features range from providing graphical user interface to low level interfaces to access the C++ data structures representing the objects.

The kernel also includes predefined object classes from ISO, such as Event Forwarding Discriminator, Log Record and Security Alarm Record. Customized applications can be written using a high level interpreted language called Perl.

16.7 Objective Systems Integrators (OSI)— Net Expert

Objective Systems Integrators (OSI) provides NetExpert, a manager platform supporting integrated management of multivendor, multiprotocol network components from a single workstation. NetExpert was designed to monitor and control a gamut of networks including computer networks, LANs, carrier networks, cellular networks and integrated networks (i.e., more than one of these types of networks at the same time). NetExpert makes use of object-oriented and expert systems technologies. NetExpert has rapid development tools to customize the product and develop new interfaces. This system can be used to support the following functions:

- Configuration management.

- Performance management.

- Data collection (e.g., traffic).

- Alarm collection and display.

- Alarm and event filtering.

- Alarm and event correlation.

- Generation of trouble tickets.

- Security control.

NetExpert conforms to ISO/OSI Network Management Forum MIB, CMIP/CMIS and CME interfaces. It also has an SNMP interface that converts MIB I and MIB II into the NMF MIB, and transforms traps into CMIP event messages for processing by NetExpert. It will conform to new standards as they evolve, and also supports IBM Netview and over 20 proprietary network interfaces. NetExpert reformats nonstandard data into encoded CMIP for processing by NetExpert. NetExpert employs expert system technology to correlate alarms and fault location. Its user interface utilizes MOTIF/Open Look graphical user interface. It runs on all major UNIX platforms (e.g., Sun Microsystems Inc. Sparcstations). OSI published a C++ API, but does not use a standard API development interface (e.g., XMP).

16.8 SunConnect—SunNet Manager

SunNet Manager is an SNMP network management system for LANs. SunNet Manager is the industry's most widely installed UNIX-based network management platform. Sun has announced that it will merge its SunNet Manager with NetLabs' management platform:

- SunNet Manager supports SNMP but not CMIP.

- SunNet Manager is used as a platform for some vendor-specific ATM management applications (e.g., Bay Networks).

- SunNet Manager is planning to license NetLabs OverLord Manager II platform.

16.9 Digital Equipment Corporation (DEC)— PolyCenter

DEC's PolyCenter NetView platform is being merged with IBM's NetView/6000. The new product is to be called PolyCenter NetView. It will combine elements of DEC's management applications with IBM's NetView/6000 engine.

16.10 Other Products

Other vendors with products include:

- Applied Computing Devices Inc. (ACD) - Network Knowledge Systems (family).

- Boole & Babbage—COMMAND/Pst (formerly NET/COMMAND).

- Digital Analysis Corp. and Data General Corp - OS/Eyenode. An integrated network, system, and application management software for OSI and TCP/IP. It runs on UNIX workstations and offers unified control of managed devices in Ethernet, Token Ring, X.25, or FDDI; and uses SNMP or CMIP.

- Novell Inc.'s NetWare Management System.

- Spider Software—SpiderCMIP. An OEM package that allows vendors develop CMIP-based network management products for users.

References

[1] D. Minoli, *Broadband Network Analysis and Design* (Artech House, Norwood, 1993).

index